AF361468

Implicit Subject and Direct Object Arguments
in Hungarian Language Use

Pragmatic Interfaces

Series Editors:
Enikő Németh T. , University of Szeged
Dániel Z. Kádár, Hungarian Academy of Sciences
Károly Bibok, University of Szeged

In the last two decades it has become increasingly clear that language and language use cannot be studied separately and independently of each other. This new approach assumes an interaction between grammar (phonology, morphology, lexicon, syntax and semantics) and pragmatics. An analysis of the interfaces between each component of grammar and pragmatics (the 'interface view') can also be applied to hard-pragmatics and soft-pragmatics research. Hard-pragmatics studies the field of language use from philosophical, linguistic and logical points of view, while soft-pragmatics explores phenomena of language use from a social and socio-cultural perspective.

The definitions hard- and soft-pragmatics, adopted around the 1980s, have become somewhat dated since pragmatics has become a field of its own, and so these two trends have merged to some extent. Also, various pragmaticians made important attempts to blend these approaches. Nevertheless, a border between these areas continues to exist: hard-pragmaticians rarely venture into socio-pragmatic issues, and, vice versa, soft-pragmatic studies rarely make use of the formal tools of hard-pragmatics.

Pragmatic Interfaces fills an important knowledge gap in the field of pragmatics as the first major publication project devoted to studying grammar–pragmatics interfaces and the merging of soft-pragmatics with hard-pragmatics. Through this merging many pragmatic phenomena could be essentially revisited. *Pragmatic Interfaces* follows an interdisciplinary approach, allowing scholars from different areas of grammar and pragmatics to collaborate.

Published:
Face and Face Practices in Chinese Talk-in-Interaction: A Study in Interactional Pragmatics
Wei-Lin Melody Chang
Impoliteness in Corpora: A Comparative Analysis of British English and Spoken Turkish
Hatice Celebi
Politeness Phenomena across Chinese Genres
Edited by Xinren Chen

Implicit Subject and Direct Object Arguments in Hungarian Language Use: Grammar and Pragmatics Interacting

Enikő Németh T.

SHEFFIELD UK   BRISTOL CT

Published by Equinox Publishing Ltd

UK: Office 415, The Workstation, 15 Paternoster Row, Sheffield, South Yorkshire S1 2BX
USA: ISD, 70 Enterprise Drive, Bristol, CT 06010
www.equinoxpub.com

First published 2019

British Library Cataloguing-in-Publication Data
A catalogue record for this book is available from the British Library.
ISBN-13 978 1 78179 595 8 (hardback)
ISBN-13 978 1 78179 596 5 (ePDF)

Library of Congress Cataloging-in-Publication Data
Names: Németh T., Enikő, 1964- author.
Title: Implicit subject and direct object arguments in Hungarian language use
  : grammar and pragmatics interacting / Enikő Németh T.
Description: Sheffield, UK ; Bristol, CT : Equinox Publishing Ltd, 2019. |
  Series: Pragmatic interfaces | Includes bibliographical references. |
  Identifiers: LCCN 2018012884 (print) | LCCN 2018020067 (ebook) | ISBN
  9781781795965 (ePDF) | ISBN 9781781795958 (hb)
Subjects: LCSH: Hungarian language--Verb. | Hungarian language--Syntax.
Classification: LCC PH2271 (ebook) | LCC PH2271 .N46 2019 (print) | DDC
  494/.5115--dc23
LC record available at https://lccn.loc.gov/2018012884

Typeset by Steve Barganski
Printed and bound in the UK by Lightning Source UK Ltd, Milton Keynes and Lightning Source Inc.,
La Vergne, TN

This book is dedicated to my mother, Irma Dancs, and to the memories of my father Endre Németh-Tóth, and my brother Mihály Németh

Contents

Acknowledgments

The research reported on in the present book has a long history. From 1994 to 1999 István Kenesei conducted a Hungarian National Scientific Research Project (Hungarian abbreviation: OTKA) on argument structure in Hungarian, which he invited me to join. In the project I attempted to investigate how the occurrence of Hungarian verbs with lexically unrealised arguments can be described from a pragmatically oriented point of view. My first project results were presented at the 6th International Pragmatics Conference in 1998 and published in 2000 in the *Journal of Pragmatics* (Németh T. 2000). I am grateful to István Kenesei for the invitation to his project, since I was able to begin a very exciting research project with great future potential.

After the completion of the project, I continued my research into implicit arguments. Firstly, I concentrated particularly on the possible occurrences of Hungarian verbs with implicit direct object arguments, before extending the examination to implicit subject arguments. My scope of interest gradually widened toward various grammatical and pragmatic factors which license the occurrence of Hungarian verbs with implicit arguments, and guide their identification mechanisms in an intensive interaction. In the course of analysing how lexical-semantic and contextual factors influence the occurrence of verbs with implicit arguments, as well as studying the role of the interaction between other grammatical properties such as indefinite and definite conjugation and pragmatic factors, I cooperated with my colleague and husband Károly Bibok, who came to very similar conclusions while investigating implicit predicates and co-composition in Hungarian. We have presented joint contributions at a number of conferences and published some papers together in various volumes and journals and also edited two books (see, e.g., Németh T. and Bibok 2001, 2010). I must express my gratitude to Karcsi for his questions, critical remarks, our heated debates about these topics, and his collaboration in the editing processes.

I wish to thank the audiences at several conferences and workshops for the questions and comments which forced me to clarify certain points. I am also indebted to Daniel García Velasco, István Kecskés, István Kenesei, and Yves Roberge as well as to anonymous reviewers of my articles and book chapters for their comments and suggestions, which helped me not only to revise the contributions involved, but also made me think further and raise new questions. My special thanks are due to András Kertész, Károly Bibok, Katalin Nagy C., Zsuzsanna Németh, Csilla Rákosi, and Zoltán Vecsey, my colleagues in the Research Group for Theoretical Linguistics at the Universities of Debrecen and Szeged. Our interesting discussions about data and evidence in linguistics, as well as linguistics theorising in general, helped me to formulate my ideas about the licensing and identifying factors of implicit arguments in Hungarian more clearly.

I would also like to express my gratitude to Károly Bibok, József Andor, Marcel den Dikken, Miklós Kontra, Valéria Molnár, and Gábor Prószéky for their valuable comments on the whole manuscript of the book.

My research was mainly conducted at the University of Szeged. My workplace, the Department of General Linguistics, provided a very friendly and inspiring atmosphere for which I would like to thank my colleagues Lívia Ivaskó, Ágnes Lerch, Márta Maleczki, and Tibor Szécsényi. I felt their support and encouragement in each phase of my work. My graduate and PhD students also gave me critical feedback, which I greatly appreciate.

In the course of writing the book I was supported by the MTA-DE-SZTE Research Group for Theoretical Linguistics, the OTKA NK 100804 project entitled *Comprehensive Grammar Resources: Hungarian*, the Hajdú Péter Research Fellowship granted by the Institute for Linguistics of the Hungarian Academy of Sciences, and the EU-funded Hungarian grant EFOP 3.6.1-16-2016-00008. I am especially grateful to the Institute for Linguistics for the five-month Hajdú Péter Research Fellowship, which lasted from February to June 2013. In this period I was free of teaching duties at the University of Szeged and was able to concentrate exclusively on the research.

Some parts of this book are based on articles and book chapters published earlier. Thanks to Elsevier for the kind permission to reuse materials from the following papers (Copyright Elsevier):

Németh T., Enikő (2000) Occurrence and identification of implicit arguments in Hungarian. *Journal of Pragmatics* 32: 1657–1683;

Bibok, Károly and Németh T., Enikő (2001) How the lexicon and context interact in the meaning construction of utterances. In Enikő Németh T. and Károly Bibok (eds.) *Pragmatics and the Flexibility of Word Meaning* 289–320. Amsterdam: Elsevier;

Németh T., Enikő and Bibok, Károly (2010) Interaction between grammar and pragmatics: The case of implicit arguments, implicit predicates and co-composition in Hungarian. *Journal of Pragmatics* 42: 501–524.

I would also like to thank John Benjamins Publishing Company for the kind permission to reprint the following papers (Copyright John Benjamins Publishing Company, https://www.benjamins.com/#catalog/books/slcs.153/main):

Németh T., Enikő (2014) Hungarian verbs of natural phenomena with explicit and implicit subject arguments: Their use and occurrence in the light of data. In András Kertész and Csilla Rákosi (eds.) *The Evidential Basis of Linguistic Argumentation* 103–132. Amsterdam: John Benjamins;

Németh T., Enikő (2017) Zero subject anaphors and extralinguistically motivated subject pro-drop in Hungarian language use. In Piotr Cap and Marta Dynel (eds.) *Implicitness: From Lexis to Discourse*. Amsterdam: John Benjamins.

And, finally, I would like to express my gratitude to de Gruyter Mouton for the kind permission to reuse the following texts (Copyright de Gruyter Mouton):

Németh T., Enikő (2010) How lexical-semantic factors influence the verbs' occurrence with implicit direct object arguments in Hungarian. In Enikő Németh T. and Károly Bibok (eds.) *The Role of Data at the Semantics–Pragmatics Interface* 305–348. Berlin: Mouton de Gruyter;

Németh T., Enikő (2012) Lexical-semantic properties and contextual factors in the use of verbs of work with implicit subject arguments in Hungarian. *Intercultural Pragmatics* 9: 453–477;

Németh T., Enikő (2017) Theoretical and methodological issues in the research into implicit arguments in Hungarian. In Stavros Assimakopoulos (ed.) *Pragmatics at its Interfaces* 149–174. Berlin: Mouton de Gruyter.

I am also grateful to Tibor Szécsényi for his help in the technical editing of the book and George Seel for improving my English.

I would also like to acknowledge my series co-editors Dániel Z. Kádár and Károly Bibok for their feedback on the manuscript, and Janet Joyce, Valerie Hall and Steve Barganski of Equinox for their assistance in the publishing process.

Finally, I would like to say a big thank you to my family, to my husband Karcsi, and our daughters Ági and Rita for their love, and for the permanent encouragement and support they provided me with in the course of the research and writing of the book. Without their love, encouragement, and support the present book might indeed have been completed much earlier, if I consider the energy and time which they always demanded I spend with them, time spent cooking for them, and having fun with them, although on the other hand, it might have taken much longer to finish it without the support, encouragement, and especially the love which they gave me during the shared activities of our family life. Without their support, encouragement, and love I could simply not live and work.

Abbreviations

1SG	first person singular
2SG	second person singular
3SG	third person singular
3PL	third person plural
ACC	accusative
ALL	allative
c	context
c_{cog}	cognitive context
c_{disc}	discourse context
c_{enc}	encyclopaedic context
c_{phys}	physical context
CAU	causal-final case
CAUS	causative
DAT	dative
DEF	definite conjugation
DEL	delative
DNC	definite null complement
DP	determiner phrase
f_{att}	attitudinal function
f_{ill}	illocutionary function
f_{ip}	interpersonal function
f_{lit}	function of literalness
GEN	genitive
IMP	imperative
INE	inessive
INC	indefinite null complement
INDEF	indefinite conjugation
ins	inscription
INS	instrumental
le_{int}	lexical entry which is an interjection or an idiom-like interjection
ls	linguistic structure
NOM	nominative

p	person
PERM	permission
pf	pragmatic function
pu	pragmatic unit
PVB	preverb
PRT	particle
SUBL	sublative
SUP	suppletive
t	time
TER	terminative
u_t	utterance-type

CHAPTER 1

Introduction

1.1 The phenomenon: the occurrence of verbs with implicit arguments

Since the well-known seminal papers by Fodor and Fodor (1980), Dowty (1981), and Fillmore (1986), a wide range of contributions have focused on the behaviour of verbs with lexically unrealised, syntactically missing constituents/arguments in English. The syntactic valence of a verb determines what syntactic constituents are needed in order to form a grammatical sentence (Cornish 2005). For instance, in a grammatical sentence, the English verb *lock* requires two syntactic constituents, a subject and a direct object. Thus, in the sentence *Mary locked the door*, *Mary* is the subject and the noun phrase *the door* is the direct object. The narrower term *verbal complement*, mostly applied in syntactically oriented approaches, indicates the syntactically required verbal constituents such as direct object and indirect object arguments (cf., e.g., Haegeman and Guéron 1999; Radford 1997a, b).

However, the term *verbal complement* is not only used in the sense of a syntactic constituent, but also a semantic one (see, e.g., Fillmore 1986; Cornish 2005). In the semantic sense, the verbal complement is a lexical-semantic entity which is determined by the semantic valence of the verb as a predicate (Cornish 2005). The semantic valence of a verb refers to the number and role of the participants of the situation (event) described by the verb. It is not necessary to have a one-to-one correspondence between the syntactic and semantic valences of a verb. For example, from the point of view of semantic valence, the verb *eat* is a two-place predicate which can be syntactically instantiated as a verb with a subject and a direct object as in the following occurrence: *John is eating an apple.* In this occurrence of the verb *eat* there is a one-to-one correspondence between semantic and syntactic valences. However, the two-place predicate *eat* can be instantiated syntactically as a verb with a subject and without a direct object as in the occurrence *John is eating.* In this occurrence the semantic and the syntactic valences of the verb *eat* diverge. The syntactic valence is reduced to one, while the semantic valence remains two, as the meaning of the verb *eat* always involves the participant of the eating event which is the object of eating, even when it is syntactically not realised.

Similarly to the twofold interpretation of *verbal complement*, another term, *verbal argument* – very often used synonymously with *verbal complement* – is also ambiguous in linguistics. Verb meanings of a language are represented in the lexicon of that particular language. The lexical-semantic representations of verbs contain information regarding their argument structure. Verbal argument structure has two sides, according to some grammatical traditions. On the semantic side, it involves the main participants in the situations (events) designated by the verb as a predicate, and on the syntactic side, it represents the syntactic constituents of the argument-taking verbal head (Bresnan 1995). In other words, in the argument structure of a verb the lexical-semantic information about the number and roles of arguments, their syntactic types, and their hierarchical organisation necessary for the mapping to syntactic structure is encoded (Rappoport-Hovav and Levin 1995; Bresnan 1995, 2001: 30). Thus, verbal argument structure can be considered an interface between the semantics and syntax of verbs.

In the present book I prefer to use the term *(verbal) argument* according to the general linguistic custom of the last two decades (Gillon 2012: 314), and by this term I refer to the lexically realisable elements of the lexical-semantic representation of a verb which make the verb meaning complete. When the syntactic appearance of a verbal argument is discussed, the adjective *syntactic* will be used before the term *argument*, and similarly, when the semantic role of a verbal argument is referred to, the adjective *semantic* will be applied with the term *argument*. Whenever the term *argument* is used without the adjectives *syntactic* and *semantic*, there is a one-to-one correspondence between the semantic and syntactic arguments and it is not important to refer separately to its syntactic and semantic characteristics.

According to the findings of investigations into occurrences of verbal arguments in English, there are cases when an argument must be realised syntactically in English. In other cases, an argument can be omitted syntactically so that the resulting sentence remains acceptable (Gillon 2012: 314), thus it is optional. For instance, in (1) the occurrence of the verb *lock* with a lexically unrealised, syntactically missing object argument is unacceptable, since the verb *lock* requires that its direct object argument be also present syntactically and expressed lexically. In contrast, in (2) the direct object argument of the verb *eat* can be left lexically unrealised and the sentence remains acceptable. The lexically unrealised syntactic argujonts are provided in square brackets.

(1) *Are you locking [the door]?

(2) Mary is eating [sandwiches].

Since the direct object in (1) cannot be omitted, the verb *lock* does not have an optional direct object. In (2) the direct object can be omitted, thus the verb *eat* has an optional direct object. If an optional argument of a verb is present in a sentence, it is explicit. If it is omitted from a sentence, it is implicit (Gillon 2012: 314). In the literature one can find several terms used to indicate implicit arguments. These terms are the following: *lexically unrealised argument, missing argument, omitted argument, zero argument, null argument, zero complement, null complement*, etc. Although these terms are used in various approaches, they can be considered synonymous and employed as terminological variants of the term *implicit argument*, since they broadly refer to the same phenomena: a verbal argument which is not explicitly present.

In English, and in languages similar to it such as Dutch, Norwegian, and German, it is strictly constrained when an argument can be omitted (see, e.g., Fillmore 1986; Goldberg 1995, 2005a, b; Groefsema 1995; Cote 1996; Rappaport Hovav and Levin 2001). At the same time, in Hungarian and in other pro-drop languages such as, e.g., Chinese, Japanese, Korean, Italian, Spanish, and Warlpiri, verbs can be used with implicit arguments far more freely than in English and in languages similar to it. Consider the following Hungarian, Spanish, and English dialogues.

(3) *Vettél*   *kávét$_i$?*
 bought.INDEF.2SG   coffee.ACC
 'Have you bought any coffee?
 Igen, vettem   *[Ø$_i$].*
 yes   bought.INDEF.1SG
 'Yes, I have bought some.'

(4) *Compraste café$_i$?*
 bought.2SG   coffee.ACC
 'Have you bought any coffee?'
 Sí, compré   *[Ø$_i$].*
 yes   bought.1SG
 'Yes, I have bought some.'

(5) 'Have you bought any coffee?'
 'Yes, I have bought some coffee.'

In (3) and (4) the direct object arguments of the Hungarian verb *vesz* 'buy' and the Spanish verb *comprar* 'buy' are left implicit. They are coreferential with the noun phrases *kávé* 'coffee' and *café* 'coffee' in the questions. The implicit direct object arguments in the Hungarian and Spanish dialogues in (3) and (4) are manifestations of the object pro-drop phenomenon. But in the English version of the dialogue in (5) the object *some coffee* cannot be omitted in spite of the fact that it has an antecedent in the context. The verb *buy* does not allow its direct object argument to be lexically unrealised. It is worth mentioning that there is a shorter, more natural answer to the question in (5): *Yes, I have bought some.* Although in this answer the noun *coffee* is omitted, the verb *buy* does not occur without a direct object; the word *some* fills the syntactic position of the direct object.

In Hungarian, it may also happen that only the verb is lexically realised and all its arguments are left implicit, as in the case of *hozat* 'to have somebody/something brought' in (6).[1]

(6) (The informant is speaking about her pregnancy and her seven-year-old daughter's opinion concerning the pregnancy.)

  Mindig vágyott   kistestvérre,   mindig is

  always desired.INDEF.3SG younger.sibling.SUB always also

  szekálták, hogy hozasson   [a gólyával].

  nagged.DEF.3SG that has.(one).brought.IMP.INDEF.3SG the stork.INS

  A gólyával.

  the stork.INS

  'She has always wanted to have a younger brother or sister. She has always been nagged to have one brought.'

  'By the stork.'

The subject argument of the verb *vágyik* 'desire' is lexically unrealised in the first utterance of the informant. Its reference (the daughter of the informant) is identifiable from the preceding discourse, being a case of subject pro-drop. Both arguments of the verb *szekál* 'nag' are left lexically unrealised in the second utterance. The subject argument of *szekál* 'nag' is not the manifestation of a subject pro-drop, since its reference disjoints with anything in the context, the identification of the subject is of no importance. As Ferenc Kiefer (personal communication) has suggested, there can be another way of analysing the verbal form *szekálták* 'be nagged'. According to this alternative analysis, the verb *szekálták* is in the impersonal form, which corresponds to the passive in English and whose function is identical to the latter. But this type of analysis is accessible only theoretically, because in the dialogue in (6) the informant knows, but does not consider it essential to tell the interviewer explicitly, who has been nagging her daughter; in this case it is her close relatives and friends. The direct object argument of *szekál* 'nag' is also left implicit in (6), and it is coreferential with the implicit subject argument of the verb *vágyik* 'desire' in the first utterance; it is a manifestation of the object pro-drop. In the case of the verb *hozat* 'to have somebody/something brought' all three arguments of the verb are lexically unrealised. The subject argument is coreferential with the subject argument of *vágyik* 'desire', and with the direct object argument of *szekál* 'nag', i.e. it is a case of subject pro-drop. The direct object argument of *hozat* is coreferential with *kistestvér* 'younger sibling' in the first utterance, so it is a manifestation of the object pro-drop. The third argument (by whom) of *hozat* is also left implicit. However, this third argument is not lexically unrealised because of the pro-drop properties of Hungarian. There is a belief in Hungarian folk thinking that children are brought by storks, therefore the stork – more exactly: the concept of the stork – is accessible mentally in a context which includes such words as *children, younger sibling, pregnancy,* etc. This mentally accessed entity can serve as the reference of the third implicit argument of *hozat*. The speaker's utterance *A gólyával* 'By the stork' is motivated by the intention to check whether the interpretation is adequate.

However, the freer occurrence of Hungarian verbs with lexically unrealised arguments does not mean that there is no control at all on how a verb can be used with implicit arguments. In their syntactic, semantic, and psycholinguistic studies (e.g. Kiefer 1990; Komlósy 1992; Pléh 1994; Alberti 1998; Pethő and Kardos 2009), some Hungarian researchers have considered questions of the occurrence of lexically unrealised, syntactically missing verbal arguments in Hungarian. However, the behaviour of implicit arguments in Hungarian, their possible occurrences as well as identification mechanisms have not yet been described and explained in detail and in their full complexity. Recently, the studies on lexically unrealised verbal arguments in various languages in different theoretical frameworks have concluded that there are various types of implicit arguments and that the factors of the licensing and interpretation of implicit arguments can only be grasped in a complex approach taking into consideration different grammatical and contextual factors together (see, e.g., García Velasco and Portero Muñoz 2002; Cummins and Roberge 2005; Goldberg 2005a, b; Scott 2006; Gillon 2012). In my previous research, I have also applied a complex approach to various kinds of implicit arguments in Hungarian, assuming an intensive interaction between different grammatical and pragmatic factors (see, e.g., Németh T. 2008a, 2010, 2012) and I attempt to do so in the present book as well.

1.2 Some metatheoretical and methodological considerations of the research into implicit arguments[2]

1.2.1 The relationship between grammar and pragmatics

If one attempts to account for the behaviour of implicit arguments in a complex approach which takes into consideration both grammatical and contextual factors, this yields some essential theoretical and methodological consequences, requires certain theoretical decisions to be made, and influences the spectrum of data to be considered. Here I intend to highlight some of the most important consequences.

Firstly, if grammatical and contextual factors license the occurrence of implicit arguments in an intensive interaction as the complex approaches to implicit arguments suppose (cf. Section 2.5), then it is plausible to assume that grammar and pragmatics are not independent of each other. Moreover, the relationship between grammar and pragmatics cannot be considered one sided, as merely a relationship between grammar and post-grammatical pragmatics; instead, pragmatic information has to be licensed to interact with grammatical information. However, the problem of the interaction between grammar and pragmatics can only be investigated within a particular theory, depending on how it conceives of the concepts of grammar and pragmatics. In the literature there are various theories with significantly different conceptions of grammar and pragmatics; therefore, it is necessary to examine, metatheoretically reflect on, and compare the different definitions very carefully in order to make clear what definitions of grammar and pragmatics are applied in a particular research concept as well as to grasp what similarities and differences the particular theories can have in the treatment of implicit arguments which assume an interaction between grammar and pragmatics.

From a metatheoretical point of view, research which attempts to solve a problem can be considered a process of plausible argumentation which aims at the gradual transformation of the problematic (incomplete and/or inconsistent) informational state into one that is not (or at least less) problematic (Kertész and Rákosi 2012: 129). Applying a plausible argumentation process, the researcher evaluates and retrospectively re-evaluates information in the context of the problem-solving process, detects the available solutions to the particular problem, and decides which of them is to be accepted (Kertész and Rákosi 2012: 129). The context of a problem includes not only the statements of the rival solutions to a problem, but all other kinds of information used in the problem-solving process. Kertész and Rákosi (2012: 122) define the notion of the context of a problem more exactly in terms of their metatheoretical model. According to their characterisation, the context for problem-solving includes (i) the accepted methodological norms, (ii) the direct and indirect sources (inferences) judged as reliable on the basis of the criteria in (i) (see Section 1.2.3), and (iii) statements and their relevant characteristics at one's disposal according to (i) and (ii), or some subset of this set.

The plausible argumentation, including the retrospective re-evaluation process, is cyclic and prismatic in nature. This cyclic nature provides the researcher with the possibility to revise the latest decisions and return to a previous stage of the argumentation in order to select another direction in the problem-solving process, while the prismatic character of the plausible argumentation makes it possible that the cycles continuously change the perspective from which the pieces of information involved in the context of the problem-solving are evaluated (Kertész and Rákosi 2012: 129).

One of the first steps in the research process designed to develop a plausible explanation for the occurrence and identification of implicit arguments is the evaluation of the previous solutions available (cf. Chapter 2). These solutions have raised the question of what kinds of information license the occurrence of implicit arguments and guide their interpretation mechanisms. The above-mentioned complex approaches assume that both grammatical and pragmatic information have an important role, therefore the starting context of the initial problem of implicit arguments, which the transformation process sets out from (Kertész and Rákosi 2012: 134), includes a sub-problem, i.e. the nature of the relationship that can be assumed between grammar and pragmatics. There are rival approaches to the relationship between grammar and pragmatics which can be classified into four groups on the basis of their similarities and differences (Németh T. 2006, 2007; Németh T. and Bibok 2010).[3] In the first group of approaches, grammar and pragmatics are not separated from each other since language and language use are not distinguished from each other. The factors considered pragmatic by other theories are included in grammar and not treated separately. This treatment is followed by holistic cognitive grammars (e.g. Langacker 1987) and functional grammars (e.g. García Velasco and Portero Muñoz 2002; Cornish 2005), as well as by construction grammars, according to which pragmatic information is either involved in the constructions, i.e. in the meaning-form pairs of the grammar, or provides the necessary motivation for the existence of a construction (e.g. Goldberg 1995, 2005a, b). Similarly, in head-driven phrase structure grammar (HPSG) pragmatic information is included in the grammar (Pollard and Sag 1994; Engdahl 1999). In HPSG, the SYNTAX-SEMANTICS (SYNSEM) attribute contains the attribute CONTEXT (CONX) in addition to the attributes CATEGORY (CAT) and CONTENT (CONT). The attribute CONX involves information that bears on certain context-dependent aspects of semantic interpretation. Since pragmatic information is included, but not separately, in the grammars mentioned here, the question of how grammar and pragmatics interact cannot straightforwardly be raised in the first group of approaches. Following on from the theoretical stances of these theories, there is no need to deal within them with the question of the relationship between grammar and pragmatics. However, this does not mean that in the study of the behaviour of implicit arguments these approaches cannot take into consideration both grammatical and pragmatic (contextual) pieces of information, as is witnessed by the complex approaches developed, for instance, in construction grammar (Goldberg 1995, 2005a, b) as well as in functional discourse grammar (García Velasco and Portero Muñoz 2002; Cornish 2005).

The second group contains frameworks which consider pragmatics a functional perspective on any aspect of language and not an additional component of a theory of language (e.g. Wunderlich 1972; Mey 1993; Verschueren 1999). Pragmatics, in this view, concerns all levels of language and examines linguistic phenomena at any level according to the motivation and effects of the linguistic choices communicators make. Pragmatics has a considerable social relevance in these frameworks. The relationship between grammar and pragmatics cannot really be examined in functional pragmatics, either. Research in functional pragmatics does not concern the questions of how an utterance meaning is constructed by a speaker according to her/his intentions and how a hearer interprets the utterance meaning intended by the speaker, but, instead, addresses the questions of why an utterance is produced, why the particular linguistic form is selected by the communicator, and also what consequences the communicator's linguistic choices have. Pragmatics as a functional perspective examines and describes linguistic phenomena at all levels of language from the point of view of the properties of use. Although pragmatics is situated outside of grammar, there is no real possibility to assume an interaction between grammar and pragmatics. As to the investigation of the possibilities of the occurrence and identification of lexically unrealised arguments, this kind of pragmatics can concern the speaker's motivations for using implicit arguments in a given context and the consequences the speaker's choice has in the flow of communication (for the speaker's motivations for using implicit arguments, cf., Chapter 7), but cannot analyse how the meaning of an utterance with an implicit argument is constructed on the basis of grammatical and pragmatic requirements.

In the third view, pragmatics is one of the components of grammar (e.g. Levinson 1983). It intrudes into the lexicon, semantics, and syntax (Levinson 2000). For example, in the lexicon some kinds of contextual information should be taken into consideration to define the meanings of lexemes. In this case we involve pragmatic information in the lexicon of grammar. The semantic component of grammar also requires pragmatic information, i.e. in order to construct the meaning of sentences with deictic and indexical phrases, we should necessarily rely on the context. Levinson (2000) convincingly argues that syntax can also rely on pragmatics. The theory of generalised conversational implicatures helps syntax to account for anaphoric relations in a more adequate way. Newmeyer (2006) also considers pragmatics a component of grammar. In harmony with the generative framework, he assumes grammar with a modular architecture, but his approach also differs from Chomsky's (1977, 1995) and Kasher's (1986), because he takes pragmatics into account as a module of grammar. Newmeyer presupposes different principles for each component of grammar, i.e. syntax, semantics, and pragmatics. However, he emphasises an intensive interaction between these modules, differently from the classical Fodorian (1983) modularity hypothesis and similarly to the latest versions of generative grammar (cf. Chomsky 1995; Engdahl 1999). To summarise approaches in the third group, it can be noted that here pragmatics as a component of grammar and other components of grammar are in a close relationship. The difference between the first and the third group of approaches appears when we consider where and how pragmatic information is situated. In the first group, the pragmatic pieces of information are not separately involved in grammar, while in the third group they are. The grammatical and pragmatic licensing and identifying factors of implicit arguments can be investigated together.

Finally, the fourth group of theories considers pragmatics a component outside of grammar. There are at least two different approaches in this group. In addition to grammar, pragmatics is either a component of a theory of language (e.g. Kasher 1986) or cognition (e.g. Sperber and Wilson 2002). In the first case, pragmatics is mainly defined with regard to semantics, which is a component of grammar. There are theories which draw a strict dividing line between semantics and pragmatics, considering semantics truth-conditional and pragmatics post-semantic, as well as non-truth-conditional (e.g. Gazdar 1979), and there are theories which allow pragmatics to contact grammar through its semantic component (e.g. Leech 1983). Grammar and pragmatics are distinguished in the research framework of generative linguistics as well, but the treatment of the relationship between them has changed in the history of generative grammatical theory. The generative framework defines grammar and pragmatics on the basis of the distinction between grammatical competence and pragmatic competence, which are two separate modules of the human mind. According to Chomsky (1977) and Kasher (1986), grammatical competence is independent of pragmatic competence, consequently grammar is independent of pragmatics. However, pragmatics as a model of the faculty of language use cannot be considered independent of grammar, since its operation is based on grammar, i.e. the model of the knowledge of language. In the latest version of generative grammar, i.e. in the Minimalist Program, Chomsky (1995) emphasises the interface character of the two interpretive components – phonetic as well as logical form – in grammar. Logical form can be related to the conceptual-intentional system of the human mind. This potential relationship makes it possible to treat grammar and pragmatics as not independent, but to assume an interface between them (Engdahl 1999), which can yield a complex approach to implicit arguments as well.

The second approach, which situates pragmatics outside of grammar, considers pragmatics a component of cognition outside of the theory of language (Sperber and Wilson 2002). Its task is to describe and explain how ostensive-inferential communication operates. Since ostensive-inferential communication does not refer only to verbal communication but also to the various types of non-verbal communication as well as to the kinds of communication without any code use, pragmatics as a theory of ostensive-inferential communication is not an exclusively linguistic discipline. Natural languages enter ostensive-inferential communication in order to make information transmission in communication more effective and reliable (see Sperber 2000; Wharton 2003; Németh T. 2005), i.e. one of the main functions of languages in ostensive-inferential communication is to fulfil communicators' informative intentions. Language and linguistic communication are not independent in verbal communication; consequently, a contact can be supposed between grammar as a theory of language and pragmatics as a theory of communication. This contact makes it possible to analyse the behaviour of implicit arguments taking into account both grammatical and pragmatic information.

On the basis of this brief evaluation of the four groups of rival approaches, as well as their comparison, it is obvious that the question of interaction between grammar and pragmatics can be dealt with in the fourth group. However, the third group of approaches, according to which pragmatics is included in grammar, is also worth taking into consideration, because it assumes a close relationship between various components of grammar including pragmatics. And, further, according to the approaches in the first group, grammar also contains pragmatic information. To summarise: the majority of the theories mentioned in this section agree on the point that grammar and pragmatics cannot work adequately without each other in the various forms of language use. So, if one decides to study implicit arguments in language use, one should necessarily consider both grammatical and pragmatic factors.

The critical evaluation of rival hypotheses about the relationship between grammar and pragmatics has helped me to formulate my views on this topic, developing mainly the ideas of the third and fourth groups of approaches. I define grammar as the explicit model of the knowledge of language, i.e. grammatical competence, which is a component of the theory of language, not independent of pragmatics, while pragmatics can be characterised as the model of the faculty of language use, i.e. pragmatic competence, which is another component of the theory of language, not independent of grammar (Németh T. and Bibok 2010). Pragmatic competence is not restricted to one module of the human mind. It contains and organises procedural and declarative knowledge concerning not only communicative but all possible forms of language use (Németh T. 2004: 385). Consequently, pragmatics as a model of pragmatic competence should describe and explain not only communicative language use, i.e. verbal communication, but other forms of language use, e.g. informative language use and also manipulative language use (Németh T. 2008b). Although implicit pieces of information have an important role in all forms of language use, in the present book I only deal with communicative language use and focus on the implicit arguments as a kind of implicit information in verbal communication.

Consequently, I consider the interaction between grammar and pragmatics to be in essence a co-operation of two separate, but not independent components of the theory of language in order to account for how the knowledge of language and faculty of language use interact in particular contexts of language use. Nevertheless, I also accept that, when detached from its particular contexts, not only does some contextual information become context-independent, i.e. general pragmatic information, but also that such encyclopaedic information or information concerning the use of language can be fixed as integral parts of semantic representations of lexical entries (see Németh T. and Bibok 2010).

It is worth noting that the above-mentioned definitions of grammar and pragmatics do not rely on the classic, strict modularity hypothesis proposed by Fodor (1983), according to which modules of the human mind are unique, independent, informationally encapsulated systems. In addition to neurolinguistic evidence, Sperber's (2000) extended modularity hypothesis has served as one of the starting points to formulate my definitions. The extended modularity hypothesis suggests that, in addition to peripheral systems, there is not only one central system in the human mind as Fodor (1983) proposes. Instead, peripheral systems are connected with more than one conceptual module. The conceptual modules themselves are not independent of each other; an intensive interaction can be supposed between them.

The cyclic and prismatic nature of the plausible argumentation process also yields that the researcher in the course of the construction of a new solution to a problem returns to the previous stages in the problem-solving, e.g. to previous alternative or rival solutions and compares them to her/his own solution in order to check whether it is more plausible than the previous solutions (Kertész and Rákosi 2012: 138). In accordance with this practice, I have also compared my view on the notions of grammar and pragmatics, as well as the interaction between them, to previous opinions. My approach to grammar and pragmatics and to their interaction can be related, firstly, to Leech's (1983) idea that pragmatics is a component of the theory of language situated outside grammar, secondly, to Chomsky's (1977, 1995) and Kasher's (1986) proposals according to which grammar and pragmatics are models of the grammatical and pragmatic competences, i.e. faculties of the human mind, respectively, and thirdly, to Sperber's (2000) and Sperber and Wilson's (2002) extended modularity hypothesis, which allows an intensive interaction between grammar and pragmatics. A possibility of the interaction between grammar and pragmatics through logical form is also provided in Chomsky's (1995) Minimalist Program. Fourthly, in connection with the appearance of encyclopaedic information or information concerning the use of language in the lexicon of grammar, I must refer to similar ideas expressed by Levinson (1983) about the intrusion of pragmatics into the lexicon of grammar.[4]

However, my views of grammar and pragmatics and the relationship between them differ from Leech's (1983), because I do not restrict the interaction between grammar and pragmatics to the relationship between semantics and pragmatics. In this respect I agree with Levinson's (2000) and Newmeyer's (2006) suggestions that pragmatics can intrude into all components of grammar, including the lexicon, semantics, and also syntax. At the same time, I do not consider pragmatics a component of grammar as Levinson and Newmeyer do. I define pragmatics as the model of pragmatic competence and grammar as the model of grammatical competence (Németh T. 2004; Németh T. and Bibok 2010). Most recent neurolinguistic and neuropragmatic research (e.g. Paradis 1998; Ivaskó 2002) supports the ideas of both the real existence of pragmatic competence and the separate location of grammatical and pragmatic abilities in the brain. While grammatical competence is located in the left hemisphere, pragmatic competence is located in the right one. In contrast with damage in the left hemisphere, lesions in the right hemisphere do not lead to grammatical (i.e. phonological, morphological, or syntactic) deficits, i.e. to a kind of aphasia, but they result in considerable systematic dysfunctions in the course of the production and interpretation of pragmatic phenomena such as indirect speech acts, conversational implicatures, metaphors, humour, discourse coherence, etc. However, grammatical and pragmatic abilities interact in language use. On the basis of these neurolinguistic and neuropragmatic results, if grammatical and pragmatic competences are conceived of as two separate but interacting abilities, it is reasonable not to take pragmatics as a component of grammar, but instead to consider it a separate component of the theory of language in addition to grammar, while assuming an intensive interaction between them.

My approach also differs from Chomsky's (1977) and Kasher's (1986), since it does not treat grammatical competence as independent of pragmatic competence, so it does not draw a strict, impenetrable boundary between grammar and pragmatics. My proposal is also different from Chomsky's (1995) solution in the Minimalist Program, because I do not restrict the interaction between grammar and pragmatics to an interface between the logical form of grammar and the conceptual-intentional system of mind. And finally, my approach also differs from Sperber's (2000) and Sperber and Wilson's (2002), because I regard pragmatics, i.e. a model of pragmatic competence, as a component of the theory of language which is responsible not only for verbal communication, but also for all forms of language use.

To summarise: in my approach both grammar and pragmatics are considered components of the theory of language, and an intensive interaction is assumed between them. I also deem an interaction between grammar and pragmatics possible in such a way that encyclopaedic information or information concerning the use of language can be fixed in the lexical-semantic representations of words. This latter assumption also has an important role in the explanation of the occurrences of implicit arguments in Hungarian (see Chapter 4). On the basis of the comparison of my view to rival hypotheses, I consider my conception a more plausible solution since (i) it integrates the features from the previous approaches which are in harmony with the latest neurolinguistic findings as well as the results of the particular analyses of language use, and (ii) it disregards the features which are inconsistent with them.

After having evaluated rival hypotheses about the relationship between grammar and pragmatics, clarified what I mean by grammar and pragmatics and what relationship I suppose between them, and compared my conception to the rival solutions, let us turn to another theoretical choice I have taken in the course of my research.

1.2.2 Utterances instead of sentences

Before starting research into lexically unrealised arguments in Hungarian, my second theoretical decision concerns where to examine implicit arguments or, to formulate this more precisely, in what units to analyse them. From theoretical decisions regarding the notion of grammatical and pragmatic competences, the conceptions of grammar and pragmatics, and the interaction between grammar and pragmatics in the language use described in Section 1.2.1, it follows that a researcher involved in a particular research programme into a given problem of the investigation of language use should apply the kind of theoretical framework, methodology, and data which are in harmony with the theoretical decisions taken. More concretely, the researcher should take into account the various manifestations of the interaction between grammar and pragmatics in language use in the practice of research. Thus, my study on the occurrences and interpretation of implicit arguments should start from the assumption that in addition to grammatical constraints, general pragmatic and particular contextual factors can influence the licensing and interpretation of lexically unrealised arguments, and, moreover, that in these processes grammatical, general pragmatic, and particular contextual pieces of information interact. Assuming such an interaction, implicit arguments cannot be described and explained only in sentential environments, i.e. in sentences which are the units of grammatical competence strictly determined by the grammar of a particular language (Chomsky 1986: 3; Németh T. 1995: 393). Instead, in the research the utterance environment of implicit arguments should be taken into account. Moreover, in most cases the utterance environment must be extended with information from a larger context, i.e. information from the previous discourse context, from the directly observable physical environment of the utterance in which the implicit argument occurs, and from encyclopaedic knowledge (see Sperber and Wilson 1986/1995: 137–142; Németh T. and Bibok 2010; and Chapter 5). Utterances are meant as units of language use, which have both grammatical and pragmatic properties. It is worth noting that not all kinds of linguistic theories distinguish between sentences and utterances. The functional or holistic cognitive grammatical approaches which do not differentiate language and language use by rejecting the Saussurean opposition of 'langue' and 'parole', as well as Chomskyan grammatical and pragmatic competence, do not distinguish between the terms *sentence* and *utterance*. Both terms are used in these frameworks in a similar meaning: 'unit of language use'. An abstract, structural unit of language independent of meanings and functions in language use is not assumed by these frameworks as it is in the formal, structural approaches.[5]

Language use can be studied from at least two perspectives. On the one hand, in Section 1.2.1 we have seen that pragmatic competence can be considered a faculty of the human mind which is responsible for language use, i.e. it contains knowledge about how to use language in particular situations to achieve different human purposes. So, language use can be studied from the perspective of pragmatic competence. On the other hand, language use can be investigated on the basis of real, particular manifestations of the knowledge of language use in various contexts, taking into consideration interactions of grammatical and pragmatic competences with other systems of knowledge, memory, and perception in particular contexts. So, language use can be studied from the perspective of performance. Utterances can be examined from both perspectives. As to the pragmatic competence perspective, utterances are examined as units of various forms of language use, i.e. as communicative, informative, or manipulative forms, and also as linguistic examples from intuition (Németh T. 2008b) referred to as utterance-types. The particular, physically observable forms of communicative language use can be analysed through the examination of discourses. In the present book, the term *discourse* without any adjective is applied not only to spoken products of language use, but also to written ones, since it refers to all kinds of discourses, i.e. monologic and dialogic discourses, and conversation. To describe discourses adequately one has to characterise the common substantive features of particular utterances and the sequences which make up coherent discourses. These features can be formulated by postulating utterance-types, which disregard any individual, accidental, or contingent filling of contextual factors and take into account only the general pragmatic and contextual categories of communicative interaction with their potential values. Therefore, utterance-types as units of pragmatic competence can be defined as (7) (Németh T. 1995: 394, 1996: 17–40).

(7) $u_t = (\text{ins } (pu, c, p, t)$

The utterance-type u_t is an inscription *ins* that a person p relates to a pragmatic unit pu at a time t in a context c. The term *inscription* refers to a realisation in a physical medium, i.e. it indicates that from the two meanings of the word *utterance*, u_t refers to the 'product' meaning and not the 'process' meaning. The definition in (7) is neutral with respect to the production and interpretation of *ins*. It says only that an utterance-type is a product of some cognitive activities. If the person p is the communicator, then the definition can be paraphrased as follows: the utterance-type u_t is an inscription *ins* that the communicator uses as a pragmatic unit pu at a time t in a context c. If the person p is the communicative partner, then the definition can be paraphrased as follows: the utterance-type u_t is an inscription *ins* that the communicative partner interprets as a pragmatic unit pu at a time t in a context c.

Since the utterance-type is conceived of as the unit of pragmatic competence, i.e. the knowledge of language use, it must be characterised from both grammatical and pragmatic points of view. The grammatical description of utterance-types can be given by relating them to the corresponding well-formed sentences. There are two basic classes of utterance-types in this respect. The members of the first class can be related to sentences – units of grammatical competence – since they have linguistic structure *ls*. Utterance-types in this class can have either a complete or an elliptical sentence structure. It can also happen that they only consist of a constituent which can be integrated into the syntactic structure of a sentence, and the missing parts of the sentence can be recovered from the context directly, rather than through an elliptical or anaphoric relation. The members of the second class either do not have any linguistic structure or they do not contain a constituent which can be integrated into the syntactic structure of a sentence, but consist only of one lexical entry le_{int}, namely, an interjection or an idiom-like interjection which cannot be integrated into the structure of well-formed sentences. Implicit arguments can only occur in the first class of utterance-types which has the linguistic structure *ls*.

(8)

$$pu = (\begin{Bmatrix} ls \\ le_{int} \end{Bmatrix}, pf)$$

The pragmatic description of utterance-types can be made by defining the pragmatic functions *pf* utterance-types play in language use with respect to context *c*. Previously, I suggested that the context *c* consists of two parts, namely, the physically observable context c_{phys} and the cognitive context c_{cog} (Németh T. 1995, 1996). In accordance with the results of my particular analyses of the occurrences of implicit arguments as well as findings in the pragmatic literature, I propose to treat encyclopaedic pieces of information and information from the preceding discourse separately, since they can have different linguistic markers (see Chapter 5). Thus, in the communicative form of language use, the context contains pieces of information from the immediately observable physical environment c_{phys}, from the encyclopaedic knowledge of communicative partners c_{enc}, and from the preceding discourse c_{disc} (Sperber and Wilson 1986/1995: 137–142; Németh T. and Bibok 2010; Németh T. 2012).

(9) $c = (c_{phys}, c_{enc}, c_{disc})$

In Chapter 3, starting with a discussion of the possibile occurrences and identification of implicit verbal arguments in Hungarian language use, I will also introduce the terms *immediate utterance context* and *extended context*. The immediate utterance context refers to the narrow linguistic utterance environment of the implicit arguments with its grammatical and encyclopaedic properties (cf. also Groefsema 1995), while the extended context refers to the broader context of utterance in which implicit arguments occur. The extended context of utterances involves further contextual information in comparison with the immediate utterance context of implicit arguments. The extended context contains information from the physical context c_{phys}, from the encyclopaedic knowledge of communicative partners c_{enc} and from the preceding discourse c_{disc} (see (9)). The distinction between these two terms helps to grasp the order of licensing and identification mechanisms of implicit arguments.

In the communicative form of language use, pragmatic functions of utterance types can have the following appropriate values in particular utterance-tokens: function of literalness f_{lit}, interpersonal function f_{ip}, illocutionary function f_{ill}, and attitudinal function f_{att}.

(10) $pf = (f_{lit}, f_{ip}, f_{ill}, f_{att})$

According to the function of literalness f_{lit}, an utterance-type can be used literally or non-literally. Non-literal uses result in implicitly conveyed pieces of information. The interpersonal function f_{ip} concerns the starting, maintaining and finishing of communicative interaction, while illocutionary function f_{ill} indicates what kind of illocutionary act can be performed by the utterance-type. And, finally, attitudinal function f_{att} refers to what speaker's attitude can be assigned to the utterance-type. The pragmatic functions of utterance-types belong to general pragmatic knowledge and can be distinguished from the particular contextual information in particular discourses, which either coincides with the predictions of general pragmatic knowledge or differs from it. In this latter case the particular contextual information can override the information from general pragmatic knowledge. This differentiation has an important role in the licensing and interpretation of implicit arguments, especially in the course of the use and recovery of zero anaphors (see Pléh 1994, 1998; Németh T. and Bibok 2010 as well as Sections 5.1 and 6.1).

The elements involved in defining the utterance-type acquire particular values in real, particular manifestations of language use, as I pointed out when I characterised the various pragmatic functions utterance-types can have. Manifestations of utterance-types in particular language use are called utterance-tokens. Since in the present book I will analyse particular manifestations of utterance-types from various data sources, henceforth I will, for the sake of convenience, use the term *utterance* in the meaning of utterance-token, and when I wish to refer to the units of pragmatic competence (and not performance) I will use the term *utterance-type*.

To summarise: on the basis of the above-mentioned theoretical considerations, I will study how Hungarian verbs can occur with various types of implicit arguments and how language users can interpret lexically unrealised verbal arguments in particular utterances of language use in a complex approach, instead of investigating implicit arguments in sentences from basically syntactic or semantic or phonological perspectives as the majority of Hungarian researchers have done in their previous studies.[6] From the two theoretical decisions I have taken, according to which I assume that grammar and pragmatics interact and implicit arguments are investigated in utterances, it follows that verbal argument structure must be regarded not only as an interface between semantics and the syntax of verbs as indicated above in Section 1.1 and with reference to some grammatical tradition (Rappoport-Hovav and Levin 1995, 2001; Bresnan 1995, 2001), but also as an interface between semantics, syntax, and pragmatics.

1.2.3 Data, data sources and the relationship between theory and data in the course of research

In the last two decades several books and articles have been published discussing the notion of linguistic data and evidence in various linguistic fields and approaches (e.g., Lehmann 2004; Penke and Rosenbach 2004; Borsley 2005;

Kepser and Reis 2005; Kertész and Rákosi 2008a, 2009, 2012, 2014; Németh T. and Bibok 2010).[7] These works have attempted to answer questions regarding the nature and functions of data and evidence and the relationship between data/evidence and the hypotheses of linguistic theories. Lehmann (2004: 191–195) discusses the role and function of data in linguistic theorising, taking into consideration both the researcher's and the audience's perspectives. As to the users of linguistic data, Lehmann distinguishes between the researcher who takes linguistic data for granted and the audience of the research. For a researcher it is her/his epistemic interest that triggers the research including the supply of data. From the point of view of a researcher, linguistic data can be used (i) as the basis of an inductive construction of a hypothesis, (ii) as a test of theorems that were deduced, and (iii) can play the argumentative role of evidence for a theory (Lehmann 2004: 191). The first two functions can be grasped in the course of the research, but the third function operates when reporting on the research. Examining these three functions of linguistic data, Kertész and Rákosi (2008b: 390–392) criticise Lehmann's approach. In their opinion, Lehmann does not clarify what relationship can be assumed between these three functions of data, which raises certain problems. According to Kertész and Rákosi, the reasons for these problems are as follows. Lehmann (2004: 208) emphasises that, on the one hand, linguistic data in the first function are theory and problem dependent, and, on the other hand, linguistic data are suitable to fulfil the second function only if they are independent of any theory and problem which is principally characteristic of raw data. Raw data which represent the whole speech situation are the most ideal type of data recorded in the form of a non-symbolic representation (Lehmann 2004: 183, 205–208). They are the kind of data which to a great extent fulfil the expectation that data should be outside of and independent of the researcher (Lehmann 2004: 181). The third function of linguistic data, i.e. the functioning as arguments for a theory in a particular argumentative process of reporting on research, is absolutely theory dependent. Kertész and Rákosi (2008b: 390–392) consider these statements controversial, because they point in the opposite direction regarding the relationship between the theory and data, or more precisely, theory and problem (in)dependence. However, two remarks seem to be necessary with regard to Kertész and Rákosi's criticism. Firstly, one has to take into account that Lehmann makes a clear, essential distinction between the roles of data in the research itself and in the reporting on the research. Secondly, if one does not assume that data can fulfil Lehmann's three functions simultaneously at the same time, which is not possible without resulting in circularity, but rather one examines the role of data in the course of the whole research, it can be established that various kinds of data from different sources have different functions according to the particular phases of the research (cf. Nagy C. 2008). Data used in the research have different functions than data used in the presentation of the results of the research. On the basis of these two remarks, it is not necessary to consider Lehmann's functions of linguistic data problematic, because it is not the case that one and the same piece of data is theory and problem dependent as well as theory and problem independent at the same time. However, it must be admitted that there is no ideal case, not even with raw data, when the researcher has no influence on the data, i.e. between the researcher and data there always exist certain theoretical considerations (cf. Nagy C. 2008).

From the point of view of the reader of a scientific report, linguistic data also have various functions (Lehmann 2004: 194). Firstly, if the reader is more interested in the theoretical achievements than in the linguistic data underlying them, then (s)he can join the author of the report in taking the data for granted. In this case, the reader's consideration of the data depends on the confidence that (s)he has in the author and her/his sources of data.

Secondly, if the reader is more interested in the linguistic data than in the theoretical results, then (s)he may want to check the author's data because either (s)he mistrusts the author or (s)he might develop an interest in the data that goes beyond the author's original intention (Lehmann 2004: 194). However, a remark seems to be in order in connection with these two functions of linguistic data. These two functions can be mixed for the reader. It can happen that the reader has an additional spectrum of data which does not seem to support the theoretical results based on the author's data. In this case, (s)he may want to check the author's data as well as the theoretical achievements based on them and to reformulate the theoretical hypothesis by considering her/his own additional data as well. Furthermore, taking into account a new spectrum of data from new sources can also contribute to the elimination of inconsistencies and contradictions in the previous and the author's own research.

According to Lehmann (2004: 194), there is a third function of linguistic data for the reader: namely, they may also fulfil the function of illustration. In this expository function, data serve as examples in the presentation of the research in order to play the argumentative role of evidence for the author's theoretical results and to persuade the reader.

On the basis of Lehmann's treatment of linguistic data and the remarks added to them above, one can conclude, firstly, that linguistic data can have various functions both from the point of view of the researcher and that of the reader, and that secondly, these functions can be mixed; thirdly, there is an apparent relationship between the functions of data for the researcher and the reader, and, fourthly, the researcher and the reader always, but not to the same extent, influence the status of those linguistic phenomena which may or may not serve as a basis for data.

After discussing the above-mentioned functions of linguistic data theoretically, three questions have to be addressed in the practice of research into the occurrence of verbs with implicit arguments in Hungarian. They are as follows: (i) what kinds of data have to be used in the research and in what functions, (ii) what relationship can be assumed between the theory and data in the research itself and the presentation of the results of the research, and (iii) can data from various data sources be integrated into the research.

The initial hypotheses of the research I report on in the present book were that, firstly, all Hungarian verbs can occur with implicit arguments, but they differ in what manner and in what contexts they can be used with lexically unrealised arguments; secondly, although the lexical-semantic properties of verbs can strongly determine the manner of the occurrence of verbs with implicit arguments in Hungarian as in other languages (see Chapter 2), the licensing and interpretation of implicit arguments are, by their nature, complex procedures, i.e. in addition to the lexical-semantic factors one also has to take into account grammatical, general pragmatic, and particular contextual factors, and even their intensive interaction (see Chapters 4–6).

In constructing these hypotheses, I relied on (i) the theoretical considerations presented in Sections 1.1, 1.2.1, and 1.2.2, (ii) definitions and data from other languages reported on in the literature (see Chapter 2), (iii) my previous results (e.g., Németh T. 2000, 2001, 2010, 2012, 2014b; Bibok and Németh T. 2001; Németh T. and Bibok 2010), and (iv) my data from the various direct data sources presented below. The theoretical considerations and my definition of implicit arguments in a complex approach (see Section 3.1) influenced my decisions concerning the selection of data. The sentence-oriented approaches to implicit arguments in Hungarian relied mostly on data from intuition and introspection. However, as indicated in Section 1.2.2, I decided, firstly, to study the occurrence of verbs with implicit arguments in utterances and not in sentences. Therefore, those occurrences of implicit arguments which were excluded because of their strong context-dependence by sentence-oriented approaches also became data for my research (see, e.g., the occurrence of the implicit argument *a gólyával* 'by the stork' in (6) in Section 1.1 as well as (18b) in Section 2.1). The use and interpretation of verbs with implicit arguments in utterances in contexts of language use can be investigated, for instance, by searching for occurrences in various written and spoken corpora (e.g., Hungarian National Corpus at corpus.nytud.hu/mnsz or various Hungarian spoken corpora, including my own 310-minute long Hungarian spoken corpus),[8] or by conducting different thought experiments in which we imagine and assign appropriate situations to implicit arguments. However, it must be emphasised that researchers also have to rely on their own intuition when searching a corpus in order to exclude those utterances which contain a performance error instead of an implicit argument. Similarly, in thought experiments the researcher starts out from her/his own intuition in the course of building or selecting a context to an utterance. Therefore, it is plausible to assume that acquiring data from intuition, corpora, and thought experiments share some common points (see Németh T. 2010: 340). Furthermore, during the design of a real experiment or a minimal-pair experiment, and evaluating their results, the researcher also uses her/his own intuition regarding the language or language use. Therefore, it can be generalised that when a researcher collects data (s)he always relies on her/his intuition, in some sense independently of what kind of data sources (s)he takes into consideration.

Thus, in my research, relying on my definition of implicit arguments (see Section 3.1) as well as my own intuition, it was also possible to exclude those utterances which contained a performance error instead of an implicit argument. Secondly, in each phase of the research the selection of data was also driven by particular aims and problems. Data selected this way always influenced the actual argumentation process, which, subsequently, influenced the subsequent data selection (Kertész and Rákosi 2009; 2012).

Data selected in this manner originated in various kinds of direct sources. However, it has to be noted that researchers do not agree on how to define the directness of data sources. On the basis of Rescher's (1976: 6) approach to plausible reasoning, Kertész and Rákosi (2012, 2014) consider perceptual experience, experiments, a theory, an application of a method, a historical document, etc. as direct data sources in their Plausible Argumentation Model. This conception of direct data sources differs from Penke and Rosenbach's (2004: 487–488) idea, according to which data from direct sources directly mirror the knowledge of her/his language. Thus, Penke and Rosenbach evaluate data from written and spoken corpora, as well as grammaticality judgments, as data from direct sources, but data from psycholinguistic experiments as data from indirect sources. In contrast, Kertész and Rákosi (2012, 2014) consider all these data sources direct. In my research I follow this latter conception of direct data sources. Taking into account data from various direct sources eliminates the disadvantages of using only a particular data source and increases the plausibility of conclusions made on the basis of the analyses (see Dörnyei 2007; Kertész and Rákosi 2009, 2012; Németh T. 2010).[9]

Furthermore, Kertész and Rákosi (2012: 169–185) propose a new interpretation of the term *datum* as well. Consider (11):

(11)   A **datum** is a statement with a positive plausibility value originating from some direct source.

(Kertész and Rákosi 2012: 169)

As it can be seen in (11), Kertész and Rákosi (2012: 169–187) do not restrict data to their informational content; instead, they assign a structure to data. Data consist of an informational content and a plausibility value. To put it the other way round, data are plausible statements and not only a pure occurrence of a linguistic phenomenon in a corpus or a sentence coming from one's intuition. Data cannot be deemed true with certainty, but they can be considered more or less reliable truth-candidates (Kertész and Rákosi 2012: 50). The plausibility of data is initially determined by their source or, more precisely, by the reliability of their source (Kertész and Rákosi 2012: 170). The more reliable the source the higher plausibility value can be assigned to the data. The initial plausibility values of data can change in the course of the research, for instance, if there are other supporting or non-supporting sources.

Let us take an example. In traditional grammars of Hungarian (cf., e.g., Keszler 2000) verbs of natural phenomena such as *hajnalodik* '[for day to] break' are considered subjectless, i.e. they cannot occur with an explicit subject. Relying on the subjectless occurrences of *hajnalodik* cited in traditional grammars of Hungarian and considering Kertész and Rákosi's (2012: 169) definition of data in (11), the structure of data in traditional grammars of Hungarian can be reconstructed as a plausible statement in (12).

(12)   The verb *hajnalodik* is a verb of natural phenomena and it cannot occur with explicit subjects.

However, in the Hungarian National Corpus (corpus.nytud.hu/mnsz) one can find a considerable number of occurrences of *hajnalodik* (and other verbs of natural phenomena) with explicit subject as, e.g., in (13).

(13)   *Hajnalodik*   *az   idő.*
       [for day] breaks.INDEF   the   time.NOM
       'The day is breaking. [lit. The time is coming to dawn.]'[10]

On the basis of the occurrence of the verb *hajnalodik* with explicit subject *az idő* 'the time' in (13), the plausible statement in (14) can be constructed.

(14)   The verb *hajnalodik* is a verb of natural phenomena and it can occur with explicit subjects.

Notice that there is a contradiction between (12) and (14). This contradiction can be eliminated if we compare the plausibility values of (12) and (14). According to traditional grammars of Hungarian, (13) is not acceptable. But on the basis of the

Hungarian National Corpus, grammaticality judgments of other native speakers of Hungarian, and my own intuition, (13) can be evaluated as acceptable. Since the datum in (14) built on the occurrences with explicit subjects is supported by more direct data sources, it is much more plausible than (12); i.e. (12) loses its plausibility.

Relying on Kertész and Rákosi's (2012) conceptions of data and data sources, the data in my research were selected from the following direct sources. One of the main sources of data in my research is various corpora. I collected data from both spoken and written corpora. I have my own 310-minute long Hungarian spoken corpus, which consists of eight interviews with eight different people who differ from each other in gender, age, education, profession, and place of residence. The interviews lasted 30–45 minutes. Two interviewers conducted the interviews, one of them conducting three interviews, the other five. Each interviewee was asked similar questions regarding her/his life, family, childhood, work, and hobbies. The interviewers let the informants speak spontaneously as much as was possible. All of the informants agreed to the use of her/his interview for the purposes of linguistic analyses.[11] I transcribed the spoken interviews and segmented them into utterances on the basis of the definition of utterance-types in (7) in Section 1.2.2 and the phonetic properties of spoken Hungarian (see Németh T. 1996). The written version of my spoken corpus is a 189-page text (22 lines per page, 57–60 characters a line). Since in the present book I do not aim to analyse this corpus from a conversation analytical point of view, I do not apply any special notation when I use occurrences from this corpus and the data built on them as illustrations.

The written corpus I used in my research was the Hungarian National Corpus (corpus.nytud.hu/mnsz). It currently contains 187.6 million words and is divided into five subcorpora by regional language variants (Hungary, Slovakia, Subcarpathia, Transylvania, and Vojvodina) and also into five subcorpora by text genres (press, literature, science, official, and personal). Texts from the news media make up almost half of the corpus, presenting a broad range of dialects, both vertically and horizontally. The literature subcorpus fully incorporates material from the Digital Literary Academy (Digitális Irodalmi Akadémia: pim.hu/dia/). The source of scientific texts is the Hungarian Electronic Library (Magyar Elektronikus Könyvtár: http://mek.oszk.hu/). Official texts include regulations, laws, by-laws, and parliamentary debates. The personal subcorpus contains discussions from Internet forums (the forums of the biggest and oldest Hungarian Internet portal: index.hu and several forums from Subcarpathia). This language variant is particularly interesting because it stands closest to spontaneous linguistic communication; moreover, in some cases it is very similar to spoken communication. The subcorpus to be studied can be chosen to include any combination of these.

The relevant characteristic of the Hungarian National Corpus is its detailed morphosyntactic annotation. Every word form is annotated with stem, part of speech, and inflectional information. This kind of information is especially useful for the study of verbs with implicit subject and direct object arguments.[12]

In addition to my spoken corpus and the Hungarian National Corpus, I also used definitions of various verbs in Hungarian monolingual dictionaries, analyses of my previous papers (see, e.g., Németh T. 2000, 2001, 2008a, 2010, 2012; 2014a, b; Bibok and Németh T. 2001; Németh T. and Bibok 2010), and comparisons with other languages treated in the literature (see Chapter 2) as a corpus.

The second main source of data in my research was intuition. My own and some other informants' intuition also provided a wide range of data. And thirdly, I also acquired data from experiments: minimal pair and thought experiments. However, this kind of classification of the direct sources of data is also problematic. For example, data from other researchers' experiments can be considered data from corpora for particular subsequent research, and data from minimal pair and thought experiments can be treated as introspective data as well.[13]

The occurrences and interpretation mechanisms of Hungarian verbs with implicit arguments were systematically analysed in my research in a complex approach, i.e. from the point of view of the lexical-semantic representations of verbs, grammatical and general pragmatic properties of utterances, as well as particular contexts. The results of the analyses support my initial hypotheses (see Chapters 3–6). In the course of research, the relationship between hypotheses, theory, and data are not linear and unidirectional (Kertész and Rákosi 2009, 2012; Németh T. 2010, 2014a). The formulation of the initial assumptions can be considered hypothesis construction by means of inductive procedures. Since among the data which serve as the basis for the induction there can also be theoretical considerations and definitions, the initial assumptions can also be evaluated as derived theoretical theses, the plausibility of which must be supported by data, i.e. which must be made plausible by linguistic data. However, data are theory and problem dependent (Kertész and Rákosi 2009, 2012; Németh T. 2010). It is always the particular requirements and steps of the research that determine the data selection. It must be particularly emphasised that among data there can occur utterances with various performance errors, but if this is not the case, then different utterances do not have equal importance and relevance as data for research. It can also occur that data used to support a hypothesis influence the theoretical considerations underlying the hypotheses at stake, which can result in modification of the hypotheses (Nagy C. 2008).

On the basis of the above-mentioned statements concerning the functions and sources of data, one can conclude that, firstly, it is not reasonable to sharply separate the process of hypothesis construction and the process of making a hypothesis plausible. Secondly, the relationship between theory and data must be thought of as cyclic and prismatic, and it is always the actual argumentation process which determines what can serve as data and in what functions (Kertész and Rákosi 2009, 2012; Németh T. 2010; Section 1.2.2).

In the course of the presentation of the analyses and results of my research in the present book, I do not rely on all data used in the research itself. Since the role of data in the reporting on the research is to serve as evidence for the theory and to persuade the reader (Lehmann 2004), I have attempted to select the kind of data used in the research itself which is most suitable to illustrate and support the theoretical theses. Data applied in the presentation of my results in this book came mostly from the following direct sources:

a. corpora including recorded interviews, the Hungarian National Corpus (corpus. nytud.hu/mnsz), the Concise Explanatory Dictionary of Hungarian, and data reported on in the literature: e.g. (6), (13), (63), (85), (150), (161)–(164), (197)–(198);

b. intuition and introspection including my own intuition and introspection and that of some other informants: e.g. (19), (70), (77), (80)–(81), (84), (101), (134)–(137);

c. experiments, including minimal pair and thought experiments:[14] e.g. (69), (89), (90)–(99), (144)–(147), (151)–(154).

One of the methodological requirements of partly pragmatically oriented research is that it also relies on spontaneous occurrences of the investigated phenomena in spoken forms of language use. According to Lehmann (2004: 183, 205–208), these occurrences count as raw data, which is the ideal type of data. However, it must be noted that Lehmann's (2004) notion of data differs from Kertész and Rákosi's (2009, 2012) data conceptions applied in the present book. Lehmann (2004) interprets *raw data* as linguistic occurrences in spontaneous spoken language use, but the term can be interpreted in the sense of (11) as statements with positive plausibility values originating from spontaneous spoken discourses. From here on I will use the term *raw data* in this meaning. Lehman emphasises that raw data are less theory-dependent data recorded in the form of non-symbolic representation and represent the whole speech situation. They are the kind of data which mostly fulfil the expectation that data should be outside of and independent of the researcher (Lehmann 2004: 181). However, the discussion on the relationship between theory and data based on Kertész and Rákosi's (2009, 2012) proposal and my previous analyses (Németh T. 2010) have revealed that there is no datum totally independent of a theory, or at least a hypothesis.

Applying raw data has several other problems as well (Németh T. 2010: 337–338). Firstly, raw occurrences in a spoken corpus have to be analysed very carefully from the point of view of the context, in order to construct the explicit and implicit meanings of utterances the speakers intend to convey. Secondly, even if we analyse the spontaneous use of language in a particular context very carefully, we cannot be quite sure whether the speakers have the same intentions, attitudes, thoughts, beliefs, and background knowledge which we as researchers attribute to them, i.e. we can never know whether the researchers' meaning construction of the speakers' utterances is correct.[15] Thirdly, even if we have very large spontaneous spoken corpora consisting of more than several hundred million words, we cannot extract from them the various, systematically changing interpretation possibilities of utterances. And, fourthly, it may happen that raw occurrences in a spontaneous spoken corpus do not involve utterances which demonstrate the phenomena studied in the research to an appropriate extent. Because of these problems, it can be fruitful to use other direct sources such as minimal pair experiments usually applied in sentence-oriented research, and thought experiments usually applied in pragmatically oriented research. As indicated above, in a thought experiment we fix the contextual factors in all phases of the experiment, including the mental states of the language users, and then we change one factor, as is widely accepted in minimal pair experiments. In this way we can construct all interpretation variations which are possible in principle and evaluate them. By applying this method, we can also study interpretation possibilities which may not occur among raw data. Thought experiments have a further advantage in reporting on pragmatically oriented research: they are extremely illustrative, i.e. they can contribute to the effectiveness of the researchers' efforts to persuade the reader.[16]

The theoretical and methodological considerations discussed so far served as background assumptions for my research into implicit arguments in Hungarian, which explains and supports the length and depth of the discussion. When evaluating rival hypotheses from the literature as well as different interpretations of various occurrences of verbs with implicit and explicit arguments, I also relied on these background assumptions. Moreover, it was also necessary to reveal those background assumptions of the rival solutions which they left invisible, but which were needed in order to decide whether their inferences were plausible. Thus, by presenting my initial theoretical decisions and their consequences here and in the previous sections, I made manifest some of the latent background assumptions of my research. These latent assumptions are needed to secure the plausibility of my final conclusions (for a more detailed discussion of the role of latent background assumptions in inference processes, see Kertész and Rákosi 2012: 85–128.)

1.3 Aims and organisation of the book

The present book is intended to summarise the results of my previous research into implicit arguments in Hungarian and to enrich them in several new respects. The main aim of my volume is to study various grammatical (including lexical-semantic and morphosyntactic), general pragmatic, and particular contextual factors which license occurrences of Hungarian verbs with implicit subject and direct object arguments in an intensive interaction and guide their interpretation mechanisms, on the basis of the analyses of data from different direct sources mentioned in Section 1.2.3. In addition to this main aim, I also intend to set up a typology of Hungarian verbs according to the possibilities of their occurrences with implicit arguments and reveal what motivations underlie the use of lexically unrealised arguments and what principles guide their interpretation mechanisms. The individual chapters have their own sub-aims, the achieving of which results in new conclusions compared to the previous treatment of implicit arguments in Hungarian. Furthermore, in some sections I also reflect on my research from a metatheoretical point of view in order to shed light on how methodological decisions can influence the process of research into implicit arguments in Hungarian and the formulation of conclusions.

The organisation of the book is as follows. After the introductory Chapter 1, in Chapter 2 I will briefly overview the previous types of explanations of occurrences of verbs with lexically unrealised arguments in various languages and different frameworks. Firstly, I will criticise purely syntactic (Section 2.1), pragmatic (Section 2.2), and lexical-semantic (Section 2.3) explanations. Secondly, I will discuss the current treatments (Section 2.4) which apply more complex approaches, taking into consideration different factors in the licensing and interpretation of lexically unrealised arguments. What these complex frameworks have in common is that they integrate grammatical and pragmatic constraints in their explanation, but they differ in their latent background assumptions and theory formation. In Chapter 2, I will not aim to provide a full review of the relevant literature; instead, I will attempt to characterise some typical treatments in order to make it manifest why purely syntactic, pragmatic, or lexical-semantic explanations cannot adequately account for the behaviour of verbs with implicit arguments, and demonstrate how current approaches argue for the necessity of a complex framework. By such a presentation of the selected literature, I aim to prepare my own approach, which I will start to introduce in Chapter 3.

In Chapter 3, I will define what I mean by implicit arguments and compare my definition to some others, indicating what approaches my conception is similar to and what approaches it differs from (Section 3.1). In Section 3.2, I will present three manners of occurrence of implicit arguments in Hungarian. In Chapters 4 and 5, I will discuss these three manners in detail.

In Chapter 4, I will concentrate on how the lexical-semantic properties of verbs influence the use of verbs with lexically unrealised subject and direct object arguments in an interaction with other grammatical requirements and contextual factors. Firstly, in Section 4.1, I will examine the occurrence of verbs with implicit subject arguments. I will provide a new explanation for the occurrences of verbs of natural phenomena with explicit and implicit subject arguments in Hungarian language use. I will rely on a wide range of data from various direct sources and demonstrate that verbs of natural phenomena are not subjectless in Hungarian as the Hungarian grammatical tradition supposes. I will propose a lexical-semantic representation for the verbs of natural phenomena on the basis of which the occurrences of these verbs with both explicit and implicit subjects can be explained in a unified way. In Section 4.1, I will also analyse another class of verbs, namely verbs of work which can be used with implicit subject arguments not only because of the pro-drop characteristics of Hungarian, but because of their lexical-semantic properties and contextual factors. In Section 4.2, I will investigate how the lexical-semantic properties of verbs license implicit direct object arguments in an interaction with morphosyntactic constraints and contextual factors. I will especially focus on the role of selection restrictions, the characteristic manners of action denoted by the verbs, and the prototypical structure of implicit arguments. Section 4.3 will provide an internal summary of Chapter 4.

In Chapter 5, I will turn to the second and third manners of occurrences of implicit arguments in Hungarian, and I will study the influence of the immediate utterance context and extended context. In Section 5.1, I will examine implicit subject and direct object arguments as zero anaphors and exophoric pronominal subjects and objects in utterance and discourse contexts, while in Section 5.2, I will analyse the role of the encyclopaedic information available in the immediate utterance context. In Section 5.3, I will deal with the way in which the context extended with information from the observable physical environment and how encyclopaedic knowledge can influence the use and interpretation of implicit subject and direct object arguments in Hungarian language use. Then, in Section 5.4, I will discuss how indefinite/definite conjugations play a role in the licensing and identification of implicit direct object arguments.

In Chapter 6, on the basis of the data, analyses, and argumentation presented in Chapters 3–5, I will summarise my results and conclusions. I will also set up a classification of Hungarian verbs according to the possibilities of their occurrence with lexically unrealised arguments. And finally, I will recover the pragmatic motivation behind the occurrence of Hungarian verbs with implicit arguments as well as the main pragmatic principle guiding the identifying mechanisms.

CHAPTER 2

Explanations of the occurrence of verbs with implicit arguments

2.1 Purely syntactic explanations

Cote (1996) overviews the extensive literature up to 1996 concerning zero subject and direct object arguments in various languages and demonstrates rather convincingly why purely syntactic, pragmatic, and lexical-semantic explanations are inadequate by themselves. Implicit arguments discussed in the literature have various subtypes, e.g. indefinite implicit object arguments, reflexive, reciprocal, and contextual (definite) implicit complements. Consider (15a–d), respectively (cf. Cote 1996; Németh T. and Bibok 2010; Gillon 2012; Section 3.1).

(15) a. I am cooking [Ø].

   b. Peter shaved [himself].

   c. Mary and Peter divorced [from each other].

   d. Bill stayed in the park$_i$ all day. He left [Ø$_i$] at sunset.

(Gillon 2012: 341)

Purely syntactic accounts analyse only those types of implicit arguments which can be explained on the basis of the syntactic structures of sentences. They underestimate the role of other factors such as constructions, lexical-semantics, and discourse constraints; some of them even ignore them (Goldberg 2005a, b, 2013). If one considers, for example, the indefinite implicit argument in (15a) and the definite, contextual implicit argument in the second sentence in (15d), purely syntactic explanations cannot provide an adequate account for them by themselves, since the occurrence of implicit indefinite and definite implicit arguments is not a purely syntactic phenomenon. Firstly, in English, not all verbs can be used with indefinite and/or definite contextual implicit arguments (Fillmore 1986).

While the verbs *cook* in (15a) and *leave* in (15d) can be used with implicit arguments, the verbs *await* in (16) and *vacate* in the second sentence in (17) cannot.

(16)   *I am awaiting. (Fillmore 1986: 99)

(17)   The protesters stayed in the park all day. *They vacated [the park] at sunset.

(Gillon 2012: 341)

Secondly, it is not easy for purely syntactic approaches to explain the behaviour of verbs such as *cook, leave, eat, drink, read, write*, etc., which can be used both with indefinite implicit objects and overt objects. When they are used without explicit objects, their object arguments are not projected into the syntax, i.e. objectless uses of these verbs are considered intransitive from the syntactic point of view. That is, purely syntactic explanations can cope with objectless uses of these verbs as if they were intransitive verbs. From this, however, a problem arises, since they can be used with explicit objects as well, as if they were transitive verbs. One and the same verb, then, behaves at one time as if it were intransitive and at other times as if it were transitive. This behaviour cannot be explained purely syntactically. However, we can also take into account semantic/pragmatic factors that the act of cooking, eating, drinking, ironing, reading, writing, etc. necessarily involve the act of cooking something, drinking something, ironing something, reading something, writing something, etc. Thus, it is reasonable to assume that the verbs *cook, leave, eat, drink, read, write*, etc. always have two arguments. The second, direct object arguments of these verbs can be left lexically unrealised with an indefinite interpretation based on the information concerning the type of the direct object arguments involved in the verbs' lexical-semantic representations. When the second, direct object arguments of these verbs are lexically unrealised with the indefinite reading, they are not represented in the syntactic structure of sentences (cf. Cote 1996; Groefsema 1995; Németh T. 2001).

Purely syntactic approaches to implicit arguments rely on a latent background assumption that the occurrence of implicit arguments is a sentence-oriented phenomenon. Thus, purely syntactic approaches are not sensitive to contextual analyses and they cannot take into consideration implicit arguments in utterances. Consider the following Hungarian examples.

(18)   a.   *Mari   vasal   [Ø].*

              Mari.NOM   irons.INDEF

              'Mari is ironing [Ø].'

        b.   **Áron   tologat   [Ø].*

              Áron.NOM   pushes.INDEF.

              'Áron is pushing [Ø] back and forth.'

According to the sentence-oriented Hungarian grammatical traditions (cf., e.g., Komlósy 1992, 1994), while *Mari vasal [Ø]* 'Mari is ironing [Ø]' in (18a) is a grammatical sentence, *Áron tologat [Ø]* 'Áron is pushing [Ø] back and forth' in (18b) is unacceptable as a Hungarian sentence. However, the judgment of unacceptability is valid only if one considers *Áron tologat [Ø]* as a sentence without any context. *Áron tologat [Ø]* may be acceptable as a Hungarian utterance if one chooses an appropriate context for it as in (19) (Németh T. 2001: 117).

(19)   (A mother is walking with her children, the baby is sitting in the pushchair, and the older brother, named Áron, is walking next to it. Suddenly the mother notices the nurse and she wants to talk to her, but the baby begins to cry.)

Ne sírj!   *Áron*   *tologat*   *[téged].*

no   cry.IMP.INDEF.2SG   Áron.NOM   pushes.INDEF   [you]

'Don't cry! Áron is going to push [you] back and forth.'

In (19) the direct object argument of the verb *tologat* 'push somebody back and forth' is lexically unrealised. The linguistic structure of the utterance *ls* which contains this implicit argument is not a complete sentence structure, but it can be completed with the information from the observable physical context c_{phys}. Since purely syntactic approaches do not take into account contextual information, e.g. from the observable physical environment, they should evaluate (18b) as unacceptable.

Cote (1996) discusses purely syntactic explanations which examine the licensing of lexically unrealised direct object arguments in English in detail and argues very convincingly why they are inadequate by themselves. According to purely syntactic approaches, implicit direct objects are represented in the syntactic structures of sentences and can be accessed through binding principles. This kind of explanation cannot be accepted for at least three reasons. Firstly, as indicated above, sometimes the implicit object is not represented in the syntactic structure of the sentence, e.g. the verbs that can be used with indefinite implicit objects behave differently in occurrences with indefinite implicit objects and overt pronominal objects as in (20a–b).

(20)   a.   Joyce ate this afternoon because the turkey was ready.
        b.   *Joyce ate it$_i$ this afternoon because the turkey$_i$ was ready.

The comparison of (20a) and (20b) shows that if the direct object argument of an *eat*-type verb, i.e. a verb which can occur with an indefinite implicit object argument, is not overt, then it is not present in the syntactic structure of the sentence. This is the same conclusion we came to above when we discussed (15a) and (15d).

Secondly, it is inconsistent with an exclusively syntactic analysis that verbs with indefinite null objects do not allow their zero objects to have an antecedent which violates the binding principles (cf. Chomsky 1981). It may be a solution that one assumes a special empty category which differs from the zero pronominal, but this proposal also raises further questions. Thirdly, in a purely syntactic analysis it is not possible to make a distinction between verbs with definite null objects and otherwise similar verbs which give thematic roles only to overt objects (cf. (21a–b)).

(21)   a.   John entered.

      b.   *John penetrated.

In the past two decades various versions of the argument realisation principle have been put forward by a number of researchers (e.g., Grimshaw and Vikner 1993; Kaufmann and Wunderlich 1998; Rappaport Hovav and Levin 2001) in order to describe general tendencies in argument realisation in languages like English.[1] According to the argument realisation principle, there must be one argument XP in the syntax to identify each subevent in the event structure template. Goldberg (2005a, 2013) demonstrates, however, that these treatments have not solved the above-mentioned three problems and fail to account for open-ended classes of counterexamples.

In his recently published book, Camacho (2013) analyses the possibility of occurrences of verbs with null subjects in various languages. On the basis of the detailed examination of different languages regarding the occurrence of verbs with null subjects in clauses, he sets up a typology according to which certain languages have very productive null subjects (e.g., Spanish, Italian, and Quechua), while others have partially null subjects (e.g., Hebrew, Finnish, and Shipibo) and others can only have overt subjects (e.g., French and English) (Camacho 2013: 31–38). This variety of the occurrence of verbs with null subjects in various languages is partly explained with the help of the revised Null Subject Parameter in a generative linguistics minimalist framework (Camacho 2013: 105). The revised Null Subject Parameter takes into account – among other things – that the inflectional properties of verbs frequently correlate with the availability of null subjects, but there is no universally determined notion of agreement-richness that could provide a sufficient condition for the use of null subjects, and there are languages in which null subjects can be identified in discourses (e.g., Chinese, Japanese, and Hindi). This latter phenomenon, i.e. the identification of null subjects in discourses within the Null Subject Parameter, which in its first formulations was derived from the idea that syntactic clauses in all languages have (overt or null versions of thematic or expletive) subjects and which was associated only with syntactic properties (Camacho 2013: 13), contradicts a widely accepted latent background assumption in the Chomskyan types of generative grammars. According to this latent background assumption, a generative grammar defines the well-formed sentences of a particular language by means of its rules (Chomsky 1957). Well-formed, grammatical sentences in this type of generative grammatical approach belong to the language, since language itself is defined as an infinite set of well-formed sentences (Chomsky 1957). In a Chomskyan type of generative grammar, discourses cannot be considered the units of a grammatical, syntactic analysis because they can only be taken into account in the investigation of language use. Since the possibility of the occurrence of null subjects constrained in discourses in some languages is involved in the revised Null Subject Parameter, there is a significant divergence from the latent theoretical requirements of Chomskyan generative grammars. In other words, the practice of the research into null subjects in various languages and the theoretical requirements differ, which attests to the fact that a purely syntactic approach in practice cannot explain all occurrences of implicit subjects in various languages.

Furthermore, there is another argument against the purely syntactic approaches which also contradicts Camacho's (2013) revised Null Subject Parameter. Camacho (2013: 2, 16, 34) assigns English to those languages which can only have overt subjects in both types of clauses, i.e. in clauses with thematic and expletive subjects. However, Cote (1996) and Scott (2013) demonstrate that there are pragmatically motivated null subjects in certain discourse contexts despite English being traditionally classified as a language which does not allow null subjects. Cote (1996) concentrates on conversational spoken English, where null subjects occur with a certain frequency and regularity in tensed, declarative, or interrogative sentences, and English native speakers find utterances including null subjects acceptable and do not evaluate them as true performance errors (for a detailed analysis of these kinds of null subjects, see Section 2.4). Scott (2013) investigates two registers in written English where null subjects can also occur, namely diary texts and journals. She mentions that in addition to these sources one can find null subjects in email messages, short text messages, telegrams, postcards, note-taking, and message boards. Scott (2013: 69–71) summarises how syntactic analysis attempts to explain these occurrences of null subjects, called diary-drops, focusing on syntactic aspects of the phenomenon (cf., e.g., Haegeman and Ihsane 1999, 2001) acknowledging the need for a pragmatic analysis as well. The syntactic treatments of diary-drops agree that the interpretation and acceptability of null subject utterances in English varies from situation to situation and they share the opinion that this variation is due to pragmatic factors (Scott 2013: 69).[2]

It is worth highlighting that if in a syntactic analysis of null subjects in a non-null subject languages such as English researchers refer to pragmatic factors, this has at least two consequences. Firstly, null subjects cannot be explained exclusively syntactically as a sentence phenomenon; instead, they should be analysed in discourses. And secondly, if one allows that in some languages null subjects can be identified in discourses as Camacho (2013: 105) argues, the classification of the English language as a non-null subject language should be revisited in the light of the occurrences of null subjects in spoken and written conversational English.

2.2 Purely pragmatic approaches

Contrary to purely syntactic explanations concerned with describing those implicit arguments which have a position in the syntactic structure of sentences on their own, purely pragmatic accounts attempt to describe all types of implicit arguments treated in the relevant literature, but cannot distinguish between them and do not rely on any grammatical information. Purely pragmatic approaches lead to analyses according to which every argument can be omitted if it is inferable. There are two main types of pragmatic accounts of implicit arguments, which differ in terms of the level of meaning they assign to implicit arguments and their inferential procedures. According to the first type of pragmatic approaches, the missing content can be inferred as a conversational implicature through Gricean maxims (Rice 1988). This type of pragmatic explanation states that verbs can optionally have lexically unrealised direct object arguments and assume a true intransitive–transitive alternation. These accounts suppose that verbs may optionally have no linguistic representations for an object, even in the lexicon. Rice (1988) argues for a basically pragmatic kind of analysis relying on the Gricean maxims. Moreover, she rejects the existence of a lexicon with definable lexical entries; instead, she proposes that there is a dynamic, interconnected network which involves semantic, phonological, and pragmatic information.

Cote (1996: 123) highlights that pragmatic explanations relying only on conversational implicatures through Gricean maxims are insufficient to account for the behaviour of verbs with implicit direct object arguments in different languages.[3] Elbourne (2008) also argues against this explanation, investigating the implicit content of utterances which include implicit verbal arguments such as the direct object argument of the verb *eat* in (22) in addition to other types of unarticulated constituents such as 'somewhere' in (23) (Recanati 2007) or 'at the dinner party' in the reply in (24) (Neale 1990: 94–95).

(22)   I haven't eaten.

(23)   It's raining.

(24)   How did your dinner party go last night?
       Everyone was sick.

Elbourne (2008) argues that the missing content in (22)–(24) seems to be part of the literal content of utterances rather than a Gricean conversational implicature.

The other type of pragmatic approach suggests that pragmatic free enrichment is responsible for the interpretation of the implicit contents of the utterances in (22)–(24) (Sperber and Wilson 1986/1995: 189; Carston 2002). According to relevance theory, the decoded meanings of the utterances in (22)–(24) are linguistically underspecified and can be enriched into fully fledged conceptual representations of literal utterance meanings by means of free enrichment. The process of free enrichment contains general-purpose inference rules (Sperber and Wilson 1986/1995: 176).

It is worth emphasising that, although the relevance-theoretic explanation considers the missing contents to be part of the literal meanings of the utterances in (22)–(24), rather than regarding them as conversational implicatures, the recovery of the missing contents is only based on pragmatic inferences and does not involve any decoding grammatical procedures. Thus, there are no syntactic or other grammatical constraints assumed in the course of free enrichment procedures. As Elbourne (2008: 287) emphasises, relevance theorists suggest only a pragmatic principle of relevance in order to arrive at an adequately disambiguated and enriched conceptual representation of an utterance with implicit content. To summarise: the missing bits of content in (22)–(24) are purely pragmatically inferred both in Gricean and relevance-theoretic proposals. The main difference between these two purely pragmatic approaches lies in whether they consider the missing content in (22)–(24) conversational implicatures or part of the literal meanings of utterances, respectively.

The idea of describing implicit arguments purely pragmatically cannot be supported for at least three reasons. Firstly, as I have noted at the beginning of this section, purely pragmatic accounts such as Gricean or relevance-theoretic ones cannot distinguish between the different types of implicit arguments (cf. various kinds of implicit arguments in (15a–d) in Section 2.1). The reason for this is that they focus mainly on the inferential mechanisms of the identification of implicit arguments, and these mechanisms by themselves are not adequate to differentiate various types of implicit arguments.

Secondly, if it were possible to clearly account for the occurrences of zero objects purely pragmatically, then there should not be any evidence for the presence of null objects in the syntax, and the occurrences of zero objects should never be lexically determined, but all information concerning them should only be pragmatically inferred (Németh T. 2010). Further, if a reading is not available for a particular utterance, purely pragmatic approaches cannot refer to syntactic constraints to explain the absence of this reading, and if this reading can be considered pragmatically plausible, there will be no tools available to account for why the reading in question is missing (Elbourne 2008: 293–294). Elbourne argues against the pragmatic free-enrichment approaches on the basis of an argument from binding. He analyses sentences containing definite descriptions made with Saxon genitives (cf. the sentences with bound reading *John fed no cat of Mary's before it was bathed* and *John fed no cat of Mary's before the cat of Mary's was bathed*). His main argument is built on sentences that lack a bound reading, cf., e.g., *John fed no cat of Mary's before Mary's cat was bathed.* The free-enrichment approaches cannot prevent the pragmatically plausible but unavailable bound reading here, since they do not have the syntactic tools to achieve this (Elbourne 2008: 293–294). (Also Fillmore's example in (25) below, where the use of an implicit direct object argument is also blocked syntactically.)

Thirdly, as Fillmore (1986) argues, to give a purely pragmatic account of the occurrence of null objects is not possible, because some arguments cannot be left lexically unrealised in spite of the fact that there is an immediately retrievable antecedent in the context, i.e. these arguments can be easily inferred from the context, but they cannot still remain implicit. Consider Fillmore's example in (25).

(25)   *Did you lock?

Although it can be quite straightforward in a particular context which door the speaker intends to refer to, in English the verb *lock* cannot be used with a lexically unrealised direct object argument.

Furthermore, verbs with indefinite and definite implicit objects show certain lexical alternations independently of pragmatic factors, and it is also allowed to refer to the lexically unrealised objects of these verbs later in discourse with overt forms that are grammatically constrained and not characteristic of pragmatic inferences (Cote 1996).[4]

2.3 Purely lexical-semantic and semantic explanations

In the literature on implicit arguments in different languages, a hypothesis that lexical-semantic properties of verbs can determine their various occurrences with lexically unrealised arguments has also been formulated. The criticism of purely lexical-semantic explanations has raised questions which have led to complex approaches, a type of explanation I also prefer to apply in my research. Thus, I will discuss lexical-semantic accounts in this section and complex explanations in Section 2.4 in more detail than I did in the case of purely syntactic and pragmatic analyses (see Section 2.1 and 2.2, respectively).[5]

Purely lexical-semantic explanations suggest that the lexical-semantic representation of verbs fully determines whether a verb can occur with implicit arguments, and if so, with what type and how. However, there is no consensus among the various proposals as to whether occurrence with an implicit argument is an idiosyncratic property of the verb in question or a predictable lexical-semantic or other property. As to English and languages similar to it, such as, e.g., German, Norwegian, and Dutch, lexical-semantic approaches agree that the licensing of the implicit arguments is the individual peculiarity of verbs. In other languages such as Hungarian, Italian, and Spanish, the occurrence with implicit arguments can be considered a predictable phenomenon (see Chapters 3–5).

In Fillmore's (1986) approach, in English the omissibility of an argument is determined by the particular, unique lexical-semantic features of verbs.[6] What argument can be left implicit is marked in the lexical-semantic representation of the given verbs. According to this view, in English there are verbs whose lexical-semantic features license the use of verbs with implicit arguments, and there are verbs whose lexical-semantic features do not. Fillmore divides the verbs which license implicit arguments into three groups in terms of the indefiniteness/definiteness of their omitted complements. Verbs in the first group can occur with indefinite null complements (INC), e.g. *eat, drink, read, sew, sing, cook,* and *bake.* In their case, the reference of the null complement is unknown or the speaker does not consider it essential to identify it exactly, thus an INC is obligatorily disjoint in reference to anything saliently present in the context. Fillmore illustrates the INC-phenomenon by means of a dialogue produced by Adrian Akmajian in a personal conversation.

(26)   A: What happened to my sandwich?

     B: Fido ate.

Fillmore and Akmajian are of the opinion that the dialogue in (26) cannot be a well-formed conversation in English. The implicit argument of the verb *eat* in B's answer cannot be coreferential with the lexically expressed definite noun phrase *my sandwich,* which has been introduced into the discourse context c_{disc} in A's question. The verb *eat* can be acceptable only with indefinite null complements according to Fillmore (1986). I will return to this dialogue later in this section.

The second group contains verbs which can be used with definite null complements (DNC), e.g. *accept, object, wait, win, lose,* and *insist.* These verbs can occur with null complements only if the missing information can be immediately retrieved from the context. The reference of the null complement can be identified with a saliently present entity of the context unambiguously, i.e. the null complement has a definite reading as in (27).

(27)   A: Why did you marry her?

       B: Because mother insisted.

Fillmore also argues that it is impossible to give a pragmatic account of when an argument of a verb belonging to the second group can be left implicit. No matter how clear and unambiguous the pragmatic context may be, only certain verbs can have definite omissible complements. To put it the other way round, although there can be a saliently present entity in the context by means of which a potential definite null complement could be identified, not all verbs license their complements to be left lexically unexpressed, i.e. not all verbs can belong to the second group. Consider Fillmore's (1986: 98) example again.

(28)   *Did you lock?

Even if it is quite clear to everyone concerned what particular door is being talked about, (28) cannot be used to refer to it. In other words, Fillmore argues that to give a pragmatic account of the occurrence of null complements is not possible, because some arguments cannot be left lexically unrealised in spite of the fact that there is an immediately retrievable antecedent in the context (see also Section 2.2). There are two problems with this argumentation. The first problem concerns the notion of context. Fillmore does not define explicitly what he means by context. The analyses of his examples may indicate that he understands the notion of context very narrowly and that he takes into account only what is called the linguistic context, i.e. the utterance context in which the implicit argument occurs, or, rarely, the preceding discourse. Unfortunately, one cannot find any preceding discourse element in the explanations of the examples, and this reduces the plausibility of Fillmore's statements to a great extent. The second problem with the impossibility of giving a pragmatic explanation is that Fillmore does not define what immediate retrievability means, either. However, some native speakers found (28) not unacceptable, but marginal or even acceptable when a particular door is clearly the focus of attention of the discourse participants (García Velasco and Portero Muñoz 2002: 17). Moreover, if the example contains the verb *lock up*, the question *Did you lock up?* is fine (cf. the title *Did you lock up?* of Episode 1, Season 1 of the TV series *Shadows of Fear* (1970–1973), retrieved on 30 October 2015 from http://www.imdb.com/title/tt0698886/). We have seen in Section 2.2 that purely pragmatic explanations are really inadequate by themselves, but not because of the factors Fillmore mentions.

Furthermore, Fillmore claims that one cannot give a semantic explanation for when an argument may be omitted with the verbs of the second group either, for at least two reasons. Firstly, closely synonymous verbs do not display the same behaviour regarding whether or not they allow their arguments to be left implicit. In (27) we have seen that *insist* can occur with a definite null complement under the appropriate conditions, but many of the verbs semantically related to *insist*, e.g. *require* and *demand*, cannot occur with an implicit argument in the same context (see (29) and (30a–c)).

(29)   Why did you marry her?

(30)   a.   Because mother insisted.
       b.   *Because mother required.
       c.   *Because mother demanded.

Similarly, the verb *accept* in (31a) and the verb *try* in (32a) allow their direct object arguments to be left implicit, but their synonymous verbs *endorse* in (31b) and *attempt* in (32b) do not.

(31)   a.   They accepted.
       b.   *They endorsed.

(32)   a.   I tried.
       b.   *I attempted.

However, Fillmore does not determine how the verbs he mentions are related semantically. He relies only on his intuition and does not make explicit what semantic relatedness means. If in English the occurrences of verbs with indefinite/ definite null complements can be lexically explained, as Fillmore claims, then this must be mirrored in the lexical-semantic representations of the verbs. Semantically related verbs must have similar lexical-semantic representations. However, semantically related verbs can behave differently with regard to indefinite or definite implicit arguments if they have different specific components, e.g. selection restrictions, or presuppositions, in their lexical-semantic representations.

Secondly, one cannot give a semantic explanation, because the omissibility of the arguments in the case of polysemous DNC-verbs is often restricted to particular meanings. Consider the examples in (33)–(35).

(33)   a.   She arrived at the summit.
       b.   She arrived.
       c.   She arrived at the answer.
       d.   *She arrived.

(34)   a.   They accepted my offer.
       b.   They accepted.
       c.   They accepted my gift.
       d.   *They accepted.

(35)   a.   They closed the shop early.

     b.   They closed early.

     c.   She closed the drawer.

     d.   *She closed.

Fillmore states that the omissibility of an argument is defined lexically. It is marked in the lexical-semantic representation of a verb what argument can be left implicit, and, furthermore, which argument can be used as an INC and which can be used as a DNC.[7]

English verbs in the third group in Fillmore's (1986) classification may have both indefinite and definite omissible complements, e.g. *contribute* and *give* 'donate'. Let us take the verb *contribute*, which has three arguments in its lexical-semantic representation.

(36)   a.   I contributed to the movement.

     b.   I contributed five dollars.

     c.   I've already contributed.

In (36a) the direct object argument of the verb *contribute* is left implicit as an INC. Fillmore assumes that when the direct object argument of *contribute* is not lexically expressed, the nature or quantity of the donation is a matter of no importance. Goldberg (2005b) argues that the verbs *contribute*, *donate*, and *give* 'donate' can be fused with the implicit theme construction, i.e. they can be used with indefinite implicit direct object arguments because this is pragmatically motivated. It is culturally preferred not to make public what kind and what amount of donation is given. Thus, there is no need to have a shared advance understanding of the identity or nature of the donation, therefore the lexically unexpressed direct object argument can have an indefinite interpretation. In (36b) the direct object argument of the verb *contribute* is lexically expressed, but the receiver complement is not. Fillmore argues that the implicit receiver complement must be a definite null complement. Its identity must be recoverable from the context. In (36c) both arguments of the verb *contribute* are omitted. The direct object argument, i.e. the donation complement, is lexically unexpressed as an INC; it is left unspecified, while the receiver complement is lexically unexpressed as a DNC, and it must be identified with an entity previously introduced into the discourse context c_{disc}.

Summarising Fillmore's proposal, one can say that in lexical-semantic representations it is not only the fact that a verb can occur with null complements which is marked, but, if this is the case, then the kind of reading – i.e. indefinite and/or definite – the null complement can have is also marked. However,

Fillmore's purely lexical-semantic approach cannot provide a sufficient account of the occurrences of verbs with implicit arguments in pro-drop languages. The pro-drop languages such as Hungarian, Italian, and Spanish allow null arguments far more freely than English does (see, e.g., (3)–(4) and (6) in Section 1.1). At the same time, this freer occurrence does not mean that an argument can be left implicit everywhere, i.e. in every utterance and context. The freer occurrence of implicit arguments in pro-drop languages can be predicted on the basis of various lexical-semantic, morphosyntactic, semantic, and contextual factors, and not only on the basis of the individual lexical-semantic peculiarities of verbs. The lexical-semantic, grammatical, and contextual factors as well as the pragmatic principles governing the freer occurrence of null complements in Hungarian will be treated in Chapters 3–6.

Furthermore, even if only English is taken under closer scrutiny, there are also problems with Fillmore's explanations. Firstly, the markedness regarding the occurrence with indefinite or definite complements in the lexical-semantic representations of verbs does not always make the right predictions about the behaviour of verbs in different contexts (Groefsema 1995: 141–142). On the one hand, the references of null complements of INC verbs do not differ very often from all entries saliently presented in the context. To identify the reference of the missing complement, the context involves the necessary information. On the other hand, definite null complements do not always have a discourse antecedent. Consider Groefsema's examples in (37)–(38).

(37)   John brought the sandwiches and Ann ate.

(38)   Martina Navratilova has won again.

Since Fillmore states that the reference of an INC must differ from everything in the context, (37) is expected to have an interpretation such as 'John brought the sandwiches and Ann ate something other than sandwiches'. However, English native speakers interpret (37) as something like 'Ann ate (some) of the sandwiches that John brought', although this leaves unspecified how many of them Ann ate. So, the null complement does not necessarily refer to all the sandwiches that John brought, nor is it disjoint in reference with the sandwiches that John brought. The null complement of *eat* in (37) refers to the sandwiches cumulatively (i.e. there is no quantitative restriction on how many objects it denotes), similarly to the reference of bare common nouns (Maleczki 1994), or the appropriate cases of noun incorporation (Kiefer 1990) in Hungarian. Hale and Keyser (2002) as well as Cummins and Roberge (2005) even propose that implicit indefinite direct objects are represented by null bare nouns (see also Scott 2006). Similarly to the verbs *lose, wait, accept, object,* and *insist,* the verb *win* in (38) licenses a definite null complement in Fillmore's classification, and the null complement should have a discourse antecedent. Analysing the behaviour of *win* and *lose*, Fillmore argues that these verbs can only occur with implicit direct object arguments if there is a concrete competition in the context of which the subject is the winner or the loser. This claim is too strong in Groefsema's opinion (1995: 144), because there is no need to mention a particular competition in the context in the case of famous sports people. Thus, in (38), if the speaker/hearer knows who Navratilova is and what she is famous for, a contextually given competition is not necessary to access the interpretation 'Martina Navratilova has won the competition in which she took part'.

Here I want to return to (26), which was mentioned by Fillmore as illustrating INC-phenomena. On the basis of the analysis of (37), it is not certain that the implicit argument of *eat* is always obligatorily disjoint in reference with *my sandwich* in (26). Although I have to admit that such a dialogue is fairly strange in English, it can be interpreted without any difficulty. What the exact reference of the implicit argument of *eat* is depends on the context in which the utterance *What happened to my sandwich?* was produced. For example, if the speaker does not find the sandwich in the place where (s)he left it, and the hearer sees Fido coming out of the room with crumbs around his mouth, then with the reply *Fido ate* the hearer may implicate that Fido might have eaten the sandwich or Fido might have eaten part of it. The hearer does not express her/his belief that Fido ate the sandwich or part of it explicitly, because (s)he did not see Fido eating the sandwich. The hearer may avoid making a mistake if (s)he does not use *it* to refer to the sandwich, or *part of it* to refer to a part of the sandwich. (S)he leaves the direct object argument of *eat* implicit, and (s)he conveys his/her insinuation by means of a conversational implicature. So, the hearer does not decode but infers the insinuation and this inference is deductive, but not demonstrative.[8] If the speaker finds a chewed, incomplete sandwich, then (s)he may imply that Fido might have eaten part of the sandwich. So, the implicit argument in the hearer's reply may refer to the missing part of the sandwich. In this case the hearer implies that Fido might have eaten part of the sandwich. One may consider these analyses of (26) too liberal. But the explanation of the example is the same as it is in the case of (37). So, if one can accept (37), then one must also accept (26). It is worth mentioning that Cote (1996: 158, note 32) analyses the following spontaneous dialogue similarly:

(39)   What happened to all the bananas?
        Well, Cheetah ate heartily today.

The second problem with Fillmore's (1986) suggestions regarding the markedness of the possibility of occurrences with INC and DNC in the verb's lexical-semantic representations is that it can also happen that the same verb behaves differently with regard to INC-DNC-phenomena in its different occurrences. Consider Groefsema's (1995: 142–143) examples again.

(40)   Ann: I don't know how to finish this letter.

       Sue: Why don't you put 'yours sincerely'?

(41)   Mary walked to the table with a book in her hand. *She put the book.

(42)   (John, Bruce and Mary were playing a game which involved putting something on the table.)

       ? John put his book, Bruce put his pipe, and Mary her glasses.

The locative argument of *put* can be left implicit in (40), but it cannot be lexically unrealised in (41) in spite of the fact that there is an antecedent immediately recoverable from the context. It may be an acceptable solution that *put* is used in two different meanings in (40) and (41). However, this does not explain why (42) is more acceptable than (41).[9]

After discussing Fillmore's account and its shortcomings, let us turn to another purely lexical-semantic approach which concentrates on the conceptual semantic representations of verbs. Jackendoff (1990) argues that verb meanings are decomposed conceptual semantic representations. The constituents of conceptual representations (THING, EVENT, STATE, PLACE, PATH, PROPERTY, etc.) belong to a small set of major ontological categories. Using these categories, for example, the verb *eat* may be represented as (43).

(43)   [Event CAUSE ([Thing]i, [Event GO ([Thing FOOD]j, [Path TO ([Place IN
      ([Thing MOUTH of ([Thing]i)])])])])]

According to Jackendoff (1990), a lexically realised verb gives access to its conceptual representation during the interpretation, and this representation involves the arguments of the verb, even those arguments which are left implicit in the utterance. Conceptual representations of verbs determine what categories of arguments verbs can occur with. One can see from (43) that there are two arguments of the category THING in the conceptual representation of the verb *eat*, they are ordered, and the second THING argument must be FOOD. Thus conceptual representations of verbs also specify what selection restrictions are placed on arguments. Verbs may constrain their arguments by means of selection restrictions that they must be of a particular type or an instance of a particular type or have a particular property, etc. Relying on Jackendoff's (1990) analysis, it can be pointed out that Fillmore's INC verbs put a selection restriction on their lexically unexpressed arguments such that they are of a particular type of THING, while DNC verbs put a selection restriction on their implicit arguments such that they are instances of a particular type of THING. This difference in selection restrictions partly causes the different behaviour of INC and DNC verbs with regard to their occurrence with implicit arguments.

Saeboe (1996) also purposes to account for the behaviour of definite zero direct object arguments in English. Since Shopen's (1973) early article on the grammatical determination/indetermination of ellipsis, it has been known that syntactically missing arguments sometimes have an existential interpretation but sometimes depend on the context, i.e. they have definite anaphoric interpretation. It has remained a mystery why some zero direct object arguments behave like anaphors. The explanations with regard to this phenomenon have a mainly lexical character. As we have seen, in Fillmore's solution whether a verb can occur with an indefinite or a definite zero argument was encoded in lexical-semantic representations of the verbs.

Saeboe (1996) agrees with Fillmore (1986) that the omissibility of an argument is an idiosyncratic lexical-semantic feature of verbs. It is not possible to predict semantically when an argument can be optional. The omissibility of an argument varies across languages, even among such closely related languages as English, German, and Norwegian. Many English verbs which allow their definite direct object arguments to be phonetically unrealised correspond to verbs requiring overt anaphors in German or Norwegian (Saeboe 1996: 193). Saeboe enumerates three possibilities with respect to the realisation of an argument. Firstly, an argument is obligatory, it can never be omitted; secondly, an argument can be left implicit with definite, anaphoric interpretation, and thirdly, an argument can have a zero form with indefinite, non-anaphoric interpretation. A fourth possibility can be added to these three cases in terms of Fillmore's argumentation. There are some verbs which can occur with both definite, anaphoric and indefinite, non-anaphoric null complements, see *contribute, give* 'donate'. The borderlines between the first and second or first and third possibilities may be partly syntactically based, subject to parametric variation across languages, and partly arbitrary. In Saeboe's opinion, it is for the borderline between the second and third kind of cases that one can provide a semantic account which predicts that the anaphoricity of zero arguments cannot vary across languages. This means that it should not be possible to find two otherwise synonymous verbs where an argument of one language can be left implicit with a definite reading but the same argument of the other language can be left implicit with an indefinite interpretation.

Saeboe connects the anaphoricity of zero arguments to presuppositions. A zero argument is anaphoric if it is involved in a presupposition triggered by the verb and is recovered in the same process in which the presupposition is verified. Thus, the context dependence of the missing complement can be described as a presuppositional effect. The relevant referent is introduced in the presupposition and the substituted referent is extended to the assertion in an updating process. The difference between indefinite/definite implicit arguments surfaces where the referent is introduced: in the case of indefinite implicit arguments the referent is introduced in the universe of the assertion, but in the case of definite implicit arguments the referent is introduced in the presupposition.[10] If a predicate with an optional argument triggers a presupposition involving the argument, the presupposition itself becomes anaphoric as soon as the argument is omitted. Consider Saeboe's (1996: 192) example.

(44)   Susan dissuades John.

Example (44) asserts that Susan dissuades John from P and triggers the presupposition that John plans P. On the basis of the anaphoric notion of the presupposition, P must be anchored to some familiar action Q in the context: John plans Q, and once it is anchored, Q substitutes P in the assertion. Thus, zero anaphors are not really anaphors. There is no need to distinguish between definite/indefinite implicit arguments in any other way than through the presence of a presupposition. For example, the occurrences of verbs triggering reactions (*agree, disagree, refuse, accept*), factive predicates (*remember, remind, forget, notice, aware*) and state transition predicates (*recover, return*) with zero arguments can be considered anaphoric. The triggering of a presupposition must be involved in the lexical-semantic representations of a verb and it must be marked in the lexicon.

However, Saeboe's proposal raises some further questions. Firstly, if a verb does not trigger a presupposition involving the lexically unrealised argument then the zero occurrence of this argument can be anaphoric. Consider (45a–b) and (46a–c).[11]

(45)   a.   When the Pope asked Galilei to renounce his theory, Galilei refused.

      b.   'When the Pope asked Galilei to renounce his theory, Galilei refused to renounce his theory.'

(46)   a.   Sue had not heard from Joe for months when, suddenly, she received a letter.

      b.   'Sue had not heard from Joe for months when, suddenly, she received a letter from him.'

      c.   'Sue had not heard from Joe for months when, suddenly, she received a letter from somebody about him.'

Examples (45a) and (46a) are utterances with a zero argument, (45b) and (46b–c) demonstrate their possible interpretations. As we have seen above, the anaphoricity of a zero argument in Saeboe's proposal can be explained by the introduction in the presupposition. The verb *refuse* triggers a presupposition, namely, that the subject has been asked to do what (s)he refuses to do. In (45a), *Galilei refused* presupposes that somebody has asked him to do P, and asserts Galilei's unwillingness to P. The variable P is present both in the presupposition and assertion. The anaphoricity of the zero argument can be explained by the introduction in the presupposition.

The verb *receive* in (46a) does not trigger a presupposition which involves the zero argument *from x*, so in (46a) the assertion structure of *Sue received a letter* contains the variable *from x*. It does not occur in a presupposition, so it cannot receive an anaphoric interpretation through the presupposition. However, native speakers prefer (46b) out of the possible interpretations, and it is quite natural for them that Sue received the letter from Joe. Example (46c) can also be a possible interpretation, but is not preferred. In (46b), the zero argument is also anaphoric, but its anaphoricity is not caused by the presupposition triggered by the verb *receive*. This zero complement acquires its anaphoricity through a pragmatically driven inference process. Relevance considerations lead to the identification of the lexically unrealised argument with a known entity of the context, independently of the semantic presupposition. Thus, (46b) demonstrates that a zero argument can also have an anaphoric reading, even if it is not involved in a presupposition triggered by the verb. In this case the anaphoricity of the null argument can be explained by other lexical-semantic features or non-lexical-semantic properties.

Secondly, it may also happen that a zero argument involved in a presupposition is not anaphoric. This case can be well illustrated by the occurrences of the German verb *erkränken* 'become sick' with zero arguments.[12] Some occurrences of the English verbs *eat* and *drink* also may be problematic in this respect, depending on the definition of presupposition.

The third question is that sometimes it is very difficult to verify the anaphoricity of a zero argument because the presupposition triggered by the verb is vague, as, for example, in the case of *come* and *go*.[13]

There is a fourth problem with Saeboe's proposal. He states that the anaphoricity of zero arguments does not vary across languages. If one takes into consideration not only languages closely related to English but also pro-drop languages, which allow their arguments to be left implicit far more freely than English does, it is not certain that Saebo's claim can be maintained. For example, in Hungarian most transitive verbs can occur both with indefinite and definite zero arguments following from the special morphosyntactic properties of Hungarian, namely, from the indefinite and definite conjugations, i.e. in addition to subject pro-drop, object pro-drop is also possible in Hungarian (see Bartos 1997; É. Kiss 2002 as well as Section 5.1.2). So, one can easily find two otherwise synonymous English, German, or Norwegian verbs, on the one hand, and Hungarian verbs, on the other, where an argument in a language of the first group can be left implicit with a definite reading, but the same argument in Hungarian can be left implicit, not only with a definite but also with an indefinite interpretation.

Although Gillon (2012) includes syntactic and model theoretic semantics elements in the way he accounts for a verb's behaviour with implicit complements, he shares Fillmore's (1986) opinion that the occurrence of implicit complements is lexically determined. Syntax and model theoretic semantics require that the possibility of the occurrence of an implicit complement be signalled by the lexical item, and that the kind of interpretation which should be assigned to the implicit complement in question should also be marked (Gillon 2012: 352). He emphasises that the use of implicit complements is a common feature in the world's languages with a range of construals such as indefinite implicit object, reflexive, reciprocal, and contextual (definite) implicit complements (see (15a–d), respectively, in Section 2.1). He argues that it is not only verbs which can occur with implicit complements, but all words denoting binary relations. These words can also be found in other major lexical classes such as, e.g., adjectives (*nearby, foreign, friendly*, etc.) and nouns (*father, mother, captain, mayor, bottom*, etc.).

On the basis of Gillon's (2012) suggestions, words admitting implicit arguments can be divided into two groups. Words in the first group are context-sensitive in the sense that they can only be used with lexically unrealised arguments if the reference of implicit arguments can be identified in the context (see Fillmore's (1986) DNC-verbs). Words in the other group are not context-sensitive, i.e. they can occur with indefinite implicit complements (see Fillmore's (1986) INC-verbs). Gillon (2012: 335–337) refers to two kinds of generally recognised context sensitivity. One kind is endophoric usage and the other exophoric. An endophoric expression (e.g., the utterances *Two is even* and *It is even* where *it* in the second utterance is endophoric) requires knowledge of another expression, namely an antecedent or postcedent in its cotext in order to have its full and appropriate interpretation.[14] An exophoric expression (e.g. *here* in the utterance *Marco Polo died here*) needs knowledge of the circumstances of its use to be fully and properly interpreted. They are also known in the philosophical, logical, and semantic/pragmatic literature as indexicals. It is worth mentioning that, although there are a few expressions which have an endophoric usage but no exophoric one (e.g. the third person reflexive pronouns and reciprocal pronouns) and other expressions which have an exophoric usage but no endophoric one (e.g. the first person singular personal pronoun), many expressions (e.g. third person personal pronoun) have both usages. Since there are expressions with both endophoric and exophoric usages, Gillon (2012: 337) introduces a new term, *ambiphoric*, to cover words which have both usages. Gillon also remarks that ambiphoric implicit arguments were considered contextual construal by Allerton (1975, 1982) and DNC by Fillmore (1986).

However, it should be highlighted that there are context-sensitive implicit arguments not mentioned by Gillon (2012) which have neither an endophoric nor an exophoric character, i.e. their use is not licensed by the preceding discourse context c_{disc}, nor by the observable physical environment c_{phys}, respectively. Their context sensitivity is connected to the encyclopaedic context c_{enc} language users have in mind. Recall the Hungarian conversation in (6) in Section 1.1, where the third argument of the verb *hozat* 'to have somebody/something brought' is lexically unrealised, not because of the pro-drop properties of Hungarian which is mirrored in an endophoric usage, nor because of the physical circumstances as in an exophoric usage. The third argument of the verb *hozat* in (6) is licensed by the shared encyclopaedic pieces of information according to which there is a belief in Hungarian folk thinking that children are brought by storks, therefore the stork – more exactly, the concept of the stork – is accessible mentally in a context which includes such words as *children, younger sibling, pregnancy*, etc. This mentally accessed entity can serve as the reference of the third implicit argument of *hozat*.

Gillon (2012) emphasises that the other type of the occurrence of verbs with implicit complements, namely with indefinite null complements which are not context-sensitive, poses a dilemma for a model theoretic treatment of natural language semantics. The dilemma is whether to assume only one verb or two verbs in occurrences with indefinite null complements and overt complements; cf., e.g., the verbs *eat, drink, bake, carve, cook, write, sweep*, and *type*. There are two emblematic accounts in formal semantics for the problem of the occurrence of verbs with indefinite null complements. Both of them agree that these verbs are ambiguous between two different lexical entries, one being intransitive and the other transitive (cf. the solution proposed by lexical-functional grammar in Section 3.1.3), but they differ in the particular solution they provide for the problem. Fodor and Fodor (1980) propose a meaning postulate, while Dowty (1981) suggests a lexical rule to suitably constrain the meanings of the intransitive and transitive entries for these verbs. Relying on the empirical difficulties these two approaches face,[15] Gillon convincingly argues for an alternative explanation, claiming that the verbs which can occur with indefinite null complements are unambiguous, i.e. there is no need to assume two lexical entries, one intransitive and another transitive. Gillon's resolution to the dilemma is based on a method familiar from HPSG (see, e.g., Pollard and Sag 1994; Engdahl 1999), according to which lexical and phrasal categories are treated as comprising two parts, namely, a part of speech category and a complement list (Gillon 2012: 322–325). For instance, the English verbs which take no complements such as, e.g., *die, sleep*, and *laugh* are assigned the category V:< >, where V means the primitive lexical category of verbs and < >

indicates that the complement list is empty. Those English verbs which take one complement, such as *greet* and *approve (of)* are assigned the categories V:<NP> and V:<PP>, respectively, where <NP> indicates that the verb *greet* takes an NP complement, while <PP> indicates that the verb *approve (of)* takes a PP complement. The English verbs which take two complements such as, e.g., *consider*, *name*, and *introduce* are assigned the categories V:<NP, AP>, V:<NP, NP>, V:<NP, PP>, respectively. Gillon (2012: 325) denotes the pairs comprising an expression and its category by writing the name of the expression on the left side of the symbol '|' and the category on the right side, as follows: *sleep*|V:< >, *greet*|V:<NP>, *consider*|V:<NP, AP>. The lexicon of English contains such pairs.[16] In order to describe the occurrence of words – including verbs – with indefinite null complements, Gillon (2012: 330) introduces a further symbol to be used in complement lists. The label *ind* is suggested for the words where a complement can be omitted with an indefinite reading. Consider Gillon's (2012: 331) examples.

(47) a. Bill read (*Le Horla*).

b. Bill perused *(*Le Horla*).

Gillon proposes the following complement lists for the verbs *read* and *peruse:* *read*|V:<{NP,ind}> and *peruse*|V:<{NP}>, respectively. The curly brackets indicate the ordered set of arguments and the presence of *ind* in the complement list in the position of direct object refers to the optionality of the direct object with indefinite interpretation.

The formation of the sentence *S* in (47a) and (47b) is as follows.

(48) a. *Bill*|N:< >   *read*|V:<{NP,ind}>

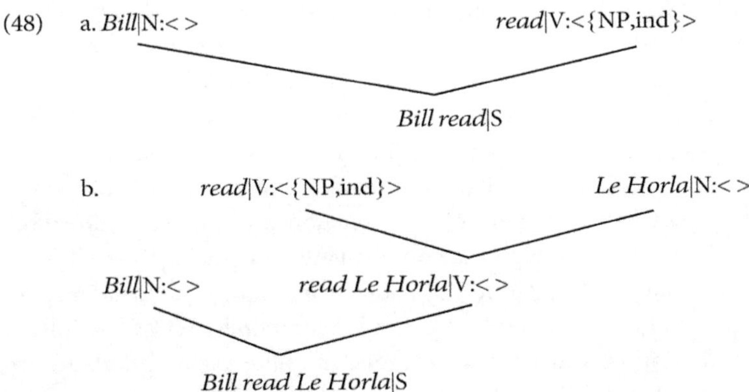

Bill read|S

b.   *read*|V:<{NP,ind}>   *Le Horla*|N:< >

Bill|N:< >   *read Le Horla*|V:< >

Bill read Le Horla|S

As to the semantic function of the label {NP,ind}, in (48b) the verb *read* should have an NP complement; the value of the VP node is then determined in the same way as is done for verbs with direct objects. But in (48a), where the verb *read* should not have an NP complement, the set of first coordinates of the set of ordered pairs assigned to the node of V is assigned to the VP node (Gillon 2012: 331–332). Gillon (2012: 333) generalises these rules and formulates a general cancellation rule formally by means of which the starting dilemma of the use of verbs with indefinite null complements can be solved. Since from the perspective of the way of thinking adopted in the subsequent chapters in the book, the presentation of the formalisation of this cancellation rule is not necessary, I do not present it here. Informally speaking, if a head word's complement is missing (as the direct object complement of the verb *read* in (48a)), then the corresponding set in the complement list includes the special sign *ind*. This condition is expressed by means of a monotonically increasing injection which pairs the categories of the word's complements with the sets of categories in the head word's complement lists. If a set in the complement list does not have a category of a complement word paired with it, then the set contains *ind*.

Gillon's non-ambiguity hypothesis makes it possible to assign values to verbs, including verbs with optional complements. It makes explicit how these values determine the values associated with the verb phrase and also sanctions the entailments arising for the verbs which license optional complements (Gillon 2012: 335). Although Gillon provides a formal semantic account for the behaviour of verbs with indefinite null complements, he emphasises that the licensing of the occurrence with an indefinite null complement is the peculiarity of individual verbs and not the result of what the verbs denote or how they are used. Licensing of implicit indefinite complements by some verbs is a purely lexical matter, as Fillmore (1986) and Saeboe (1995) suppose and not a matter of pragmatics as Groefsema (1995) suggests or a matter of metaphysics as Iten et al. (2005) propose (Gillon 2012: 335).[17] If it is so, one should examine what kind of lexical-semantic properties of verbs licenses the use of verbs with indefinite implicit arguments.

Although the non-ambiguity hypothesis is well argued in Gillon's (2012) article, there are two points to be discussed here. Firstly, if one considers the context-sensitive occurrences of implicit complements, a latent background assumption must be supposed according to which the phenomena of lexically unrealised endophoric, exophoric, or ambiphoric complements must be analysed in context-sensitive utterances of language use and not in context-independent sentences of language. But this latent background assumption contradicts Gillon's (2012: 314) definition of implicit complements. In Gillon's conception, a word can have an optional complement if the omission of the word's complement from an acceptable simple declarative sentence leaves the resulting sentence acceptable. An optional complement of a word is called an implicit complement when it is omitted, and an explicit complement when it is not. Furthermore, as we have seen above, Gillon also says that other types of implicit complements, i.e. indefinite null complements, are not context-sensitive, which means that a latent background assumption can be recovered again, i.e. the occurrences of verbs with indefinite implicit arguments must be examined in sentences. Using these two latent background assumptions as premises, it can be concluded that definite/contextual implicit arguments and indefinite ones are considered in Gillon's (2012) theory at two different levels, i.e. the utterance-level and the sentence-level, respectively. However, this cannot be an intended conclusion in Gillon's explanation, since it means that, while context-dependent implicit complements are assigned to language use, the indefinite null complements are assigned to the language itself. This conclusion is inconsistent with Gillon's (2012: 314) definition.

Moreover, there are verbs in English which can be used with both definite and indefinite implicit complements such as *contribute* and *give* 'donate', as we have seen when discussing Fillmore's (1986) approach (see (36a–c)). It is not plausible to suppose that the occurrences of these verbs with implicit complements must be examined once in language use if the implicit complement has a definite reading and once in language if the implicit complement has an indefinite interpretation, as would follow from Gillon's (2012) explanation. In the criticism of Fillmore's (1986) approach, we have seen that the context-independency of indefinite null complements in some cases does not hold. References of indefinite null complements do not differ very often from all entries saliently presented in the previous context. To identify the reference of the missing complement, the context involves the necessary information (see the occurrences of implicit arguments in (36)–(37)).

Gillon's (2012) non-ambiguity hypothesis proposes that there is only one lexical entry for both kinds of use of verbs with explicit complements and implicit indefinite complements in the case of verbs which can be used with indefinite null complements. The use of verbs with an indefinite null complement, e.g. an indefinite direct object, can only be considered a lexically determined possibility, and the actual occurrence depends on a particular language user. Since a particular language user is involved in the context, the indefinite null complements can also be evaluated as context-sensitive, i.e. the real occurrences of indefinite implicit arguments are also utterance-level-phenomena which are embedded and anchored in language use. Assuming this kind of context sensitivity for indefinite implicit complements resolves the inconsistencies (cf. Kertész and Rákosi 2012: 34–36, 130) which have emerged in Gillon's (2012) account.

The second problem which is worth discussing in Gillon's argumentation concerns the notion of context. Although context sensitivity is one of the main concepts in his theory, Gillon does not treat explicitly the notion of the context. He also applies the terms *cotext* and *circumstance*, but he does not make explicit what relationships can be assumed between these terms. As we have seen above, he refers to two universally recognised kinds of context sensitivity, i.e. endophoric and exophoric. In an endophoric kind of context sensitivity an expression requires for its full and proper interpretation knowledge of other expressions in its surrounding text or cotext, while in an exophoric kind of context sensitivity an expression needs knowledge of the circumstances of its use for a full and proper interpretation. Gillon also mentions that there are many expressions which have both kinds of usage. Cotext and circumstance can be conceived of as two subsets of context and, consequently, two kinds of context sensitivity can be assumed, namely, cotext-sensitivity and circumstance-sensitivity. In terms of the present volume, cotext is the discourse context c_{disc}, while circumstance is the physical context c_{phys}. As we have seen in Section 1.1 and 1.2.2, a third subset of context, namely encyclopaedic context c_{enc} must be assumed to account for the behaviour of verbs with implicit arguments. As I have referred to above in this section as well, in (6) in Section 1.1 one has to rely on the common encyclopaedic knowledge in Hungarian folk thinking concerning the stork, on the basis of which the implicit argument of the verb *hozat* 'to have somebody/something brought' can be left lexically unrealised. Recall also the utterance in (38) in which the English verb *win* is used with an implicit direct object argument, and, as Groefsema (1995) argues, the direct object argument can be left lexically unrealised in the example *Martina Navratilova has won again*, because we know who Martina Navratilova is and what she is famous for, i.e. there is no need to explicitly mention a particular competition in the discourse context, as Fillmore (1986) suggests. Thus, in (38), if the speaker/hearer has these pieces of information, a contextually given competition is not necessary to access the interpretation 'Martina Navratilova has won the competition in which she took part'. These pieces of information which license the use of the verb *win* with an implicit direct object argument in (38) are not included in the cotext or in the circumstances, but are instead involved in the speaker/hearer's encyclopaedic knowledge. Therefore, it is reasonable to extend Gillon's notion of context sensitivity reconstructed here with the encyclopaedic kind of information, i.e. with pieces of information from c_{enc} and to introduce a third kind of context sensitivity, namely encyclopaedic context sensitivity.

To summarise: the lexical-semantic approaches discussed in this section agree that lexical-semantic representations of verbs determine the possibility of the occurrence with indefinite and definite implicit arguments. Whether a verb can be used with implicit arguments and, if so, with what types of argument is marked in its lexical-semantic representation. Although Saeboe (1996) and Gillon (2012) suggest a formal semantic account for the occurrence with indefinite implicit arguments, they also share Fillmore's (1986) opinion regarding lexical-semantic determinacy. However, as we have seen above, various problems arise with these explanations, and some elements of inconsistency can be revealed between the latent background assumptions underlying these solutions. Three problems are worth emphasising again. On the one hand, these explanations are not consistent as to where to examine the occurrence of verbs with implicit arguments, in context-independent language or context-dependent language use. On the other hand, their predictions concerning the behaviour of verbs with lexically unrealised arguments cannot always be sustained in English and languages similar to it, since other factors also influence the occurrence of verbs with implicit arguments. And finally, the lexical-semantic accounts by themselves cannot provide adequate explanation for the freer occurrence of verbs with implicit arguments in pro-drop languages, as I have indicated when criticising Fillmore's (1986) and Gillon's (2012) accounts.

After discussing the lexical-semantic approaches to the occurrence of verbs with implicit arguments, let us turn to the complex explanations.

2.4 Complex approaches: interaction between lexical-semantic, grammatical, and pragmatic factors

To avoid the insufficiency of purely syntactic, pragmatic, or lexical-semantic explanations, recent proposals assume an interaction between lexical-semantic, grammatical, and pragmatic factors in the licensing of the occurrence of verbs with implicit arguments and also in their interpretation processes (see, e.g., Groefsema 1995; Cote 1996; García Velasco and Portero Muñoz 2002; Cummins and Roberge 2005; Goldberg 2005a, b; Iten et al. 2005; Scott 2006, 2013; Bibok 2008; Pethő and Kardos 2009; Németh T. 2008a, 2012, 2014a, b; and Németh T. and Bibok 2010). Although these different proposals in diverse theories emphasise the role of various factors to a different extent, they share the view that implicit arguments can be adequately accounted for only by assuming an interaction between the various factors.[18]

Groefsema (1995) investigates occurrences of English verbs with implicit (in her terminology: understood) direct object arguments from a discourse perspective. She explains her examples relying on Jackendoff's (1990) conceptual semantics and Sperber and Wilson's (1986/1995) relevance theory. I attempt to sketch out briefly those relevance-theoretic theses which are necessary to understand Groefsema's accounts, before discussing her solution.

According to relevance theory (Sperber and Wilson 1986/1995), the hearer must fulfil two tasks in verbal communicative interactions during the interpretation of utterances to recover information which the speaker wanted to communicate, i.e. to construct mental representations which are very similar to, or are the same as, the speaker's representations. On the one hand, the hearer must process explicatures, i.e. (s)he must set up semantic representations encoded linguistically in utterances and must enrich them into the fully fledged conceptual representation, i.e. fully propositional form, which the speaker intended to convey. On the other hand, the hearer must reconstruct the explicatures as well as recover implicatures carried by utterances and intended by the speaker. The hearer uses both decoding and inferential procedures for establishing explicatures, and inferential processes for implicatures. The linguistic decoding processes very often lead to an incomplete logical form (i.e. an incomplete conceptual representation), and to an otherwise non-fully propositional form because of the incompleteness or underdetermination of utterances. These incomplete forms must be enriched. The appropriate values have to be assigned to points at which the logical form is incomplete from the context. In relevance theory the context may include representations of the elements in the physical environment which contains the given utterance itself and the preceding discourse as physical stimuli, as well as the representations of the cognitive environment that contain the assumptions represented earlier by the communicative partner. These three kinds of information are involved in (9) in Section 1.2.2, and referred to as c_{disc}, c_{phys}, and c_{enc}, which define the term *context c* in the definition of utterance-type u_t in (7) in Section 1.2.2. Groefsema (1995) distinguishes between the immediate and extended contexts within the notion of context. The immediate context refers to the narrow linguistic utterance environment, while the extended context refers to the broader context of utterance. The extended context of utterances involves further contextual information in comparison with the immediate utterance context (see Section 1.2.2). What relevance theory means by assumptions are thoughts, i.e. conceptual representations, as opposed to sensory or emotional representations treated by an individual as representations of the actual world (as opposed to fiction, desires, or representations of representations). The context is not given and determined in advance of the comprehension process, as was previously assumed in the pragmatic literature. But the context is chosen by the hearer during the interpretation processes in such a way that the expectation of the hearer concerning the relevance of the utterance can be satisfied. In the choice of the context, extensions of the context through adding further assumptions to it are always made step by step. An assumption is immediately accessible (i.e. it is retrievable in one step) during extensions of the context if it is accessible from more than one conceptual address currently accessed (i.e. conceptual addresses already present in the context and in the logical form of the utterance being processed; Groefsema 1995: 150). Immediate accessibility is also valid for concepts and is fully in harmony with Jackendoff' s (1990) proposal (see Section 2.3). Applying this to verbs, we can say that a lexically realised verb gives access to its conceptual representation, which involves the arguments of the verb together with selection restrictions, even those arguments which are lexically unexpressed in the utterance. The assignment of values to points at which the logical form – which comes from the linguistic input – is incomplete is done in accordance with the communicative principle of relevance. The communicative principle of relevance asserts that every act of ostensive communication communicates the presumption of its own optimal relevance (Sperber and Wilson 1986/1995: 158). Ostensive communication is a kind of behaviour of the communicator which attracts the partner's attention and shows the communicator's intentions. So, the communicator behaves ostensively to make her/his partner observe her/his intention to make manifest something to her/him, namely, the intention to give her/him some information. The communicative partner takes the context and the ostensive behaviour of the communicator into account and tries to infer the communicator's intentions (Németh T. 1996: 12–16). Every speaker intends to form her/his utterances so that they are optimally relevant in the verbal communication, i.e. to form the utterances in such a way that they enable the hearer to derive an adequate number of contextual effects for no unjustifiable processing effort. An assumption represented in an interpretation process of an utterance may have three types of contextual effects: (i) contextual implications: the newly represented assumption made during the contextualisation (i.e. in the context of the old assumptions) results in further new assumptions; (ii) contextual strengthening: a newly represented assumption causes an already existing assumption to be held more strongly; (iii) contradiction elimination: the newly represented assumption resolves a contradiction between two already existing assumptions (Sperber and Wilson 1986/1995: 108–137, 142–151). Below, I use the first type of contextual effects, namely, contextual implications.

On the basis of conceptual semantic and relevance-theoretic considerations, Groefsema (1995: 152–160) gives two cases in which a verb can be used with implicit arguments. Firstly, an argument can be left implicit if the verb puts a selection restriction on the argument that provides an interpretation in accordance with the principle of relevance. In (49), which is originally Fillmore's (1986) example, one can arrive at the correct (relevant) interpretation by means of selection restrictions without any extension of the context. The selection restrictions, which the verbs *eat* and *drink* put on their second THING arguments, are: to be of the type FOOD (see (43) in Section 2.3) and to be of the type LIQUID, respectively.

(49)   When my tongue was paralysed I couldn't eat or drink.

In (49) it is not only the assumptions about what is involved in eating and drinking as physical activities that become immediately accessible, but also the grammatical information about the verbs *eat* and *drink*, including the selection restrictions which these verbs put on their direct object arguments. All these in the context of (49) yield the contextual effect that the communicator was hungry and thirsty at the time her/his tongue was paralysed. It is also possible that a further new assumption can be derived, namely, that the communicator was fed intravenously.

Secondly, a verb can be used with an understood argument if the rest of the utterance makes immediately accessible an assumption which yields an interpretation in accordance with the principle of relevance. Consider (50a–c).

(50)   a.   Paul gave to Amnesty International.

      b.   ?Paul gave to Ann.

      c.   I always give books on birthdays.

The direct object argument of *give* is left implicit in (50a). The verb *give* does not put any selection restrictions on its direct object argument, the omissibility of the direct object argument is permitted because of the fact that the interpretation of *give* and *Amnesty International* make immediately accessible an assumption that decent people donate money to Amnesty International. So, from this the hearer can infer that what Paul gave to Amnesty International was some money. The acceptability of (50b) is questionable, because the missing direct object argument does not become immediately accessible by the interpretation of *Paul, give* and *Ann*. In (50c) *give* and *birthdays* make immediately accessible the information that friends and relatives give presents to each other on birthdays. Using this assumption one can infer that the reference of the implicit argument in (50c) is the people to whom the speaker gives presents on their birthdays. Thus, the adequate interpretations of implicit arguments in (50a–c) are based on the lexical-sematic properties of the verb *give* as well as the encyclopaedic pieces of information in the context c_{enc} accessible under the conceptual addresses of the other lexemes in utterances in (50a–c).

Undoubtedly, it is true that Groefsema's (1995) proposal can account for a wider domain of the occurrence of English verbs with implicit arguments, and it has more explanatory force than the purely syntactic, pragmatic, or lexical-semantic solutions. However, according to her, if neither a selection restriction nor an immediately accessible assumption constrains the interpretation of the argument then it cannot be left implicit. Thus, the freer occurrence of implicit arguments in pro-drop languages cannot be explained entirely by Groefsema's (1995) explanation either.

Various discourse factors can also influence the occurrence of implicit arguments (Cote 1996). If a speaker does not realise verbal arguments lexically, (s) he considers these arguments to be at the centre of the hearer's attention. The interpretations of the previous utterances, the organisation of the discourse or the situation, and also encyclopaedic knowledge make it possible to access these arguments very easily without any explicit mention.[19] Cote (1996) investigates the behaviour of zero subjects as well as zero objects in English. Zero subjects generally occur in tensed, declarative, or interrogative sentences in conversational spoken English. Since utterances with null subjects occur with a certain frequency and regularity, and furthermore English native speakers find these utterances acceptable, it is necessary to contrast them with true performance errors. Null subjects in conversational English are used only if certain syntactic, semantic, or discourse properties exist.[20] Utterances with zero subjects cannot be evaluated as elliptical sentences or parts of sentences. Neither do they involve phonological or syntactic deletion. Analysing a fairly large spoken language corpus, Cote has demonstrated that the structure and the organisation of discourses constrain the appearances of null subjects. Null subjects refer to the saliently present entities in the centre of the context. Cote classifies the salience of the discourse entities and their position relating to the centre of the context on the basis of centering theory (cf., e.g., Brennan, Friedman, and Pollard 1987, Gordon, Grosz, and Gilliom 1993) and Jackendoff's (1990) lexical conceptual semantics. The placements of discourse entities relating to the centre of the discourse may change from utterance to utterance, depending on what element the speaker wants to saliently present or what element the speaker thinks of as being at the centre of the hearer's attention. In an utterance, the most salient entity of the context stays at the centre, but this position can be established only subsequently in the course of the interpretation process as a result of a comparison of the ongoing utterance with the previous one. centering theory also investigates the relative salience of entities at the centre of attention and how the ordering of entities affects the coherence of a discourse. A lexically realised verb makes access to its ordered arguments. The ordered elements of Jackendoff's (1990) conceptual semantic representation and the comparison of these elements with the lexically expressed elements serve as an input for the organisation of discourse entities relating to the centre of the context. As indicated above, if the speaker does not realise verbal arguments explicitly, (s)he considers these arguments to be at the centre of the hearer's attention. The interpretations of the previous utterances and the organisation of the discourse make it possible to access these arguments without any explicit mention. In terms of these considerations, it is not surprising that null subjects occur more often in discourses at turn boundaries (see (51)), with the speaker change at discourse segment boundaries (see (52)), and with the topic change at discourse package boundaries (see (53)).[21]

(51)   Was I on time?
        Seemed to be.

(52)   Can we talk now?

Shouldn't take long. You need any help?

Need any help?

(53)   (Break in first discourse package.)

Just a second. (Talking to child in background.) Sorry. Child.

That's all right.

(End 'aside' package – begin new discourse package)

[   ] Sounds like you have a little one there.

(Cote 1996: 84)[22]

In (51) the null subject appears at the turn boundary at the beginning of the answer in a question–answer sequence. It can be identified easily (*you*), it is coreferential with the referent of the personal pronoun *I* in the first turn. In the question the speaker refers to her/himself; (s)he marks, by the use of *I* that her/his person is the most salient among the discourse entities. To answer the question, the partner also must refer to the person in question. It must be noticed that in such dialogues the centre in the answer has not been established subsequently, as one might expect in centering theory. Following from the nature of a question–answer sequence, it can be established exactly what the centre in the answer is, therefore it should not be lexically realised. In (52) the first null subject (it refers to the dialogue itself) appears at the turn boundary at the beginning of the utterance replying to the question, which also functions as an indirect question. The second zero subject (*I* referring to the speaker) occurs at the turn boundary at the beginning of a rhetorical question, which can be taken as the first utterance of a new discourse segment: the partner wants to express why (s)he needs some help. In (53) the zero subject (*it*) occurs at the beginning of the first utterance of a new discourse package. This zero subject refers to the entity (baby's cry) at the centre of the situation. The baby's cry interrupts the first discourse package, and subsequently begins a new one which is connected to the interruptions.

In Cote's opinion, null subjects in spoken English are generated as non-overt pronominal subjects; they are the constructions most similar to pro-drop or zero pronominal subjects in discourse-oriented languages, and their occurrences are governed by discourse constraints. Unfortunately, Cote does not deal with the underlying causes of discourse constraints. Therefore, the pragmatic principles which explain the occurrences of null subjects and make it possible to identify them are not manifested.

Cote (1996) also studies the occurrences of zero objects in English. As we have seen in Section 2.3, lexical-semantic explanations also treat the licensing factors of the use of verbs with implicit direct object arguments, but they do not take the discourse constraints into consideration at all. Cote attempts to eliminate these shortcomings applying centering theory to the conceptual semantic representations of verbs as inputs. Consequently, she relies on the lexical-semantic properties of verbs as well as on discourse constraints in the treatment of zero objects.

The occurrences of zero objects in English are not restricted to the conversational spoken language. Cote (1996: 114) defines null objects as non-overt internal arguments of any verb that may also take overt pronominal internal arguments with the same semantic role. The presence of null objects must be supported by syntactic or discourse evidence. Instead of a purely syntactic definition, null objects are alternatively defined as instances of non-overt reference to a particular (though perhaps new or ambiguously determined) discourse entity. Cote divides verbs which allow their direct object arguments to be left implicit into six groups. The first group involves salient object alternation verbs (SOA-verbs), i.e. Fillmore's (1986) DNC-verbs and Gillon's (2012) context-sensitive verbs, e.g. *call, enter, leave, attend, win,* and *answer.* Lexically unrealised arguments of these verbs require saliently present discourse antecedents with which they can be coreferential. Further, as Cote claims, the discourse referents of zero objects cannot be at the centres of the subsequent utterances. The second group contains indefinite object alternation verbs (IOA-verbs), i.e. Fillmore's INC-verbs and Gillon's (2012) verbs with indefinite implicit arguments, e.g. *eat, drink, dance, write,* and *sing.* Zero objects of these verbs do not need any discourse antecedent, they themselves introduce new entities into the discourse.[23] Generic object alternation verbs (GOA-verbs), e.g. *dream, sleep, laugh,* and *weep,* belong to the third group. GOA-verbs can occur only with overt full cognition objects very restrictively in marked contexts. These verbs are very often classified as true intransitive verbs.[24] The verbs in the fourth group are arbitrary object alternation verbs (AOA-verbs), e.g. *shock, warn, caution, advise,* and *amuse.* The objects of AOA-verbs can be left implicit only if they are arbitrary in reference and the clause involving them has a generic time reference (see (54a–b)). The null objects of AOA-verbs – similarly to the zero objects of IOA-verbs – do not have an intended antecedent.[25]

(54)   a.   That movie always shocks [ ].

          b.   The instructions caution [ ] about possible electric shocks.

The fifth group in Cote's classification involves reflexive object alternation verbs (ROA-verbs), e.g. *dress, wash,* and *shave.* These verbs allow their objects to be left implicit only if they refer to the subjects of the activities, as in (55).

(55)   Greg dressed [ ] after his shower.

And finally, the sixth group contains habitual object alternation verbs (HOA-verbs), which can be used with null objects only in the case of repeated or habitual activities, as in (56a–b).

(56)   a.   What do you do when you don't know the answer?
             I guess [ ].
         b.   Shake [ ] well before using [ ]

Based on the broad idiosyncratic cross-linguistic variation and the results of the investigation of null subjects and objects in English, Cote (1996) establishes that the only absolute and universal constraint on null arguments is the interpretability of discourses that involve implicit arguments. There are various ways to reach interpretability in different languages, e.g. grammatical properties of utterances, lexical properties of verbs, and discourse constraints can be taken into account. Of these cues, the lexical properties of verbs and discourse constraints are the most important ways in English to ensure the interpretability of implicit arguments.

Among the latest approaches to lexically unrealised arguments, in a functional discourse grammar framework, García Velasco and Portero Muñoz (2002) investigate the licensing factors of implicit direct objects in English. They claim that the licensing of the occurrence of an implicit direct object argument with an indefinite reading is basically determined by lexical-semantic factors, i.e. it depends on the semantic class which the verb at stake belongs to and also on the type of the direct object argument. But implicit arguments with a definite interpretation are licensed by lexical-semantic, structural and pragmatic factors co-operatively. In both cases, the starting point is the abstract meaning definition of a verb, which determines the necessary number of participants. Following this, the predicate frames provide the syntactic environments which the lexical entries can enter according to the linking rules. The same lexical entry can join more than one predicate frame, which results in a syntactic alternation. For example, in the abstract meaning definition of the verb *eat*, two participants are involved. If *eat* enters a transitive predicate frame, then both participants in its abstract meaning definition are projected into the syntactic structure. In this case the second participant is also expressed explicitly as the syntactic object. The speaker wants to emphasise the object of the eating activity (see Section 1.1). If the speaker wants to transfer the focus of attention from the object of the eating activity to the eating activity itself, then the abstract meaning definition of the verb *eat* joins an intransitive predicate frame which does not contain a direct object position to be filled in. However, a selection restriction in the abstract meaning definition of *eat* makes it possible to interpret the direct object argument omitted in this way with an indefinite reading as a kind of food (see (43) in Section 2.3). In the case of the occurrence of verbs with definite implicit arguments, the speaker intends to identify the reference of lexically unrealised arguments from the preceding discourse or from the physical environment.

However, it must be noted that the definite implicit arguments can be identified not only with the help of information from the preceding discourse c_{disc} and physical environment c_{phys} (see above), but also by considering some pieces of encyclopaedic information c_{enc}. Furthermore, it can also happen that an indefinite implicit argument has an antecedent in the preceding discourse (see (37) in Section 2.3). In this case, the indefinite implicit argument is not only lexically determined, as García Velasco and Portero Muñoz (2002) suggest.

In construction grammar, the explicit or implicit realisation of arguments are determined by two interacting factors, i.e. by lexical semantics and constructions (Goldberg 2005a, b, 2013). The lexical-semantic representations of individual verbs involve frame-specific participant roles, while constructions, i.e. the conventional pairings of form and meaning, which are independent of individual verbs, have general argument roles capturing generalisations over individual verbs' participant roles. Not all of the participant roles of individual verbs and argument roles of constructions are profiled. To be lexically profiled is a stable aspect of lexemes. Profiled participant roles are usually obligatorily expressed or receive a definite interpretation in a language like English. The profiled argument roles usually appear syntactically as subject, object, or the second object of ditransitives, and there are also certain types of argument roles, e.g. animate roles, which are more likely to be inherently profiled than others and, therefore, are obligatorily expressed. A participant role of an individual verb must be fused with an argument role of a construction in order to be explicitly realised. The possibility of this fusion is constrained by the semantic coherence principle and the correspondence principle. The semantic coherence principle predicts that the participation role of the verb and the argument role of the construction to be fused must be semantically compatible. The correspondence principle requires that lexically profiled participant roles will be fused with profiled argument roles. An exception arises if a verb has three profiled participant roles and one of them can be fused with an unprofiled argument role. The correspondence principle is a default principle which can be overridden by the specifications of particular constructions. Taking into account all these requirements, in construction grammar verbs can occur with implicit arguments in the following two manners. Firstly, there are constructions which override the correspondence principle and de-emphasise a normally profiled participant role. In English such constructions are, for example, the implicit theme construction and the deprofiled object construction. Verbs of bodily emission, e.g. *sneeze, blow, cry, spit, ejaculate, piss*, and *vomit*, and verbs of donation, e.g. *contribute, donate*, and *give* 'donate' can be fused with the implicit theme construction. In the deprofiled object construction, the patient argument normally explicitly expressed as a syntactic object loses its emphasised status; it becomes de-emphasised instead of the action itself becoming particularly emphasised, e.g. *Pat gave and gave, but Chris just took and took. Owls only kill at night.* (see also García Velasco and Portero Muñoz 2002). Secondly, a non-profiled participant role is omitted in the intransitive use of transitive verbs, e.g. *drink, eat, sing, dance,* and *smoke.* In both manners, the lexical-semantic properties of individual verbs are crucial to determine whether a verb can be fused with a construction licensing an implicit argument, i.e. a profiled participant role can be de-emphasised or a non-profiled participant role can be omitted. The issue of what exactly these lexical-semantic properties are, and which semantic classes of verbs can participate in the occurrence with implicit arguments, requires further empirical research.

The lexical-constructional approach treats the occurrence of transitive verbs with explicit vs implicit direct object arguments as a syntactic alternation which can only be explained by considering both lexical-semantic and constructional factors (Bibok 2008, 2010). This approach assumes a general meaning representation of syntactically alternating verbs, which is encyclopaedically and pragmatically rich enough to serve as a basis for constructional meanings which come about when these verbs change their patterns of syntactic government. Thus, the constructional meanings of a verb are condensed into one lexical meaning. In other words, in the lexicon, verbs have underspecified representations and not those that are as specific as constructional meanings. From the point of view of syntactic alternations, it can be stated that verbs participate in them if they have a general meaning which is compatible with all the meanings occurring in the alternations. The occurrence of verbs with implicit arguments originates in this encyclopaedically and pragmatically rich general meaning. The lexical-semantic representation of verbs which can occur with implicit direct object arguments can be interpreted in two ways. Either only the physical activity denoted by the verbs is the focus of attention (*A gyerek iszik* 'The kid is drinking') or their object is as well (*A gyerek tejet iszik* 'The kid is drinking milk'). When only the physical activity is the focus of attention, the direct object arguments can be left lexically unrealised (see also García Velasco and Portero Muñoz 2002; Goldberg 2005b), but this argument remains available as background information in the lexical-semantic representation. Furthermore, if the direct object argument is also the focus of attention, the direct object arguments must be explicitly expressed. However, since there are various types of implicit arguments which have different licensing factors, this analysis should be extended by taking into account further grammatical and pragmatic constraints (see Chapters 3–6).

As has already been referred to in Section 2.1, Scott (2013) investigates in detail two registers in written English where null subjects can occur, namely diary texts and journals, and she also emphasises that in addition to these sources one can find null subjects in email messages, text messages, telegrams, postcards, note-taking, and message boards. Scott (2013: 69–71) briefly summarises how syntactic analyses attempt to explain these occurrences of null subjects known as diary-drops (see, e.g., Haegeman and Ihsane 1999, 2001). She highlights the fact that all of them agree that the interpretation and acceptability of utterances with null subjects in English vary from situation to situation, which is the result of pragmatic factors (Scott 2013: 69). This contradicts the generative grammatical background assumption concerning the relationship between grammar and pragmatics (see Section 1.2.1). Scott intends to recover pragmatic factors driving the use of null subjects in these registers and attempts to take up where the syntactic analyses leave off. In other words, Scott aims to provide the underlying pragmatic principles and discourse constraints of the use and interpretation of null subjects. In a relevance-theoretic approach (see also Groefsema 1995 above), Scott argues that communicators create extra or different effects by the use of null subjects in certain discourses of these registers, i.e. by using utterances with this type of null subject, speakers produce highly relevant stimuli. Scott (2013: 75–81) divides null subjects into three groups: (i) informal null subjects where the omission results in extra cognitive effects by inducing a casual, intimate tone of discourses (e.g. *Probably wants you to reply to his message* (personal email message) vs *He probably wants you to reply to his message*), (ii) pressured null subjects in discourses where there is a restriction on time or space (e.g. notes for minutes of a meeting to discuss updating a database system: *Can be integrated. Needs investigation*), and (iii) ostensively vague null subjects which can save hearers the effort of resolving a reference when this does not influence the relevance of the utterance (e.g. signs on a pile of trash outside a university department: *To be collected. Spoke to waste service*). At the same time, Scott (2013: 81) notes that with these three categories she is not offering an exhaustive taxonomy of English null subjects. With this presentation she only intends to illustrate how speakers use null subjects as referring expressions in their own right and make their utterances optimally relevant.[26] Replacing standard overt referring expressions with a diary-style implicit subject is an option for the speaker when constructing utterances. Since English is traditionally considered a non-null subject language (cf. the criticism of the non-null-subjectlessness of English in Section 2.1), the speakers are expected to use overt referring expressions according to the sentence-grammatical requirements. However, when speakers want to set an informal, intimate tone for their discourses or are under time and space pressure or a referent can be left ostensively vague or speakers aim to create literary effects, they can choose to use null subjects. In these cases, null subjects interact with the discourse context and speakers' intentions. This cannot be explained from the point of view of a purely sentence-oriented treatment; it needs a more complex approach.

To summarise: on the basis of the critical overview of some characteristic approaches to implicit arguments presented in Sections 2.1–2.4, it can be concluded that the syntactic and pragmatic factors as well as the lexical-semantic properties of verbs have a very important role by themselves in the licensing and interpretation of implicit arguments, but this role is not exclusive. It is not sufficient to consider these factors individually, independently of each other. There are various types of implicit arguments whose occurrences are guided by the interaction between these different constraints. For example, in Section 2.3 we have seen that the idiosyncratic lexical properties of individual verbs cannot license by themselves the occurrence of verbs with lexically unrealised arguments, since these idiosyncratic lexical properties are only the necessary but not sufficient prerequisites for the occurrences of verbs with implicit arguments. For the real, particular occurrences of lexically unrealised arguments, in addition to the lexical-semantic factors, one also has to take into account certain grammatical/constructional, discourse, general pragmatic as well as particular contextual factors, and even their interaction. The proposals briefly overviewed in Section 2.4 attest that grammatical/constructional, discourse, general pragmatic as well as particular contextual properties which license the occurrence of verbs with implicit arguments can be grasped and formulated in various theories, and these rival explanations can be compatible in some respect.

In the following part of the book I intend to examine how Hungarian verbs can occur with implicit subject and direct object arguments and how the lexically unrealised subject and direct object arguments can be interpreted in Hungarian language use. In Chapter 4, I will focus on which elements of the lexical-semantic representation of verbs license the occurrence with implicit subject and direct object arguments in Hungarian and how they do so. However, since the lexical-semantic properties are only necessary but not sufficient conditions of the licensing of lexically unrealised subject and direct object arguments in Hungarian language use, I will also take into account other, mainly grammatical, discourse, general pragmatic, and particular contextual constraints. Then, in Chapter 5, I will continue the investigation of the occurrence of Hungarian verbs with implicit subject and direct object arguments by the examination how the elements of the immediate utterance context and extended context with their grammatical requirements influence the behaviour of verbs with lexically unrealised subject and direct object arguments in Hungarian language use. I will devote special attention to the role of the indefinite/definite conjugations in the licensing and interpretation of implicit direct object arguments. The analyses in Chapters 4 and 5 will lead to a typology of Hungarian verbs regarding their occurrence with various types of implicit subject and direct object arguments and help to reveal the motivation of the use of verbs with these kinds of implicit arguments as well as principles guiding the identification mechanisms of lexically unrealised arguments in Hungarian language use. The concluding Chapter 6 will address these questions.

Before starting the particular analyses in Chapters 4 and 5, in the next chapter I attempt to clarify what I mean by implicit arguments, and in what manners I assume Hungarian verbs occur with lexically unexpressed arguments as well as the identification mechanisms of their implicit arguments in Hungarian language use.

CHAPTER 3

Occurrences of implicit arguments in Hungarian

3.1 Definition of implicit arguments

3.1.1 Implicit arguments at the grammar–pragmatics interface

In Hungarian linguistics research, the problem of the licensing and interpretation possibilities of lexically unrealised arguments has not so far been a widely investigated question, although there have been some works which deal with this topic by concentrating only on some types of implicit arguments, above all, those types of lexically unrealised arguments which can be explained on the basis of the pro-drop characteristics of Hungarian in sentence environments (see, e.g., Bartos 1997; É. Kiss 2002; Kiefer 1990; Komlósy 1994). Following on from this interest, this research line has especially focused on syntactic and semantic kinds of licensing factors. However, the results of psycholinguistics experiments on the behaviour of overt as well as zero anaphors[1] in Hungarian initiated by Csaba Pléh and his colleagues (see, e.g., Pléh 1994; 1998: 164–94; Pléh and Radics 1978; Pléh and McWhinney 1987; Dankovics 2005) have revealed that the recovering of zero anaphors in utterances requires both grammatical (decoding) and pragmatic (inferential) procedures. The evaluation of the findings of Pléh and his colleagues has supported the hypothesis that, on the one hand, grammar cannot account for all pro-form relations, and, on the other hand, the encyclopaedic information as well as particular contextual factors can override the use or interpretation predicted by grammar. The research by Pethő and Kardos (2009), Bibok and Németh T. (2001), and Németh T. and Bibok (2001, 2010) as well as my own investigations (e.g., Németh T. 2000, 2001, 2008a, 2012, 2014a, b) have also led to a conclusion that the occurrence and interpretation of implicit arguments in Hungarian language use are guided not only by syntactic and semantic constraints, but by lexical-semantic, grammatical, discourse, general pragmatic, and particular contextual factors taken together. In accordance with this conclusion, implicit arguments can be defined as follows.

(57)   Implicit arguments: arguments involved in the lexical-semantic representations of verbs but which are lexically unrealised, and whose implicit presence in utterances is attested by lexical-semantic, grammatical (phonological, morphological, syntactic, and semantic), discourse, and/or
pragmatic evidence.[2]

These kinds of evidence indicate the implicit presence of an argument and attest
that the particular utterance does not have a performance error. This definition
makes it possible to consider phonetically not realised, empty, or covert pronouns
(*pro* and even PRO) as implicit arguments. But, unlike the other types of implicit
arguments which are not represented in the syntactic structure of sentences, pronouns without overt phonetic form have a well-defined position on their own in
the syntactic structure. So, the conception of implicit arguments in (57) obviously
differs from the definition widely accepted in the generative grammatical tradition (cf. Radford 1997a).

Another conclusion of the previous investigations on implicit arguments is
that in Hungarian, as in other pro-drop languages, verbs can occur with implicit
arguments more frequently and in ways controlled differently than is the case
in languages without pro-drop phenomena (Németh T. 2000, 2001; Bibok and
Németh T. 2001; Németh T. and Bibok 2010). In Hungarian, verbs do not vary as
to whether they can occur with implicit arguments at all, but they vary as to the
manners or the contexts in which they occur. Thus, in Hungarian there are various types of implicit arguments, and their occurrence in utterances is licensed by
various interacting factors. The separate mention of these various factors in the
above-mentioned definition of implicit arguments indicates the diverse character
of different types of implicit arguments. However, although possibilities of the
occurrence of implicit arguments in Hungarian language use can be explained by
various factors, their intensive interaction should be emphasised.

3.1.2 Compatible alternative and non-compatible rival approaches to implicit arguments

The definition of implicit arguments in (57) is compatible with the idea of relevance theory (Groefsema 1995) and centering theory (Cote 1996), according to
which an argument involved in the conceptual-semantic representation of a verb
should not be lexically realised if certain lexical-semantic and contextual requirements are fulfilled (see Section 2.4). Functional grammars define implicit arguments similarly and propose an optional expression of an argument in the predicate frames (Dik 1985; de Groot 1985). For example, they always consider the
verb *eat* to be transitive, and as having a second (object) argument position which
may be left unspecified, thus rendering an activity meaning. Functional discourse
grammar replaces the notion of the predicate frame applied as a unique explana-

tory tool in functional grammars with a combination of the predicate template, the abstract meaning definition of lexemes and a linking mechanism joining them together (García Velasco and Portero Muñoz 2002: 19–20). The realisation and omission of an argument of a lexical item is allowed in functional discourse grammar if the abstract meaning definition of the lexical item can be connected with more than one predicate template. So, in functional discourse grammar the occurrence of verbs with implicit arguments can be treated as syntactic alternations of the particular verbs (see Section 2.4). In this regard, functional discourse grammar makes the same proposal as construction grammar (Goldberg 1995, 2005a, b) and the lexical-constructional approach (Bibok 2008, 2010; see Section 2.4). The definition in (57) is also similar to that suggested by Gillon's (2006, 2012) relational approach to verbs with implicit arguments. According to Gillon's proposal, the term *implicit argument* includes several kinds of lexically unexpressed arguments, such as PRO, missing subjects of verbs in the imperative mood, zero subjects in any pro-drop language, and missing direct object arguments in the intransitive use of transitive verbs (e.g. *eat, drink, cook,* and *read*; see Section 2.3).

However, the definition of implicit arguments in (57) differs from the definition widely accepted in the generative grammatical tradition (cf. Rizzi 1986; Roeper 1987; Radford 1997a; Bartos 2000; see also Section 2.1). According to the definition in (57), phonetically unrealised empty pronouns (i.e. *pro* and even PRO) can be considered implicit arguments which have a position on their own in the syntactic structure of a sentence, differently from the other kinds of implicit arguments (cf. Bibok and Németh T. 2001; Németh T. 2001, 2012; Gillon 2006, 2012). The definition in (57) also differs from the approach of lexical-functional grammar. Lexical-functional grammar assumes two lexical items in the case of, e.g., *eat, drink, read,* and *bake,* a transitive and an intransitive one, and there is a lexical rule which relates these two items of *eat, drink, read,* and *bake* to each other by changing their argument structure in order to account for the verbs' occurrence with or without a direct object argument (Komlósy 1994). In their formal semantics treatment, Fodor and Fodor (1980) as well as Dowty (1981) agree with the solution of lexical-functional grammar, according to which these verbs are ambiguous between two different lexical entries, one intransitive and the other transitive. However, as we have seen in Section 2.3, Fodor and Fodor (1980) and Dowty (1981) differ in the particular solution they offer to the problem. Fodor and Fodor (1980) propose a meaning postulate for the problem of the occurrence of verbs with indefinite null arguments, while Dowty (1981) suggests a lexical rule to constrain suitably the meanings of the intransitive and transitive entries for verbs which can be used with indefinite implicit arguments.[3]

The definition of implicit arguments suggested in (57) also differs from the definition applied in purely pragmatic accounts, since its starting point is the lexical-semantic representation of verbs, and it does not restrict the licensing factors to the pragmatic properties of the context in which lexically unrealised arguments occur (see Section 2.2).

Finally, the definition of implicit arguments in (57) does not distinguish terminologically between implicit arguments and the unarticulated constituents recently discussed in the semantics and pragmatics literature. The notion of the implicit argument in the literature on unarticulated constituents has a narrower scope than the definition in (57). While, according to the literature on unarticulated constituents, implicit arguments are those phonologically unrealised arguments which are generated in the syntax (*pro* and PRO), but do not have explicit expressions in the surface form of utterances, unarticulated constituents are those parts of propositions communicated by particular utterances which are necessarily assumed in order to assign a truth value to the utterances and at the same time do not correspond to any part of the linguistic utterances at issue.

Although in the present book I do not aim to overview the vast literature which discusses various kinds of unarticulated constituents and their interpretation mechanisms from very different points of view (see, e.g., Perry 1998; Stanley 2000; Carston 2002; Recanati 2004, 2007; Borg 2005; Martí 2006, Ariel 2008, 2010; Vicente and Groefsema 2013), here I intend to clarify that some kinds of unarticulated constituents can be considered implicit arguments according to the definition of implicit arguments in (57).

Recently, Vicente and Groefsema (2013: 109) have summarised and exemplified what kinds of unarticulated constituents are assumed in the literature so far. According to their summary, the following can be considered unarticulated constituents:

i.   adjuncts (e.g. *It is raining [in London]* (Perry 1986)),

ii. focusing adverbials (e.g. John has *[exactly] four children* (Bach 1994; Carston 2002)),

iii. noun modifiers (e.g. *She has a [high functioning] brain* (Carston 2009) and *Every student [in my class] passed the exam* (Hall 2008)),

iv. complements for indefinite null complement verbs such as *eat* (e.g. *I have eaten [supper]* (Wilson and Sperber 2002)),

v.   adjectives such as *ready* (e.g. *Tipper is ready [for what]* (Bach 1994)),

vi. determiners/pronouns such as *enough* (e.g. *Mark didn't get enough credit units [for what] and can't continue [with his studies]* (Carston 1988)),

vii. aspectual verbs such as *finish/continue* (e.g. *Al has finished [speaking]* (Bach 1994)), see also (vi),

viii. information in subsentential environments to construct a full proposition (e.g. *[The letter is] from Spain* (Stainton 2006)),

ix. temporal, causal, and other readings of conjunctions such as *and, if* (e.g. *Mary left Paul and [as a consequence] he became clinically depressed* (Carston 2002)),

    x.   cases of transferred reference (e.g. *[The person who ordered] The ham sandwich left without paying* (Recanati 2004)), and

   xi. multimodal ostensive stimuli such as, e.g., *I didn't see the [imitation of frightening grumpiness] woman today* (Carston 2010).[4]

It must be noted that the examples of various types of unarticulated constituents cited here can be found in the same or slightly modified versions in other works as well, e.g. Borg 2005; Martí 2006; Recanati 2007; Zouhar 2011. Thus, they can be considered typical examples of the literature on unarticulated constituents. However, from time to time new types of unarticulated constituents appear with the broadening of the literature on unarticulated constituents, and, consequently, there is no consensus in the literature on unarticulated constituents as to what phenomena can be included in the set of unarticulated constituents as well as what mechanisms can be assumed in the course of their identification.

From Vicente and Groefsema's (2013: 109) list it can be seen that the various types of unarticulated constituents are very different: the only common property they have is that they are needed for constructing a full proposition in the course of interpretation of the utterances they are involved in but not explicitly presented in. Examining these different types of unarticulated constituents from the point of view of whether the definition of implicit arguments provided in (57) can be applied to them, it can be concluded that the types of unarticulated constituents in (i), i.e. adjuncts, in (iv), i.e. complements for indefinite null complement verbs such as *eat*, in (v), i.e. adjectives such as *ready*, in (vii), i.e. aspectual verbs such as *finish/continue*, and in (viii), i.e. information in subsentential environments to construct a full proposition, are worth examining as to whether they should be involved in the set of implicit arguments as they are defined in (57).

Let us start with (iv) and (v). The verbs belonging to (iv) which can occur with indefinite null complements (e.g. *eat, drink, read,* and *write* in English and their Hungarian equivalents *eszik, iszik, olvas,* and *ír,* respectively, and also other Hungarian verbs in (106) in Section 4.2.2) as well as aspectual verbs in (v) such as *finish* and *continue* absolutely fit the definition of implicit arguments in (57). These verbs have in their lexical-semantic representations an argument, namely a direct object argument which can be left lexically unrealised if their implicit presence in utterances is attested by lexical-semantic, grammatical (phonological, morphological, syntactic, and semantic), discourse, and/or pragmatic evidence. When the literature on unarticulated constituents refers to the verbs occurring with indefinite null complements and analyses their indefinite null complements as unarticulated constituents, it excludes these lexically unrealised constituents from the notion of implicit arguments as they are conceived in the literature on unarticulated constituents, since they are not projected into the syntactic structure of utterances or, to put it the other way round, they do not have a position on their own in the syntactic structure of utterances.

However, according to a broader definition of implicit arguments in (57) the treatment of a lexically unrealised argument as an implicit argument can be licensed not only by syntactic factors. Without being involved in the syntactic structure of utterances, lexically unrealised arguments can be considered implicit arguments if other grammatical (including lexical-semantic or semantic), discourse, and/or pragmatic factors license their implicit presence in utterances (cf. also García Velasco and Portero Muñoz 2002; Goldberg 2005a, b; Bibok 2008; Gillon 2012; and Section 4.2.2). Similarly, the occurrences of aspectual verbs such as *finish/continue* with unarticulated constituents can also be analysed as implicit arguments according to the definition of implicit arguments in (57), on the same basis as occurrences of verbs with indefinite null complements.

As to adjectives such as *ready* in (i) or Hungarian *büszke* 'proud', *féltékeny* 'jealous', and *irigy* 'envious', they can also be analysed as having an argument position in their lexical-semantic representation which can be left lexically unrealised if the context contains the necessary information to construct a full proposition. The construction of a full proposition in these cases is based on the division of labour between linguistically realised and contextually inferable information. The definition of implicit arguments of verbs in (57) can naturally be modified in such a way that it can be valid for such adjectives, i.e. implicit arguments can be considered those arguments which are involved in the lexical-semantic representations of verbs or adjectives but which are lexically unrealised, and whose implicit presence in utterances is attested by lexical-semantic, grammatical (phonological, morphological, syntactic, and semantic), discourse, and/or pragmatic evidence.[5]

On the basis of the cited works, Vicente and Groefsema (2013: 109) categorises unarticulated constituents as adjuncts in the following examples: *It is raining [somewhere]* (Perry 1986; Recanati 2007), *She took out the gun, she went into the garden, and she killed her father [with the gun] [in the garden]* (Carston 2002), *Jack and Jill went up the hill [together]* (Carston 2002). However, if one examines these constituents more thoroughly, one notices that they are different in terms of how closely they are connected to the verbs on the basis of their participant role in the structure of events the verbs denote. In the syntactic and semantic literature, several tests are suggested to distinguish between arguments and adjuncts (e.g., the *do so* test, ellipsis test, ordering test, or *X-happen* test; cf., e.g., Radford 1988; Haegeman 1991; Jackendoff 2002; Culicover and Jackendoff 2005), but there is no clear division assumed between these constituents. Overviewing the literature and exploring how the distinction between arguments and adjuncts can be handled in Natural Language Processing applications, Hwang (2012) concludes that there is no one recommended set of criteria that suffices for this distinction across all verbs. Dowty (2003) goes even further, assuming that all elements in the sentence can be given both an argument and an adjunct analysis. Therefore, the quest to clearly identify the distinction between arguments and adjuncts might be misguided in his view (Hwang 2012).

But if one relies on the lexical-semantic representations of particular verbs to make a distinction between arguments and adjuncts, it can be said that arguments are those constituents which express necessary participants of the situation denoted by a verb. These participants are indicated in the argument structure of the lexical-semantic representation of verbs (Mel'čuk 2012: 195). And following from this, adjuncts are additional constituents providing information typically concerning, e.g., circumstances, goals, and manners, which are, therefore, not included in a verb's lexical-semantic representations. The main point of such a lexical-semantic view on the distinction between arguments and adjuncts is that a verb is stored with an argument structure which indicates how it combines syntactically with its dependents (Müller and Wechsler 2014).

Let us return to the verbs *rain* and *kill* in the above examples. On the basis of the lexical-semantic view on the distinction between arguments and adjuncts, we can say that the verb *rain* has not only a subject argument but also a second argument which refers to a location, and the verb *kill* has not only a subject and a direct object argument but also a third argument that refers to an instrument. The latter argument also expresses a participant of the event at issue without which one cannot think of killing. Starting out from the lexical-semantic representations of the verbs *rain* (see (58)) and *kill* (see (59)), the lexically unrealised locative phrase *somewhere* and instrumental phrase *with the gun* can be analysed as locative and instrumental arguments of the verbs *rain* and *kill* which are left lexically unrealised.

(58)   rain: 'x which is rain[6] falls in y which is place'

                [[x FALL_IN y] : [[RAIN x] & [PLACE y]]] [7]

(59)   kill: 'using z, x causes that y becomes not alive'

                [[x USE z] CAUSE [BECOME [not ALIVE y]]] [8]

At the same time, the lexically unrealised constituent *in the garden* cannot be evaluated as an argument since it is not involved in the lexical-semantic representation of the verb in question. Instead, it can be handled as an unarticulated adjunct.[9] Since the lexically unrealised locative constituent *somewhere* and the instrumental constituent *with the gun* can be considered the locative argument of the verb *rain* and instrumental argument of the verb *kill*, respectively, they are also covered by the definition of implicit arguments in (57).

Finally, it is worth reflecting on unarticulated constituents in a subsentential environment. Although the majority of examples of subsentential fragmental utterances include nominal or prepositional phrases as in Stainton's (2006) example cited by Vicente and Groefsema (2013: 109; see also Stainton 2004; Hall 2009; Gregoromichelaki, Cann, and Kempson 2013), fragmental utterances should not be reduced only to these phrases. The linguistic description of utterances in the definition in (7) and (8) in Section 1.2.2 indicates that utterances which have a linguistic structure *ls* can have a complete or an elliptical structure in comparison with well-formed sentences or they can consist only of a constituent which can also be integrated into the syntactic structure of utterances; however, the missing parts of these utterances can be recovered from the context directly, i.e. not through an elliptical or anaphoric relation. The subsentential environment can be the verb or verbal phrase itself, as can be seen in the utterance *Mindig vágyott kistestvérre, mindig is szekálták, hogy hozasson* 'She has always wanted to have a younger brother or sister. She has always been nagged to have one brought' in (6) in Section 1.1. The three-argument verb *hozat* 'to have somebody/something brought' occurs with three lexically unrealised arguments in (6). While the subject and direct object arguments are manifestations of subject and object pro-drops, the third, adverbial argument of *hozat* occurs on the basis of the encyclopaedic context c_{enc} which contains a piece of information according to which children are brought by storks. The mentally accessed entity of stork can serve as the reference to the third argument of *hozat*. This lexically unrealised argument of *hozat* can be evaluated as an implicit argument, i.e. a missing argument in a verbal subsentential environment according to the definition of implicit arguments in (57).

After discussing what other approaches to lexically unrealised constituents are compatible or non-compatible with my definition of implicit arguments in (57), let us turn to the particular manners of the occurrences of implicit arguments in Hungarian language use.

3.2 Three manners of occurrences of implicit arguments in Hungarian

As I have noted in Section 3.1.1, in Hungarian language use there is a wide spectrum of possibilities for verbs to be used with lexically unrealised arguments. Various factors and their interaction can license occurrences of different types of implicit arguments in Hungarian language use and guide their identification mechanisms. These possible occurrences and interpretations can be ordered on the basis of what kind of information should be taken into account in the course of the use and identification of implicit arguments. An argument can be left implicit in Hungarian utterances in the following three cases (for earlier formulations of these three cases, see Németh T. 2000, 2001, 2008a, 2012; Bibok and Németh T. 2001; Németh T. and Bibok 2010):

A. if some element of the lexical-semantic representation of a verb licenses the lexically unrealised occurrence of an argument involved in it, according to the cognitive principle of relevance: (1) *Júliusban már aratnak [ARATÓ/PARASZT]* 'In July [the harvesters/the peasants] already harvest.' (= (81b) below in Section 4.1.2), (2) *János iszik [FOLYADÉK]* 'János is drinking' (= (103) below in Section 4.2.2);

B. if the rest of the utterance, i.e. immediate utterance context with its contextual factors including encyclopaedic pieces of information and grammatical requirements, provides a typical interpretation, in accordance with the cognitive principle of relevance: (1) *Ági [pénzt] adott a koldusnak* 'Ági gave [money] to the beggar' (= (179) below in Section 5.2), (2) *A férj$_i$ elkísérte a feleségét$_j$ az orvoshoz$_z$, mert [Ø$_{i/j/z}$] nagyon izgult* 'The husband accompanied his wife to the doctor, because [(s)he] was very nervous' (= (144) below in Section 5.1.1);

C. if extending the immediate utterance context of the argument results in an interpretation consistent with the cognitive principle of relevance: (1) *A Mikulás$_i$ odament a kisfiúhoz$_j$. Cukrot adott [Ø$_{i/j}$] neki$_{j/i}$.* 'Santa Claus went up to the little boy. [He$_{i/j}$] gave him$_{j/i}$ candy.' (= (147a) below in Section 5.1.1), (2) *Szeretlek [téged/titeket].* 'I love [you.SG.ACC/you.PL.ACC]' (= (149c) below in Section 5.1.2).

Four remarks seem to be in order in connection with these three possibilities. Firstly, it is obvious that these generalisations are formed on the basis of the kind and 'size' of the context in which the verb with an implicit argument occurs. In case A, the possibility of a use with a lexically unrealised argument is built into the lexical-semantic representation of the particular verb. However, this does not mean that the utterance context and grammatical requirements, including grammatical morphemes (e.g. inflectional morphemes of indefinite conjugation), do not influence the occurrence of verbs with implicit arguments in case A. In case B, in addition to the lexical-semantic and grammatical information, general pragmatic and encyclopaedic information stored under the conceptual addresses of the lexemes in the utterances in which the implicit arguments occur should be considered. And, in case C, the immediate context should be extended with information from the previous discourse or from the physical environment or with further pieces of encyclopaedic knowledge. Taking into account the kinds of information which should be considered in cases A–C, it is obvious again that implicit arguments are phenomena situated at the grammar/pragmatics interface (see Section 1.2.2).

Secondly, the definition of implicit arguments in (57) itself and the formulation of the three cases above are suitable for describing the various possible ways in which a Hungarian verb can occur with implicit arguments and how implicit arguments can be interpreted.

The third point is that these three possibilities neither predict that every verb can be used with implicit arguments only in one manner or that every verb can be used in all three manners, nor restrict which argument of a verb can be left lexically unrealised. According to the manners of their occurrences with implicit arguments, Hungarian verbs can be classified into three groups. Verbs in the first group can be used with lexically unrealised arguments in all three manners (e.g., *eszik* 'eat', *lát* 'see', *takarít* 'clean', *szánt* 'plough', and *foltoz* 'patch'). The second group contains verbs which can occur with implicit arguments in the second and third manners (e.g., *ad* 'give', *ajándékoz* 'give a present', *győz* 'win', *büntet* 'punish', and *gyűjt* 'collect'). And the third group includes verbs which can be used with implicit arguments only in the third manner (e.g., *tologat* 'push', *lakik* 'dwell', *felpróbál* 'PVB.try on, *tesz* 'put', and *bízik* 'trust').

An interesting implication which follows is that if a verb can be used with an implicit argument in the first manner, then it can also occur with it in the second manner, and since an implicit argument of a verb of the second type can also be identified in the third manner, it can be used in this latter manner as well, i.e. A → B → C. Here it must be emphasised that, although there are Hungarian verbs which can be used with implicit arguments only in the third manner, the third manner is the one in which every Hungarian verb can be used appropriately with lexically unrealised arguments in appropriate contexts.

Finally, the fourth remark concerns the cognitive principle of relevance. The cognitive principle of relevance forms a generalisation according to which human cognition tends to be geared to the maximisation of relevance (Sperber and Wilson 1986/1995: 260), i.e. to achieve more and more cognitive effects with less processing effort. This cognitive principle of relevance guides the licensing and interpretation of implicit arguments in a twofold way. Firstly, if an argument can be used implicitly in one of the above-mentioned three manners in a context, it should be left lexically unrealised in that particular context, since with the use of the implicit form a speaker can achieve the same effects as with the explicit form, but with less processing effort. Secondly, in the course of interpretation the hearer attempts to form an adequate interpretation in a particular context starting from the lexical-semantic representation of the verb. If this does not result in a relevant interpretation, then (s)he turns to the second and after that to the third manner. It must be emphasised that this order of interpretation mechanisms also involves important implications: ~A → B, ~B → C. These implications indicate that the use and interpretation of implicit arguments are under the control of an economy balance, i.e. they are guided by the requirement to take into account lexical-semantic, grammatical, and contextual information only to a necessary extent. In Chapter 6, when I characterise the three classes of Hungarian verbs regarding their occurrences with implicit arguments in detail, I will further discuss the motivation behind the use of implicit arguments and the guiding factors of their identification mechanisms.

After having offered a clarification of what I mean by implicit arguments and a brief characterisation of the three manners in which they occur and can be identified, let us continue with a detailed analysis of these three manners in Chapters 4 and 5. Firstly, in Chapter 4, the first (A) manner, then, in Chapter 5, the second (B) and the third (C) manners will be examined in detail. Now, let us start the investigation of the role played by lexical-semantic representations of verbs in the licensing and identification of implicit subject and direct object arguments in Hungarian language use.

CHAPTER 4

First (A) manner: the role of the lexical-semantic representation of verbs

4.1 Occurrence of verbs with implicit subject arguments

4.1.1 Verbs of natural phenomena with implicit and explicit subject arguments

Hungarian verbs of natural phenomena have been considered subjectless by widely accepted traditional Hungarian descriptive and theoretical grammars up until the present (the only exception to this tradition is Tóth 2001), although there is a considerable amount of data from different direct sources such as written corpora, intuition, introspection, and spoken discourses which testifies to occurrences of verbs of natural phenomena with explicit subjects. To eliminate the inconsistency between the previous explanations and the data regarding the occurrences of Hungarian verbs of natural phenomena with explicit and implicit subjects, I want to argue for a new approach developed in my previous research into Hungarian verbs of natural phenomena (Németh T. 2008a, 2014a), according to which these verbs do indeed have subject arguments in their lexical-semantic representations which can (or even should) be left implicit in certain circumstances, while in others they can be lexically realised. Assuming such a lexical-semantic representation as well as taking into consideration particular contextual factors, the occurrences of Hungarian verbs of natural phenomena with explicit and implicit subjects can be accounted for in a unified way.

Verbs of natural phenomena, e.g. *esteledik* '[for evening to] close in', *alkonyodik* '[for dusk to] set in', *sötétedik* '[for dark to] grow', *hajnalodik* '[for day to] break, dawn', *virrad* 'dawn', *tavaszodik* '[for spring to] come', *fagy* 'freeze', *olvad* 'thaw', *villámlik* '[for lightning to] strike', *havazik* 'snow' are evaluated as subjectless in the *Magyar értelmező kéziszótár* (Concise Explanatory Dictionary of Hungarian, Pusztai 2003). The feature of subjectlessness is assigned not only to the above-mentioned verbs, but also to those which can be used quite easily with explicit subjects, e.g. *dereng* 'dawn' (*dereng az ég/a hajnal* 'the sky/the dawn gets lighter'), *zuhog* 'pour' (*zuhog az eső* 'the rain pours'), *szakad* 'pour' (*szakad az eső* 'the rain pours'). Furthermore, while items like the verbs *borul* 'cloud over', *dörög* 'thunder', *sötétedik* '[for dark to] grow', and *be-sötétedik* 'PVB-[for dark to] grow' contain the evaluation 'subjectless', verbs such as *be-felhősödik* 'PVB-cloud over' and *tisztul* 'clear up' are not considered subjectless in *Magyar értelmező kéziszótár*, although both groups of verbs can occur with the same explicit subject, *az ég* 'the sky'. The verbs *ki-tisztul* 'PVB-clear up' and *pirkad* 'dawn' are evaluated as 'also subjectless' in the dictionary. In the case of verbs with meanings expressing the way the rain falls, the lexical items of *szemerkél* 'drizzle', *csepereg* 'sprinkle', *csorog* 'trickle', *ömlik* 'pour' do not include the evaluation 'subjectless', while the verbs *zuhog* 'pour' and *szakad* 'pour' are considered subjectless, although all of these verbs can occur with an explicit subject, i.e. *az eső* 'the rain'. And, finally, among verbs with meanings concerning the wind such as *fúj* 'blow', *fújdogál* 'blow gently', *fuvall* 'blow gently', *lengedezik* 'blow gently', *süvít* 'bluster', *fütyül* 'whistle', only the verb *fúj* 'blow' is evaluated as 'also subjectless', although all of the named verbs can be used without an explicit subject.

In the lexical entries of the above-mentioned verbs of natural phenomena, there is no explicit clarification of the notion of subjectlessness, and because of the confusing evaluations regarding the subjectlessness of verbs of natural phenomena, there is no possibility to reconstruct this notion on the basis of the evaluations of the dictionary. Consequently, on the basis of *Magyar értelmező kéziszótár*, one cannot make a plausible statement about the subjectlessness of Hungarian verbs of natural phenomena, i.e. this dictionary cannot be considered a reliable or usable data source in this respect (Kertész and Rákosi 2014: 24).

In *Magyar grammatika* (Hungarian Grammar, Keszler 2000) Lengyel (2000: 85, 90–91) and Kugler (2000a: 409) divide Hungarian verbs of natural phenomena into two groups. The first group contains verbs which are considered subjectless by the grammar, e.g. *hajnalodik* '[for day to] break', *pirkad* 'dawn', *alkonyodik* '[for dusk to] set in', *tavaszodik* '[for spring to] come', *havazik* 'snow', *villámlik* '[for lightning to] strike', *esteledik* '[for evening to] close in'. The second group involves verbs with an optional explicit subject, e.g. *esik az eső* 'the rain falls', *szemerkél az eső* 'the rain drizzles', *dörög az ég* 'the sky thunders', *be-borul az ég* 'the sky PVB-clouds over', *ki-derül az ég* 'the sky PVB-clears up', *sötétedik az ég* 'the sky darkens', *ki-világosodik az ég* 'the sky PVB-clears up'.

According to *Magyar grammatika*, the filling of the subject argument position is not permitted in the first group of verbs. It is argued that the meanings of the verbs in the first group concern elements of the general natural environment; therefore, there is no need or interest to name them explicitly. Furthermore, in some cases the subject is missing because it is incorporated into the stem of the verb of natural phenomena. However, it is not clear how to interpret the constraint of not filling the subject argument position: either the verbs in the first group do not have a subject argument position at all or they have such a position but its filling is prohibited. In my previous work (Németh T. 2014a) I reconstructed the structure of the data on the basis of this dilemma. In the first case, the structure of the data concerning verbs of natural phenomena in the first group can be reconstructed as follows:

> The verbs *hajnalodik* '[for day to] break', *pirkad* 'dawn', *alkonyodik* '[for dusk to] set in', *tavaszodik* '[for spring to] come', *havazik* 'snow', *villámlik* '[for lightning to] strike', *esteledik* '[for evening to] close in' are verbs of natural phenomena and they do not have a subject argument position.

And, in the second case:

> The verb *hajnalodik* '[for day to] break', *pirkad* 'dawn', *alkonyodik* '[for dusk to] set in', *tavaszodik* '[for spring to] come', *havazik* 'snow', *villámlik* '[for lightning to] strike', *esteledik* '[for evening to] close in' are verbs of natural phenomena; they have a subject argument position but the filling of the subject argument position is prohibited.

On the basis of these reconstructions, inconsistency can be explicitly established in *Magyar grammatika* which cannot be eliminated on the basis of the following further argumentation. *Magyar grammatika* emphasises that verbs of natural phenomena which are considered subjectless can and even must occur with explicit subjects in their metaphorical uses –e.g., *havazik az élet* 'life is snowing', *az egész világ havazik* 'the whole world is snowing', *csend havazik* 'silence is snowing', *a szeme villámlik* 'her/his eyes flash', *villámlik a fekete nappal* 'the black daytime flashes [like lightening]'.[1] If verbs of natural phenomena are subjectless, i.e. if one selects the data structure first proposed in the previous paragraph, it must be explained how a subject argument position arises in the metaphorical use. If one assumes that these verbs always have a subject argument position, i.e. their data structure can be reconstructed along the lines of the second proposal in the previous paragraph, which must not be filled in non-metaphorical uses, then what constraints predict the subjectless uses must be accounted for. It is obvious that these two assumptions are inconsistent, and this inconsistency cannot be eliminated in the framework of *Magyar grammatika*.[2]

As to the verbs in the second group, *Magyar grammatika* allows them to be used with explicit subjects, i.e. they certainly have a subject argument position. But this position can be filled optionally, i.e. the verbs in the second group can have an explicit subject argument, and they can also be used without it. According to this, the structure of data concerning the verbs in the second group can be reconstructed, as follows:

> The verb *esik* '[for precipitation to] fall' is a verb of natural phenomena and it has a subject argument position which can be filled optionally.

Now, a question arises as to what plausibility value can be assigned to the above reconstructed data. If one accepts *Magyar grammatika* as a relatively reliable authoritative source, then the plausibility value of the above reconstructed data is relatively high. But if one decomposes and analyses the information content of the reconstructed data, as has been done in this section, one can explicitly identify inconsistencies. Because of these inconsistencies *Magyar grammatika* cannot be considered a reliable or even a usable source.

In a lexical-functional approach, Komlósy (1994) also considers Hungarian weather verbs[3] to be subjectless. In Komlósy's (1994) proposal the lexical-semantic representation of weather verbs contains an internal semantic argument which cannot be expressed syntactically. Thus, weather verbs are not regents, they cannot occur with explicit subjects, and they do not allow even expletive, formal subjects. Komlósy (2001) also emphasises that weather verbs are not predicates either. They are lexical items which do not require any semantic arguments. Relying on the requirements of grammatical interpretability, semantic arguments cannot include internal arguments which form a necessary, inherent element in the meaning of lexical items of weather verbs, and therefore cannot be explicitly realised (see Komlósy's (1994: 160–161) lexical-semantic representations in (60a–c)). Since weather verbs have only internal arguments and do not have semantic arguments at all, they are neither regents nor predicates. Komlósy (2001) considers Hungarian weather verbs to be similar to Russian weather verbs, which do not have a controllable subject relation either. Both Hungarian and Russian weather verbs differ from English weather verbs, which do require a formal subject, i.e. they are regents (e.g. *It is raining, It is snowing*). However, it must be noted that the meaningless expletive subject *it* in English is not a semantic argument either, i.e. *rain* and *snow* are not predicates, and their syntactic subject satisfies only formal grammatical requirements.

Consider Komlósy's (1994: 160–161) examples in (60).

(60) a. *Hajnal-od-   ik.*

       dawn-SFX-   INDEF.3SG

       'dawn is coming'   → 'ARISE (DAWN)'

b.   *Villám-l-*   *ott.*

lightning-SFX-   PAST.INDEF.3SG

'there was lightning'   → 'APPEAR (LIGHTNING)'

c.   *Sötét-ed-*   *ik.*

dark-SFX-   INDEF.3SG

'it is getting dark'   → 'ARISE (DARKNESS)'[4]

The weather verbs in (60a–c) have a morphologically complex structure, as do most weather verbs in Hungarian.[5] They are derived from the nouns *hajnal* 'dawn' and *villám* 'lightning', as well as from the adjective *sötét* 'dark'.[6] The meaning of the nominal or adjectival stem can be factored out as an internal argument in the lexical-semantic representation of the weather verb derived from the stem at stake, which is why a weather verb may be given a motivated full function-argument structure without any slot to be filled in in syntactic derivation. According to Komlósy's (1994: 161) proposal, the relation between nominal or adjectival stems and affixes in the lexical-semantic representation of morphologically complex weather verbs can be thought of as a relation between a subject and a predicate. The subject slot of affixes is filled with the nominal or adjectival stem; consequently, the resulting verbs ought to be subjectless.

Although Komlósy (1994) aims to provide an explicit explanation of the subjectlessness of weather verbs in Hungarian, there are questions which cannot be answered by his proposal. Firstly, on the basis of Komlósy's (1994) work as a direct source, the following plausible statement can be formulated:

> The verbs *villámlik* '[for lightning to] strike' and *sötétedik* '[for dark to] grow' are weather verbs which cannot occur with an explicit subject and do not license a formal subject either.

From this plausible statement one can infer that the expressions *villámlik az ég* 'the sky is lightning' and *sötétedik az ég* 'the sky is getting dark' are ill-formed. However, according to my and others' linguistic intuition this statement is implausible. My and others' intuition as a direct source supports the plausibility of the following statement:

> The expressions *villámlik az ég* 'the sky is lightning' and *sötétedik az ég* 'the sky is getting dark' are well-formed expressions in which *villámlik* '[for lightning to] strike' as well as *sötétedik* '[for dark to] grow' are weather verbs and *ég* 'sky' is an explicit subject.

If these weather verbs are subjectless, i.e. they do not have a subject slot in their lexical-semantic representation, it should not be possible to use them with overt, syntactically realised subjects in metaphorical (see above: *a szeme villámlik* 'her/ his eyes are flashing', *villámlik a fekete nappal* 'the black daytime flashes [like lightning]') and non-metaphorical senses (*villámlik az ég* 'the sky is lightning', *sötétedik az ég* 'the sky is getting dark').[7] From this analysis it can be concluded that if we take into consideration these latter data as well, and confront them with Komlósy's (1994, 2001) lexical-functional approach to Hungarian weather verbs, Komlósy's proposal becomes inconsistent, and this inconsistency cannot be eliminated in terms of his lexical-functional explanations.

The generative grammatical analysis proposed by Tóth (2001) does not accept the views of lexical-functional grammar that weather verbs are subjectless in Hungarian, and 3SG agreement in the verbs is taken to be the morphological reflex of default agreement. On the basis of theoretical considerations, as well as relying on the various occurrences of weather verbs with subjects in other languages (see also Camacho 2013: 16–20), Tóth (2001) argues that in null subject languages weather verbs are not subjectless but instead have null-quasi-argumental subjects, their 3SG agreement is real agreement, and they can take part in control relations. Tóth's suggestion can be considered an extension of Chomsky's (1981: 323–325) proposal on weather-verb expletives like *it* to null subjects of weather verbs in null subject languages. According to Chomsky's suggestion, weather verb expletives like *it* are quasi-argumental because they can control an infinitival subject. Thus, similarly to the weather verb expletives in non-null subject languages, weather verbs' null subjects in null subject languages have a quasi-argumental nature.

Tóth (2001) assumes that strong evidence for the non-subjectlessness of weather verbs in Hungarian is provided by their behaviour in participial adjunct clauses. According to Kertész and Rákosi (2012: 178), evidence in linguistics research can be a datum whose function is to contribute to the evaluation and comparison of the plausibility of rival, incompatible hypotheses. They distinguish between three types of evidence (2012: 178–185), i.e. weak evidence, relative evidence, and strong evidence. Weak evidence is a datum on which one can build an inference that makes the given hypothesis plausible (weak evidence for a hypothesis) or implausible (weak evidence against a hypothesis). It is worth noting that weak evidence can support other, rival hypotheses as well. Relative evidence is a stricter concept. A datum can be relative evidence for a hypothesis if it is weak evidence for it and the inference built on it makes it possible to assign a higher plausibility value to the hypothesis at stake than to the rival hypotheses. A datum can be relative evidence against a hypothesis if it is weak evidence against it and the inference built on it makes it possible to assign a higher plausibility value to a rival hypothesis than the hypothesis at stake. Thus, while a datum as weak evidence may support more than one rival hypothesis, as relative evidence a datum supports only one of the rival hypotheses. Finally, a datum is strong evidence for a hypothesis if it is weak evidence for it and at the same time it is not weak evidence for any other rival hypotheses, and a datum is strong evidence against a hypothesis if it is weak evidence against it and at the same time it is not weak evidence against the rival hypotheses. To put it another way, a datum as strong evidence for a hypothesis makes only this hypothesis plausible. In this sense the behaviour of Hungarian weather verbs in participial adjunct clauses serves as strong evidence for the non-subjectlessness of weather verbs in Hungarian.

Participial adjunct clauses in Hungarian either contain *va*-participles or *ván*-participles. Tóth (2001: 63) emphasises that although these two forms have a number of common syntactic properties, there is an important difference between them. *Va*-participles cannot have a lexical subject due to lack of case, while a *ván*-participle can have a nominative marked DP or a pronominal subject, see (61)–(62).

(61)   *János   megérkez-vén/*ve,*   pro *elindultunk   hazafelé.*
       János.NOM   PVB.arrive-VÁN/-VA   PVB.started.1PL   towards.home
       'János having arrived, we started for home.'

(62)   *Hajnalod-ván/*va,* pro *elindultunk   hazafelé.*
       dawn-VÁN/-VA   PVB.started.1PL   towards.home
       'Dawn coming, we started for home.'

The utterance in (62) makes it possible to form the following plausible statement:

> The *va*-participle **hajnalodva* formed from the weather verb *hajnalodik* 'dawn' is ill-formed, but the *ván*-participle form of it, *hajnalodván*, is well-formed.

According to Tóth's intuition, as a direct source, *hajnalodik* can grammatically be combined with *-ván*, and only with *-ván*. This contrast is unpredictable and inexplicable for the approaches in which weather verbs cannot have a subject, but is accommodated under Tóth's (2001: 63) quasi-argumental subject analysis, according to which *ván*-participles assign nominative case to the quasi-argumental *pro* and thus make it licit, while *va*-participles cannot license *pro* because no case is available. Consequently, since weather verbs select *-ván* constructions, i.e. they can be combined with *-ván* resulting in well-formed utterances, the plausible statement about (62) serves as strong evidence against the hypothesis that weather verbs are syntactically subjectless in the context of Tóth's (2001) generative grammatical analysis.[8]

It must be noted that some native speakers of Hungarian cannot accept or find it difficult to accept weather verbs in *-ván* constructions. According to their intuition, *ván*-participle forms from weather verbs are ill-formed. Sárik (1998: 426) also shares this opinion.

To consider *ván*-participle forms formed from weather verbs ill-formed contradicts Tóth's (2001) argumentation, i.e. data concerning the ill-formednes of the utterances containing *ván*-participle constructions formed from weather verbs causes further inconsistency in the context of the research. However, my own intuition as well as the intuition of other Hungarian native speakers support Tóth's intuition. My intuition licenses even the sentence *Hajnalodván az idő, elindultunk hazafelé* 'Dawn coming, we started for home', where the weather verb with the *ván*-participle form *hajnalodván* occurs with an explicit subject *az idő* 'the time'. The utterance *Hajnalodván az idő, elindultunk hazafelé* 'Dawn coming, we started for home' has the same structure as *János megérkezvén, elindultunk hazafelé* 'János having arrived, we started for home' in (61), which also supports the non-subjectless analysis of the weather verbs.

Since the statement about the well-formedness of *ván*-constructions formed from weather verbs is plausible, while the statement about the ill-formedness of *ván*-constructions formed from the weather verbs is implausible for me and other native speakers, I will rely on the former statement in the subsequent argumentation.

If we continue thinking in the way suggested by Tóth (2001) and also reverse the direction of the argumentation in lexical-functional grammar concerning the relationship between internal arguments, semantic arguments, and syntactic complements, the following statements can be made. If weather verbs have a syntactic subject, it cannot be an expression of an internal semantic argument, because internal arguments cannot be syntactically realised. Syntactic subjects of weather verbs cannot be considered realisations of (external) semantic arguments, either. There are cases when lexical items grammatically require syntactic constituents which are not expressions of semantic arguments (see *rain* and its expletive formal subject *it*: *It is raining*). However, the comparison of (61) and (62) convincingly testifies that Hungarian weather verbs occur with syntactic subjects which are not empty expletives. Therefore, the conclusion of Tóth's (2001) argumentation that weather verbs take a quasi-argumental subject is more plausible than the conclusion of previous approaches according to which weather verbs are subjectless in Hungarian.

The thorough investigation of the rival approaches to the subjectlessness of Hungarian verbs of natural phenomena in the previous paragraphs reveals that the context of the research is problematic, since it contains incompleteness and inconsistencies (cf. Kertész and Rákosi 2012: 130–134). Firstly, *Magyar értelmező kéziszótár* and *Magyar grammatika* have inconsistent evaluations regarding the occurrence of Hungarian verbs of natural phenomena without and with an explicit subject. Komlósy's (1994, 2001) proposal in lexical-functional grammar is also problematic because of its incompleteness. Secondly, there is an inconsistency between, on the one hand, *Magyar értelmező kéziszótár*, *Magyar grammatika*, and Komlósy's (1994, 2001) lexical-functional grammatical proposal and, on the other hand, Tóth's (2001) generative syntactic analysis. The first three consider Hungarian weather verbs subjectless, while the fourth non-subjectless.

Magyar értelmező kéziszótár and *Magyar grammatika* have collected their examples mainly from various corpora: previous dictionaries, grammars and works of fiction,[9] while Komlósy's (1994, 2001) proposal in lexical-functional grammar and Tóth's (2001) is a generative grammatical analysis through intuition. These approaches all regard their own sources of examples reliable and unquestionable. On the basis of their examples, *Magyar grammatika* and Komlósy (1994, 2001) consider the hypothesis that the verbs of natural phenomena are subjectless acceptable with a high plausibility value, while Tóth's (2001) analysis argues for the opposite hypothesis, according to which verbs of natural phenomena are not subjectless. In order to resolve this contradiction, I have taken into account a new spectrum of data based on various new direct sources, such as *Magyar Nemzeti Szövegtár* (Hungarian National Corpus, corpus.nytud.hu/mnsz), my own and other Hungarian native speakers' intuition, discourses from my spoken corpus characterised in Section 2.1.1, as well as observation of spoken spontaneous discourses. The aim of the extension of the context of the research with new data from these direct sources is to examine whether we can find more evidence for and against one or the other rival hypothesis.

The data regarding the subjectlessness of verbs of natural phenomena referred to above seem to be counterintuitive on the basis of my own intuition, therefore I consider them implausible. If the *Magyar Nemzeti Szövegtár* (Hungarian National Corpus, corpus.nytud.hu/mnsz) is also taken into account as a direct data source in addition to my intuition, it turns out that a great number of occurrences of verbs of natural phenomena with explicit subjects can be found; see, e.g., (63).

(63) a. *esteledik/*   *alkonyodik*
          [for evening].closes.in.INDEF   [for dusk].sets.in.INDEF

          a   nap
          the   day.NOM
          'the day is coming to the evening/the day is coming to dusk'

      b. *sötétedik*   *a   látóhatár/*   *az   ég*
          [for dark].gets.INDEF   the   horizon.NOM   the   sky.NOM
          'The horizon/sky is getting dark.'

c. *hajnalodik*   *az*   *idő*
    [for day].breaks.INDEF   the   time.NOM
    'The day is breaking. [lit. The time is coming to dawn.]'

d. *virrad*   *a*   *nap/*   *az*   *éjszaka/*   *a*   *fény*
    dawns.INDEF   the   day.NOM   the   night.NOM/   the   light.NOM
    'The day/night/light is dawning.'

e. *villámlik*   *az*   *ég*
    [for lightning].strikes.INDEF   the   sky.NOM
    'The sky is lightning.'

f. *zuhog*   *az*   *eső*
    pours.INDEF   the   rain.NOM
    'Rain is pouring down.'

g. *szakad*   *az*   *eső*
    pours.INDEF   the   rain.NOM
    'Rain is pouring down.'

h. *szakad*   *a*   *hó*
    pours. INDEF   the   snow.NOM
    'It is snowing heavily.'

Based on the occurrences of verbs of natural phenomena with explicit subjects in the Hungarian National Corpus, a high plausibility value can be assigned to the following statement:

> The verbs *esteledik/alkonyodik* '[for evening to] close in/[for dusk to] set in', *sötétedik* '[for dark to] grow', *hajnalodik* '[for day to] break', *virrad* 'dawn', *villámlik* '[for lightning to] strike', *zuhog* 'pour', *szakad* 'pour' are verbs of natural phenomena and they can occur with explicit subjects.

Of course, one can say that the Hungarian National Corpus is not a reliable source of data, or that occurrence in a corpus cannot be evaluated as sufficient positive evidence (Bibok 2009). However, my own intuitions, as well as the result of the testing of data by other native speakers have made the following statement plausible:

> Hungarian verbs of natural phenomena can occur with explicit subjects.

Furthermore, examining spoken everyday discourses, I have also collected occurrences of verbs of natural phenomena with explicit subjects (see, e.g., (64b), (69a), and (69c) subsequently in this section). Relying on these occurrences with explicit subjects and taking into consideration my own intuition, I have also assigned a high plausibility value to the above statement. Consequently, on the basis of data from these various new direct sources, a high plausibility value can be assigned to the hypothesis that:

Hungarian verbs of natural phenomena are not subjectless.

If we also take into account metaphorical uses, then all verbs of natural phenomena can occur with explicit subjects. Let us consider only two verbs – *havazik* 'snow', *villámlik* '[for lightening to] strike'– in their metaphorical uses found in the Hungarian National Corpus: *havazik az élet* 'life is snowing', *az egész világ havazik* 'the whole world is snowing', *csend havazik* 'silence is snowing', *a szeme villámlik* 'her/his eyes are flashing [like lightning]', *villámlik a fekete nappal* 'the black daytime is lightning'.

In the light of the data introduced newly into the discussion of the subjectlessness of Hungarian verbs of natural phenomena, it can be seen that those verbs of natural phenomena which are considered subjectless by *Magyar grammatika* can also occur with explicit subjects. Thus, one can conclude the following: (i) verbs of natural phenomena considered subjectless by the Hungarian grammatical tradition are not subjectless; instead, they can occur with explicit subjects, and, consequently, (ii) Hungarian verbs of natural phenomena cannot be divided into two groups in terms of whether they can occur with explicit subjects or not.

If we assume lexical-semantic representations for verbs of natural phenomena similar to the ones proposed by Komlósy's (1994, 2001) lexical-functional approach (see (60a–c)), i.e. lexical-semantic representations without a subject argument position, then we cannot account for the uses of verbs of natural phenomena with explicit non-metaphorical and metaphorical subjects.

However, on the basis of data from the above-mentioned new direct sources, we can go even further than Tóth's (2001) quasi-argumental analysis in her generative grammatical approach. Since the hypothesis that verbs of natural phenomena can occur with explicit, lexicalised non-metaphorical and metaphorical subjects is plausible, their subject can be thought of as a real (external) semantic argument which must be indicated somehow in their lexical-semantic representation. In other words, instead of Tóth's quasi-argumental analysis, a real-argumental analysis can be suggested which can be considered more complete and plausible than Tóth's analysis, since it can also account for the occurrence of weather verbs with explicit non-metaphorical and metaphorical subjects. As it was indicated earlier in this section, the utterance in (62) can also contain a lexically realised explicit subject argument, see *Hajnalodván az idő, elindultunk hazafelé* 'Dawn coming, we started for home'.

By confronting new data with rival approaches, it has been revealed that the use of verbs of natural phenomena with explicit non-metaphorical and metaphorical subjects cannot be accounted for by these approaches. Consequently, the extended and coordinated context of the problem of the subjectlessness/non-sub-jectlessness of Hungarian verbs of natural phenomena has remained incomplete. At the same time it is also inconsistent. There is an inconsistency inherited from the starting context of the problem between the rival approaches, and there is a new inconsistency in the extended context of the problem between the previous approaches and the newly introduced data. Finally, at this stage of the argumen-tation it can be concluded without any doubt that the hypothesis according to which Hungarian verbs of natural phenomena are subjectless is less plausible, and the opposite hypothesis, i.e. that the verbs of natural phenomena in Hungarian are not subjectless, is more plausible.

In a further argumentation cycle, let us start from the hypothesis that verbs of natural phenomena previously considered subjectless in Hungarian grammars are not subjectless. As we have seen at the end of the previous argumentation cycle, this hypothesis can be formulated on the basis of the theoretical conclu-sions of the evaluation of the rival explanations of the behaviour of Hungarian verbs of natural phenomena with and without subject arguments as well as rely-ing on various kinds of data from different direct sources. Although Hungarian verbs of natural phenomena can all occur with or without explicit subjects, they differ in what manner and in what context. The default use of the verbs *esteledik* '[for evening to] close in', *be-esteledik* 'PVB-[for evening to] close in', *alkonyodik* '[for dusk to] set in', *be-alkonyodik* 'PVB-[for dusk to] set in', *hajnalodik* '[for day to] break', *tavaszodik* '[for spring to] come', *ki-tavaszodik* 'PVB-[for spring to] come', *fagy* 'freeze', *olvad* 'thaw', *villámlik* '[for lightning to] strike', *havazik* 'snow', *be-havazik* 'PVB-snow in', *virrad* 'dawn', *pirkad* 'dawn', etc. is the occurrence with-out an explicit, lexicalised subject. However, this does not necessarily mean that these verbs are null-argument verbs, as is widely assumed in the literature (see Keszler 2000; Pusztai 2003). On the contrary, these verbs have an (external) argu-ment position in their lexical-semantic representation which can be filled with an explicit, lexicalised syntactic subject, although what lexemes can appear in this subject position is strictly constrained. In the literature concerning implicit object arguments in various languages, a hypothesis has been formulated accord-ing to which if a verb can have only one specific object or a very limited number of specific objects, then the object(s) can be predicted on the basis of the particu-lar verb meaning, and, therefore, be easily omitted (Rice 1988; García Velasco and Portero Muñoz 2002). For example, in English the verbs of bodily emission such as *sneeze, blow, cry, spit, ejaculate, piss*, and *vomit*, and verbs of contribution such as *contribute, donate*, and *give* 'contribute' can occur with implicit direct object arguments in this manner. In construction grammar, Goldberg (2005b) argues that these verbs can be fused with the implicit theme construction since their second argument position can be filled by a unique object. The omitted syntactic object can be identified with a particular kind of bodily emission or contribution which is indicated in the lexical-semantic representation of these verbs as selection restrictions. Pragmatic factors, especially politeness considerations, also motivate leaving these arguments lexically unrealised. Lexical-functional grammar also applies a unique selection restriction to account for idioms such as *to crane one's neck* (Komlósy 2001: 121).[10]

There is no theoretical argument against the extension of this hypothesis to syntactic subject arguments. By means of selection restrictions, the lexical-semantic representation of verbs of natural phenomena listed above unambiguously and uniquely determines those kinds of natural phenomena (e.g. the Hungarian equivalents of *sky*, *dawn*, *day*, and *horizon*) that can occupy the syntactic subject position in non-metaphorical uses. To put it the other way around, it follows directly from the selection restriction what kinds of natural phenomena can serve as syntactic subjects with verbs of natural phenomena; therefore, there is no need to express them explicitly. Thus, if the verbs in question occur without an overt, lexically realised subject, then this implicit subject can unambiguously and exclusively be identified with the information about the particular kind of natural phenomenon involved in the selection restriction. Consider (64).

(64) a. *Nagy   a   vihar.   Villámlik   [ég].*
          big   the   storm.NOM   [for lightning].strikes.INDEF   sky.NOM
          'The storm is big. It is lightning.'

      b. *Nagy   a   vihar.   Az   egész   ég   villámlik.*
          big   the   storm.NOM   the   whole   sky.NOM   [for lightning].strikes.INDEF
          'The storm is big. It is lightning [in the entire sky].'

In (64a) the verb *villámlik* '[for lightning to] strike' occurs with an implicit subject argument, while in (64b) it occurs with a lexically realised one. The occurrence of the verb *villámlik* with an implicit subject argument is licensed by the unique selection restriction on argument x in its lexical-semantic representation: argument x must be *ég* 'sky' among existing natural phenomena (see (65)). Similarly, in the lexical-semantic representation of the verbs *esteledik* '[for evening to] close in' and *hajnalodik* '[for day to] break, dawn' the argument x must be *nap* 'day'/ *idő* 'time' and *idő* 'time', respectively, which can be realised as a syntactic subject: *esteledik a nap/az idő* 'the day/time is coming to the evening',[11] *hajnalodik az idő* 'The day is breaking. [lit. The time is coming to dawn]'(see (66)–(67)).

(65)   *villámlik* '[for lightning to] strike':   'x which is sky is showing very
                                                          bright flashes of light'

(66)   *esteledik* '[for evening to] close in':   'x which is day (24 hour time unit) or time is approaching evening time'

(67)   *hajnalodik* '[for day to] break, dawn':   'x which is time is approaching daybreak'

The possibility of using the verbs *villámlik, esteledik, hajnalodik* with implicit subject arguments follows from the double interpretability of their lexical-semantic representations. If they occur with an explicit subject, then the subject argument is also the focus of attention, while if these verbs are used with an implicit subject, only the particular natural (weather) event is the focus of attention, but the lexically unrealised subject argument can also be accessed by means of the unique selection restriction as background information. The two kinds of occurrence of these verbs with an overt or covert subject argument can be considered a syntactic alternation similar to occurrences of transitive verbs with or without an explicit object argument (Bibok 2008, 2010; Németh T. 2010, 2014a; Section 4.2). Because of the uniqueness of the selection restriction put on argument *x* and also the permanent accessibility of argument *x* in the lexical-semantic representation as background information, the other verbs *be-esteledik* 'PVB-[for evening to] close in', *alkonyodik* '[for dusk to] set in', *be-alkonyodik* 'PVB-[for dusk to] set in', *tavaszodik* '[for spring to] come', *ki-tavaszodik* 'PVB-[for spring to] come', *fagy* 'freeze', *olvad* 'thaw', *havazik* 'snow', *be-havazik* 'PVB-snow in', *virrad* 'dawn', *pirkad* 'dawn' can also be used with implicit subject arguments very economically, which is why their occurrence with a lexically unrealised subject argument can be considered their default use.

In the semantic literature the meaning of the utterance *Villámlik* 'It is lightning' in (64a) is accounted for as a thetic statement (Maleczki 2001; Martí 2006; Recanati 2007). Thetic statements are about a particular situation, they have no topic constituent. But if a component of a particular situation, e.g. a temporal or locative constituent, becomes prominent enough, then it can play the role of the sentential topic (Maleczki 2001: 169, 179–180). Cf. (68).

(68)   a.   *Tegnap   havazott.*
              Yesterday   snowed.INDEF
              'Yesterday it snowed.'

        b.   *Galyatetőn   havazik.*
              Galyatető.SUP   snows.INDEF.
              'At Galyatető it is snowing.'

The utterances in (68) are already categorical judgments which make a predication on the prominent temporal and local components of the particular situation which are now in the sentential topic position. Similarly, in (64b) in the course of the occurrence of the verb *villámlik* '[for lightning] to strike' with the explicit subject argument *az ég* 'the sky', the participant required by the verb's unique selection restriction becomes prominent. Therefore, it can occupy the topic position in the sentence, and, consequently, the statement can be considered a categorical judgment.

Now, let us turn to the metaphorical use of the verb *villámlik* in (69).

(69)   (In the family there is a big row between the father and kids because of the kids' bad behaviour, when the mother enters the room and says:)

    a.   *Látom,*   *nagy*   *a*   *vihar,*   *villámlik*
       see.DEF.1SG big the storm.NOM [for lightning].strikes.INDEF
       apa   *tekintete.*
       father.NOM glance.NOM
       'I can see that there is a big storm, father's glances are flashing (like lightning).'

    b.   **Látom,*   *nagy*   *a*   *vihar,*   *villámlik*
       see.DEF.1SG big the storm.NOM [for lightning].strikes.INDEF
       [apa   *tekintete].*
       father.NOM glance.NOM

    c.   (Later, kids among themselves.)
       Láttad,   *milyen*   *volt* *apa*   *tekintete?*
       saw.DEF.2SG what.kind was father.NOM glance.NOM
       'Did you see what father's glances were like?'

       Igen. *Villámlott*   *[apa*   *tekintete]*
       yes [for lightning].stroke.INDEF.3SG father.NOM glance.NOM
       'Yes. They [= father's glances] were flashing (like lightning).'

In (69a) the expression *apa tekintete* 'father's glances' serves as an explicit subject of the verb *villámlik* '[for lightning to] strike' used metaphorically. The metaphorical use of *villámlik* with an explicit subject is also supported by the metaphorical use of *vihar* 'storm' in the utterance context. On the basis of (65), it is obvious that by means of its selection restriction the verb *villámlik* requires a unique subject argument (*ég* 'sky'). The lexically realised subject argument in (69a) is not identical with the one required by the selection restriction. Consequently, it cannot be left implicit, which is why (69b) is not grammatical; (69b) cannot be used with an implicit subject argument metaphorically either. In *Magyar grammatika* Kugler (2000a: 409) referred to this phenomenon by formulating a constraint according to which in the metaphorical uses weather verbs must be supplied with explicit, lexically realised subjects. However, in (69c) one can see that the verb *villámlik* can occur with an implicit subject argument in a metaphorical sense. But this occurrence is not licensed by the verb's unique selection restriction on argument *x* and, consequently, by the possibility of double interpretability. Instead, it is licensed by discourse grammatical factors, it is a kind of zero anaphor.

Let us also examine another group of verbs of natural phenomena, namely, verbs with meanings expressing how rain, snow, etc. falls. With the verbs *szemerkél* 'drizzle', *csepeg/csöpög* '[for rain to] fall in drops, drip', *csepereg/csöpörög* 'sprinkle', *eseget* 'rain sporadically', *csorog/csurog* 'trickle', *zuhog* 'pour', *szakad* 'pour', *ömlik* 'pour', the noun *eső* 'rain' can serve as an explicit, lexically realised subject. The explicit subject of the verb *szállingózik* 'fall softly/snow softly' can be the noun *hó* 'snow', while the explicit subject of the verb *szitál* 'mizzle' can be the nouns *köd* 'haze' and *eső* 'rain'. The verb *hull* 'fall' can occur with the nouns *eső* 'rain', *hó* 'snow' as well as *zúzmara* 'rime' as explicit, lexically realised subjects. However, the verb *esik* '[for precipitation to] fall' can be used with a range of other nouns in the subject position, e.g. *eső* 'rain', *hó* 'snow', *hódara* 'hoar-frost', *dara* 'sleet', *jégeső* 'hail', *jég* 'hail', *köd* 'haze', *permet* 'fine rain', *harmat* 'dew', *dér* 'frost', and *zúzmara* 'rime'. The verbs expressing meanings describing how rain, snow, etc. fall can occur with implicit subject arguments in various ways. Consider (70).

(70)   *Milyen   az   idő?*
         What.like   the   weather.NOM
         'What is the weather like?'

    a.   *Szemerkél   [eső].*
           drizzles.INDEF   rain.NOM
           'It is drizzling'.

           Csepeg/csöpög   [eső].
           drips.INDEF   rain.NOM
           'It is dripping rain'.

           Csepereg/csöpörög   [eső].
           sprinkles.INDEF   rain.NOM
           'It is sprinkling rain.'

  Eseget   *[eső].*
  falls.INDEF   rain.NOM
  'It is raining sporadically'.

  Csorog/csurog   *[eső].*
  trickles.INDEF   rain.NOM
  'It is trickling rain.'

  Zuhog/szakad/ömlik   *[eső].*
  pours.INDEF   rain.NOM
  'It is pouring with rain'.

b. *Szállingózik*   *[hó]*
    falls.INDEF.softly snow.NOM
    'It is snowing softly.'

c. *Szitál*   *[{köd, eső}]*
    mizzles.INDEF {haze.NOM, rain.NOM}
    'It is mizzling'.

d. **Hull.*
    falls.INDEF

e. *Esik*   *[CSAPADÉK].*
    [for precipitation].falls.INDEF   precipitation
    'It (i.e. precipitation) is falling'.

Let us examine the utterances in (70) which answer the question *Milyen az idő?*
'What is the weather like?' The answers in (70a) contain verbs with implicit subject arguments. In all of them the implicit subject argument can be identified
unambiguously and uniquely with the noun *eső* 'rain'. The verbs in (70a) have
a shared meaning component in their lexical-semantic representation, namely,
a selection restriction which predicts that their argument x must be 'rain'. This
unique selection restriction licenses the verbs' occurrences with implicit subject
arguments in (70a). There are native speakers of Hungarian who can use the verbs
zuhog 'pour' and *szakad* 'pour' in (70a) with the explicit subject *hó* 'snow' as well.
Zuhog a hó 'It is pouring with snow' and *Szakad a hó* 'It is pouring with snow' are
well-formed Hungarian utterances, many occurrences of which can be found in
the reports on the weather in the newspapers and on the various news portals on
the Internet. Cf. (71).

(71)   a.   *Zuhog*   *a*   *hó*   *Budapesten.*

pours.INDEF   the   snow.NOM   Budapest.SUP

'It is pouring with snow in Budapest.'

(Retrieved on 14 April 2014 from http://hirek.animare.hu/zuhog_a_ho_budapesten+1746873.html)

b.   *Szakad*   *a*   *hó*   *Kelet-Magyarországon.*

pours.INDEF   the   snow.NOM   east.Hungary.SUP

'It is pouring with snow in east Hungary.'

(Retrieved on 14 April 2014 from http://frisshir.tk/hirek.php?id=13661484&kategoria=Belfold)

If, on the basis of native speakers' intuitions and occurrences in newspaper corpora, we accept that the verbs *zuhog* 'pour' and *szakad* 'pour' can be used with both explicit subjects *eső* 'rain' and *hó* 'snow', then their lexical-semantic representation must contain a unique selection restriction constraining the subject argument which can be selected from a two-element-set according to contextual requirements: {'rain', 'snow'}. (Cf. also the lexical-semantic representation of the verb *szitál* 'mizzle' below.)

Let us turn back to the meanings of verbs in (70a), which also differ from each other. The differences concern the manner in which the rain falls. While in the case of *szemerkél* 'drizzle' this is 'lightly falling in fine drops', in the case of *zuhog* 'pour' it is 'raining very heavily'. There are various proposals in the literature regarding the status of this kind of information relating to the lexical-semantic representations of verbs. Conceptual semantics (Jackendoff 1990) and the theory of a generative lexicon (Pustejovsky 1995, 1998) do not distinguish between linguistic and encyclopaedic knowledge in lexical (conceptual)-semantic representations, thus the pieces of information related to the manner of actions and events must be built into them. Two-level conceptual semantics (Bierwisch 1983, 1996), as its name suggests, however, makes a difference between these two types of knowledge and, consequently, between the linguistic and conceptual meanings. In this theory the characteristic manner of 'falling events' can be captured by the lexical stereotype belonging to encyclopaedic knowledge. Although in relevance theory (Sperber and Wilson 1986/1995) linguistic and encyclopaedic types of information are distinguished, they are treated in the same way, rather than being provided with a separate, independent status. In relevance theory the conceptual node of a verb involves three types of information: lexical, encyclopaedic and logical. If the verbs' conceptual node becomes active, all these three kinds of information can be accessed simultaneously. The encyclopaedic information on the characteristic manner of actions or events is added to the lexical information in the course of its use or interpretation. In functional discourse grammar (García Velasco and Portero Muñoz 2002) the encyclopaedic information is included in the cognitive component of the grammar. When a verb appears in a sentence, the representational level and the cognitive component interact with each other, so both the linguistic and encyclopaedic information is taken into account.

In this brief overview we have seen that the rival solutions differ as to whether they distinguish between linguistic knowledge and encyclopaedic knowledge or not. But it is indisputable that the lexical-semantic representation of verbs must be extended by this information, or that such information must somehow be added to it (cf. Bibok 2004; Bibok and Németh T. 2001: 296; Németh T. 2014a). So, it is plausible to conclude that the information concerning the typical, characteristic manner of actions or events forms a necessary part of the verb meanings.[12]

Now, let us return to the answers to the question *Milyen az idő?* 'What is the weather like?' In (70b) the verb *szállingózik* 'fall softly/snow softly' also puts a unique selection restriction on its subject argument: it must be *hó* 'snow'. This unique selection restriction makes it possible to use the verb *szállingózik* without an explicit subject. At the same time, in (70c) it is not unambiguous what the exact reference of the lexically unrealised subject argument is. According to my and others' intuition, the verb *szitál* 'mizzle' can occur with the nouns *köd* 'haze' and *eső* 'rain'. Thus, in the lexical-semantic representation of the verb *szitál*, we can assume a unique selection restriction concerning argument x which must be selected from a two-element set in particular contexts: {'haze'; 'rain'}. The particular occurrence of the verb *szitál* with an implicit subject is licensed by the interaction between the verb's lexical-semantic representation which includes the selection restriction and information from the observable physical context c_{phys}. If one does not know the physical environment, then one cannot select from the two possibilities predicted by the selection restriction. However, this does not mean that (70c) becomes a syntactically ill-formed utterance, but that two meanings can be assigned to it. There are Hungarian native speakers according to whose intuition the acceptability of (70b) and (70c) is questionable. Their intuition always requires an explicit subject with the verbs *szállingózik* 'fall softly/snow softly' and *szitál* 'mizzle' without a specific context. In this case the lexical-semantic representation of the verbs *szállingózik* and *szitál* does not contain a unique selection restriction requiring the particular kind of precipitation they can occur with. In other words, this piece of encyclopaedic information has not yet been built into the lexical-semantic representation of these verbs. It must be noted that this compulsory-subject analysis supports the plausibility of the hypothesis that weather verbs can occur with explicit subjects to a great extent. However, if we consider the occurrences of *szállingózik* in various newspapers or on news portals on the Internet we can find several occurrences of this verb without an explicit subject argument. These examples, which can be considered occurrences in corpora (and not performance errors), make the analysis based on the assumption of a unique selection restriction involved in the lexical-semantic representation of the verb *szállingózik* more plausible. Cf. (72).

(72)　a.　*Budapesten　　is　　szállingózik.*
　　　　　　Budapest.SUP　also　snows.softly.INDEF
　　　　　　'It is snowing softly in Budapest.'
　　　　　　(Retrieved on 14 April 2014 from http://index.hu/belfold/2014/01/24/havazas/budapesten_is_szallingozik/)

　　　　b.　*Szegeden　　még　csak　szállingózik,　　　Baranyában　erősen*
　　　　　　Szeged.SUP　still　only　snows.softly.INDEF　Baranya.INE　heavily
　　　　　　havazik.
　　　　　　snows.INDEF
　　　　　　'In Szeged it is still only snowing softly, in Baranya it is snowing heavily.'
　　　　　　(Retrieved on 14 April 2014 from http://szeged.hir24.hu/szeged/2012/12/08/szegeden-meg-csak-szallingozik-baranyaban-erosen-havazik/)

As to the verb *szitál* 'mizzle', in various newspapers or on news portals on the Internet we can find occurrences of this verb not only with the nouns *köd* 'haze' and *eső* 'rain', but also with the noun *hó* 'snow'. The verb *szitál* occurs with *hó* even in some poems and songs. Cf., e.g., (73).

(73)　　*Szitál　　　a　　hó　　　　és　　minden　　jégvirág.*
　　　　　mizzles.INDEF　the　snow.NOM　and　everything　snow frost.NOM
　　　　　'The snow is mizzling and there is snow frost everywhere.'
　　　　　(Retrieved on 14 April 2014 from http://www.youtube.com/watch?v=dg71MwbjYis)

If one can accept the occurrences of the verb *szitál* with the noun *hó*, then its lexical-semantic representation must contain a unique selection restriction which is a three-element set including not only *köd* 'haze' and *eső* 'rain', but *hó* 'snow' as well: {'haze'; 'rain'; 'snow'}.

Let us continue with the examination of the answer in (70d) to the question *Milyen az idő?* 'What is the weather like?' The utterance in (70d) is not grammatical. Although in the use of the verb *hull* '[for precipitation to] fall' as a weather verb, it is obvious what kind of precipitation can fall, e.g. *eső* 'rain', *hó* 'snow', and *zúzmara* 'rime', it cannot be used without an explicit subject in a sentence environment. It can be assumed that there is no unique selection restriction built into the lexical-semantic representation of *hull* which can predict what precipitation can fall. Therefore, it cannot occur with an implicit subject argument in the first (A) manner (see Section 3.2), only by relying on its lexical-semantic representation. However, if one answers the question *Milyen az idő?* 'What is the weather like?' with the utterance *Nagy pelyhekben hull [a hó]* 'It is snowing in large flakes', then the use of *hull* '[for precipitation to] fall' with an implicit subject argument becomes acceptable. The encyclopaedic information stored under the conceptual address of *hull* and the other lexemes in the utterance license the omission of the subject argument *a hó* 'the snow'. In other words, *hull* can occur with an implicit subject argument in the second (B) manner. *Hull* can be used with an implicit subject argument in the third (C) manner as well, see (74).

(74)   (The weather forecast predicts snow.)

   Szállingózik   *már*   *[a*   *hó]?*

   snows.softly.INDEF   already   the   snow.NOM

   'Is it (i.e. the snow) snowing softly yet?'

   Már   *hull*   *[a*   *hó].*

   already   falls.INDEF   the   snow.NOM

   'It (i.e.the snow) is falling already.'

In (74), in the question the verb *szállingózik* 'snow softly' occurs with an implicit subject argument in the first (A) manner by means of the selection restriction.[13] This question and the implicit subject argument [*a hó* 'the snow'] in it provide the discourse context for the answer to the question. In the answer the implicit subject argument [*a hó* 'the snow'] occurs with the verb *hull* '[for precipitation to] fall' in the third (C) manner as a zero anaphor, coreferential with the implicit subject argument in the question (see also Section 5.1).

Let us continue our analysis of the utterance in (70e). The lexical-semantic representation of the verb *esik* '[for precipitation to] fall' does not place a unique selection restriction on its subject argument. Instead, the selection restriction constrains the type of the subject argument. Verbs may prescribe to their arguments by means of selection restrictions that they must be of a particular type or an instance (token) of a particular type or have a particular, unique property, etc. The terms *type* and *instance* refer to super- and subcategories. Type as supercategory is more general and has only a few properties, whereas instance (token) is subordinated to a type and has more specific properties. The unique selection restriction requires a particular, unique entity to occupy the argument position in question. While the lexical-semantic representation of the verbs of natural phenomena discussed above, e.g. *villámlik* '[for lightning to] strike', *szállingózik* 'fall softly/snow softly', and *havazik* 'snow', includes a unique selection restriction imposed on the subject argument, the verb *esik* '[for precipitation to] fall' requires that its subject argument be of the type PRECIPITATION. Cf. (75) and also (58) in Section 3.1.2.

(75)   *esik* 'rain':   'x which is precipitation falls in y which is place'

                    [[x FALL_IN y] : [[PRECIPITATION x] & [PLACE y]]]

In (70e) the lexically unrealised subject argument can be identified with the type PRECIPITATION. If a particular token of this type, i.e. a specific kind of precipitation, is referred to, then it must be lexicalised, see (76).

(76)   *Esik*   *az*   *eső/*   *hó/*   *jégeső/*

        falls.INDEF   the   rain.NOM   snow.NOM   hail.NOM

        hódara/   *köd/*   *permet/*   *harmat/*

        hoar-frost.NOM   haze.NOM   sprinkle.NOM   dew.NOM

        dér/   *zúzmara.*

        frost. NOM   rime.NOM

        'Rain/snow/hail/hoar-frost/haze/a sprinkle of rain/dew/frost/rime is falling.'

The enumerated particular kinds of precipitation in (76) show that the type PRECIPITATION has a prototypical structure. This prototypical structure also influences the occurrence of the verb *esik* '[for precipitation to] fall' with implicit subject arguments. The more typical the precipitation, the easier it is to use the verb *esik* with an implicit subject argument without a specific physical or discourse context. Since in Hungarian geographical circumstances the prototypical PRE-CIPITATION is rain, without a specific physical or discourse context the reference of the implicit subject argument in (70e) can be identified with *az eső* 'the rain'.[14]

    Finally, it is worth analysing the verb *havazik* 'snow' in further detail. The verb *havazik* can occur with an explicit subject argument as well, see (77).

(77)   a.   *?A*   *hó*   *havazik.*

        the   snow.NOM   snows.INDEF

        'The snow is snowing.'

b. *?Havazik   a   hó.*
    snows.INDEF   the   snow.NOM
    'The snow is snowing.'

c. *A   rég   várt   hó   megállás   nélkül,*
    the long awaited   snow.NOM stop.NOM   without

    gyönyörűen   havazik.
    beautifully   snows.INDEF
    'The long awaited snow is snowing beautifully and continuously.'

d. *A   múlt   századi   hó   még   nagy   pelyhekben*
    the last   century   snow.NOM still large   flakes.INE

    havazott.
    snowed.INDEF.3SG
    'The snows of the last century snowed in large flakes.'

While the acceptability of (77a–b) is questionable, (77c–d) are acceptable. There is an old observation in connection with the behaviour of cognate objects according to which if a cognate object or the verb itself is modified by some constituents, then the emerging constructions become acceptable. Cognate objects, or in other terminology inner objects or inner accusatives, can be considered a special type of object, since (i) the verbs they are used with behave as if they were intransitive verbs, i.e. they occur without a lexicalised direct object (e.g., the English verbs *smile*, *live*, *laugh* as well as Hungarian *ebédel* 'have dinner', *vacsorázik* 'have supper', *reggelizik* 'have breakfast', *él* 'live', and *hal* 'die', (ii) they are not referential but instead eventive, and (iii) their lexical head is identical to the verbs (e.g. the English noun *smile* and verb *smile*) or is derived morphologically (cf. the English pairs *live/life*) or sometimes semantically (cf. English *laugh/cackle*) from the verbs of which they are cognate; Glaude and Zribi-Hertz 2014: 242).[15] In Hungarian it can also occur that the verbs are derived from the stem of the object morphologically, e.g., the verb *ebéd-el* 'have lunch-SFX.INDEF.3SG' from the noun *ebéd* 'lunch', and the verb *vacsorá-z-ik* 'have supper.SFX.INDEF.3SG from the noun *vacsora* 'supper'. From these properties of cognate objects it follows that, while the utterance in (78a) is rather strange, because the verb *ebédel* 'have dinner' occurs with its pure cognate object, the utterance in (78b) is quite acceptable, because the verb *ebédel* 'have dinner' occurs with its modified cognate object. Similarly, (78c) is questionable but (78d) is quite acceptable, since the cognate object *élet* 'life' of the verb *él* 'live' is modified.

(78) a. *?József   ebédet   ebédel.*
          József.NOM   dinner.ACC   has.a.dinner.INDEF
          '?József has a dinner for dinner.'

      b. *József   meleg   ebédet   ebédel.*
          József.NOM   hot   dinner.ACC   has.a.dinner.INDEF
          'József has a hot dinner for dinner.'

      c. *?Mari   életet   élt.*
          Mari.NOM   life.ACC   lived.INDEF.3SG
          '?Mari lived life.'

      d. *Mari   önpusztító   életet   élt.*
          Mari.NOM   self-destructive   life.ACC   lived.INDEF.3SG
          'Mary lived a self-destructive life.'

Glaude and Zribi-Hertz (2014: 289) support Pereltsvaig's (1999) general theory on cognate verbs on the basis of their analyses of Haitian verb cognates. According to this theory, verb cognates are noun phrases which either behave like direct objects (see (78a–d)) or like predicative adjuncts, in other words cognate adverbials (Pereltsvaig's (1999: 51) Russian example *Ego nagradili samoj vysokoj nagradoj* 'They rewarded him with the highest reward' cited by Glaude and Zribi-Hertz (2014: 289)). Thus, the concept of cognates has been viewed as including cognate adverbials as well. The lexical head of cognates, both cognate objects and adverbials, is morphologically related to the corresponding verbs.

This analysis can be extended to the verb *havazik* 'snow' and the noun *hó* 'snow', which can be assumed to be a cognate subject of the verb at issue. In its lexical-semantic representation, the verb *havazik* puts a unique selection restriction on its argument *x*: 'x is snow'. Consider (79).

(79)   *havazik* 'snow':   'x which is snow falls in y which is place'
                             [[x FALL_IN y] : [[SNOW x] & [PLACE y]]][16]

Since the verb *havazik* is morphologically derived from the noun *hó*, predicted by the selection restriction to be the unique subject argument of the verb in question, the verbal morphological structure is absolutely transparent. This transparent morphological structure as well as its phonetic form easily recall the subject argument *hó*, predicted by the selection restriction. Therefore, the explicit occurrence of *hó* is disturbingly redundant with the verb *havazik*, with which the noun *hó* can henceforth appear only as an implicit subject. However, if the cognate noun *hó* is modified by an adjective (and the verb by an adverb) as in (77c–d), we get an acceptable utterance containing both the verb *havazik* and the noun *hó*.

Of course, in metaphorical uses the verb *havazik* also occurs with explicit subjects as we have seen above: *havazik az élet* 'life is snowing', *az egész világ havazik* 'the whole world is snowing', *csend havazik* 'silence is snowing' (*Magyar Nemzeti Szövegtár* (Hungarian National Corpus, corpus.nytud.hu/mnsz)).

Consider also (80).

(80)   *Havazik*   *[a   hó$_i$]*   *Nagyon szépen esik*
           snows.INDEF the snow.NOM very   nicely   falls.INDEF

           [a   hó$_i$].
           the snow.NOM

           '[Snow] is snowing. [The snow] is falling very nicely.'

The possibility that in the second utterance in (80) one can refer to *a hó* by a zero anaphor supports the plausibility of the analysis assuming an implicit subject argument occurring with the verb *havazik* as in the first utterance of (80). At the same time it weakens the plausibility of the widely accepted analysis in the Hungarian grammatical tradition according to which the noun *hó* is incorporated into the verb *havazik* (see also (72b)).

To summarise: starting out from a wide spectrum of data neglected by previous approaches, in this section I have proposed a lexical-semantic representation with a subject argument position for the verbs of natural phenomena analysed as subjectless verbs in the Hungarian grammatical tradition as well as in lexical-functional grammar. The verbs of natural phenomena constrain their subject argument very strictly by means of the elements in their lexical-semantic representation such as selection restrictions, information on the characteristic manner of natural events, and the prototypical structure of the categories. The lexical-semantic representation of these verbs can be interpreted in two ways. Either only the natural events denoted by the verbs are the focus of attention, or their subject is as well. When only the natural events are the focus of attention, the subject arguments can be left lexically unrealised. Verbs give access to their lexical-semantic representations with their argument structure. If the subject argument is left implicit in the first (A) manner, it can be identified with the information provided by the constraints the selection restriction imposes on the subject argument as background information. Since in the case of verbs of natural phenomena what can fill in the subject position is strictly or even uniquely constrained by the selection restrictions, the subject argument should not be lexically realised. Therefore, the economical and default occurrence of verbs of natural phenomena is use without an explicit subject, i.e. with implicit subjects. At the same time, if the subject argument is also the focus of attention or the particular subject argument is not the prototype of the category required by the selection restriction or the speaker wants to refer to a specific token of the category, then the subject argument must be explicitly expressed. Similarly, in metaphorical uses, the verbs of natural phenomena cannot occur with a lexically unrealised subject argument in the first (A) manner, either. Sometimes the background information in the lexical-semantic representation of a verb of natural phenomenon by itself cannot license an argument to be left implicit. In these cases the lexical-semantic representation of the verb interacts with the context.

The main advantages of the proposed solution are as follows. Firstly, it can explain the occurrences of verbs of natural phenomena both with and without an explicit subject argument in a unified way. Secondly, it can account for a wider spectrum of data than the rival approaches in the starting context of the problem can, i.e. it cancels some inconsistency. Thirdly, assuming a subject argument position in the lexical-semantic representation of verbs of natural phenomena, metaphorical uses can be handled in the same way as non-metaphorical occurrences, i.e. further inconsistency and incompleteness can be eliminated. Fourthly, the occurrences of verbs of natural phenomena with implicit subject arguments can be treated similarly to the uses of verbs with implicit direct and indirect/oblique objects (see Sections 4.2 and 4.3). And, fifthly, the occurrences of verbs of natural phenomena with explicit and implicit subjects can be considered syntactic alternations similarly to the non-objectless and objectless uses of transitive verbs (see Sections 4.2 and 4.3). This supports the proposal of such a lexical-semantic representation for verbs of natural phenomena from a syntactic point of view. All these advantages increase the explanatory power of the implicit subject argument analysis of verbs of natural phenomena.

Confronting the implicit subject analysis developed in the present section with the rival approaches in the starting context of the research into the subjectlessness/non-subjectlessness of Hungarian verbs of natural phenomena, it can be established that the new analysis is more plausible than the previous ones on the basis of the newly introduced data from various direct sources, as well as on the basis of theoretical statements listed above as advantages. Therefore, the new solution can be considered a resolution of the problem in the starting context, and the newly introduced data from different direct sources serve as strong evidence for this.

After our analysis of the behaviour of Hungarian verbs of natural phenomena with and without explicit subjects, let us turn to another class of Hungarian verbs which can occur with implicit subject arguments in the first (A) manner, namely verbs of work.

4.1.2 Verbs of work with implicit subjects

In Hungarian there are verb classes which can occur with lexically unrealised subject arguments not only because of the pro-drop property of Hungarian and an interaction between grammatical constraints and pragmatic factors, but rather on the basis of the interaction between lexical-semantic representations of verbs and contextual information. In the previous section I proposed an analysis for Hungarian verbs of natural phenomena occurring with implicit and explicit subject arguments relying on the lexical-semantic representation of verbs of natural phenomena as well as contextual factors. In the present section I aim to investigate how another particular verb class, namely, verbs of work, can be used with implicit subject arguments in the first (A) manner. When verbs of work occur with implicit subject arguments in the first (A) manner, they cannot be considered zero anaphors, because they do not have an antecedent in the utterance or discourse context that they can be coreferential and co-indexed with. It must be emphasised again that zero anaphors are zero pronouns that have an antecedent in the utterance or discourse which they can be coreferential with. However, not all zero pronouns can be considered zero anaphors. If the referent of a zero pronoun does not explicitly appear in the utterance or discourse, it is called a non-anaphoric zero pronoun. A non-anaphoric zero pronoun typically refers to an extralinguistic entity (e.g. the first or second person) or its referent is indefinite and unspecified in the context (cf., e.g., Fillmore 1986; Cote 1996; Saeboe 1996; Iida, Inui, and Matsumoto 2006; Németh T. 2010). Investigating implicit direct objects, Hale and Keyser (2002), as well as Cummins and Roberge (2005), suggest that indefinite implicit direct objects are represented by null bare nouns. On the basis of these considerations, as well as the definition of implicit arguments in (57) (Section 3.1.1), the implicit subject arguments of verbs of work in Hungarian which occur in the first (A) manner cannot be treated as zero anaphors. The occurrence and interpretation of verbs of work with implicit subjects in the first (A) manner can be analysed similarly to the behaviour of verbs of natural phenomena without explicit subjects.

The group of verbs of work involves verbs such as *vet* 'sow', *arat* 'harvest', *szánt* 'plough', *takarít* 'clean', *operál* 'operate on', *gyógyít* 'treat', *ápol* 'care for', *szerel* 'mend, repair', *kézbesít* 'deliver', and *oktat/tanít* 'teach'. It must be noted that several verbs of work can occur not only with implicit subject arguments, but also with implicit direct object arguments, as can be seen in (106) below in Section 4.2. In the present section I do not intend to analyse implicit direct object arguments; therefore, in the Hungarian examples I do not indicate them – I provide only implicit subject arguments in square brackets. The implicit subject arguments indicated by capital letters can be identified with the help of selection restrictions in the lexical-semantic representations of the relevant verbs of work. These verbs constrain the type of their subject arguments, similarly to the verb *esik* '[for precipitation to] fall' which requires that its subject argument be of the type PRECIPITATION. Consider (81).

(81) a. *Ősszel   és   tavasszal   is   vetnek   [PARASZT]   gabonát.*
          in.autumn   and   in.spring   also   sow.INDEF.3PL   peasant   grain.ACC
          'In fall and also in spring [the peasants] sow grain.

      b. *Júliusban   már   aratnak   [ARATÓ/PARASZT].*
          July.INE   already   harvest.INDEF.3PL   harvester/peasant.
          'In July [the harvesters/the peasants] already harvest.'

      c. *A   heves   esőzések   miatt   napokig   nem*
          the   heavy   rains.NOM   because.of   days.TER   not
          szántottak   [PARASZT].
          ploughed.INDEF.3PL   peasant
          'Because of the heavy rains [the peasants] have not been ploughing for days.'

      d. (In the morning an office worker says to his colleague at the office:)
          Poros   az   asztalom,   tegnap   se   takarítottak
          dusty   the   my.table.NOM   yesterday   no   cleaned.INDEF.3PL
          [TAKARÍTÓ]   rendesen.
          cleaner   properly
          'My desk is dusty, yesterday [the cleaners] did not clean [the office] well.

      e. *Az   új   műtőben   sokat   operálnak   [SEBÉSZ]*
          the   new   operating.theatre.INE   much.ACC   operate.INDEF.3PL   surgeon
          '[The surgeons] operate a lot in the new operating theatre.'

      f. *Az   orvosi   fakultáson   nemcsak   tanítanak,*
          the   medical   faculty.SUP   not.only   teach. INDEF.3PL

          hanem   gyógyítanak   is   [ORVOS].
          but   treat.INDEF.3PL   also   doctor
          'At the medical faculty [the doctors] not only teach [students], but also treat
          [patients].'

      g. *Ebben   a   kórházban   naponta   ezer   beteget*
          this.INE   the   hospital.INE   a.day   thousand   patient.ACC

          ápolnak   [ÁPOLÓ].
          care.for.INDEF.3PL   medical.staff
          'In this hospital [the medical staff] care for a thousand patients a day.'

      h. *A   Mercedes   új   gyárában   régi   autókat   is*
          the   Mercedes.NOM   new   factory.INE   old   cars.ACC   also

    szerelnek   *[SZERELŐ].*

    mend.INDEF.3PL   mechanics

    'In the new Mercedes factory [the car mechanics] also mend old cars.'

i.   *Vasárnap   nem   kézbesítenek   [POSTÁS]   csomagot.*

    Sunday   not   deliver.INDEF.3PL   postman   package.ACC

    'On Sunday [the delivery men] do not deliver packages.'

j.   *Egyetemünkön   több   száz   tárgyat   oktatnak*

    our.university.SUP   several   hundred   subjects.ACC   teach.INDEF.3PL

    [TANÁR].

    teacher

    'At our university [the instructors] teach several hundred subjects.'

The occurrence of the verbs *vet* 'sow', *arat* 'harvest', *szánt* 'plough', *takarít* 'clean', *operál* 'operate on', *gyógyít* 'treat', *ápol* 'care for', *szerel* 'mend, repair', *kézbesít* 'deliver', and *oktat/tanít* 'teach' with implicit subject arguments in (81) can be explained in two ways. The first possible explanation can be based on the first (A) manner of the occurrence of Hungarian verbs with implicit arguments. According to this analysis, the lexical-semantic representation of these verbs puts a selection restriction on the type of subject argument by means of which it can license the use of these verbs without an explicit subject with a generic reading. In each case, the type of the subject argument must be a particular set of persons occupied in the profession in question.[17] For example, the lexical-semantic representation of the verbs *vet* 'sow' and *takarít* 'clean' in (82) and (83) constrain the type of the subject argument by means of a selection restriction according to which the subject argument must be PEASANT and CLEANER, respectively.

(82)   *vet* 'sow':   'action of x who is a peasant causes that y which is seed goes into z which is field'

    [[[ACT x] : [PEASANT x]] CAUSE [[GO y] : [[SEED y] & [[FIN [LOC y] ⊂ LOC z] : [FIELD z]]]]]

(83)   *takarít* 'clean':   'action of x who is a cleaner causes y to become clean'

    [[[ACT x] : [CLEANER x]] CAUSE [BECOME [CLEAN y]]]

This kind of lexical-semantic representation in (82) and (83) can be interpreted in two ways (cf. García Velasco and Portero Muñoz 2002; Goldberg 2005a, b; Bibok 2008; Németh T. 2008a, 2010, 2012; and also Section 4.1.1). Either only the actions themselves denoted by verbs of work are the focus of attention in a context, or their subject is as well. As I have discussed in Section 4.1.1, in the case of Hungarian verbs of natural phenomena occurring with implicit subject arguments, verbs give access to their lexical-semantic representations with their argument structure. If the subject argument is left implicit, it can be identified with the information provided by the constraints which the selection restriction imposes on its type as background information. Since, on the basis of the general encyclopaedic knowledge about the various kinds of work built into their lexical-semantic representations, verbs of work strictly or even uniquely (e.g., *Gyóntatnak* '[Priests] confess [penitents]') constrain what can fill the subject position, therefore the subject argument should not be lexically realised. In (81) the actions themselves are the focus of attention; agents syntactically realisable as subjects are available as background information provided by the selection restrictions. This kind of analysis is also supported by the utterances in (84) involving the same verbs of work but with explicit subjects.

(84) a. *Ősszel   és   tavasszal   is   vetnek   az*
          in.autumn   and   in.spring   also   sow.INDEF.3PL   the

          alföldi   parasztok   gabonát.
          plain   peasants.NOM   grain.ACC
          'In fall and also in spring the peasants of the plain sow grain.'

     b. *Júliusban   már   aratnak   a   katonák.*
          July.INE   already   harvest.INDEF.3PL   the   soldiers.NOM
          'In July the soldiers already harvest.'

     c. *A   heves   esőzések   miatt   napokig   nem*
          the   heavy   rains.NOM   because of   days.TER   not

          szántottak   a   asszonyok.
          ploughed.INDEF.3PL   the   women.NOM
          'Because of the heavy rains the peasant women have not been ploughing for days.'

     d. (In the morning an office worker says to his colleague at the office:)
          Poros   az   asztalom,   tegnap   se   takarítottak
          dusty   the   my.table.NOM   yesterday   no   cleaned.INDEF.3PL

          rendesen   a   diákok.
          properly   the   students.NOM
          'My desk is dusty; yesterday the students did not clean [the office] well.

     e. *Az   új   műtőben   sokat   operálnak   a*
          the   new   operating.theatre.INE   much.ACC   operate.INDEF.3PL   the

nőgyógyászok.
gynaecologists.NOM
'The gynaecologists operate a lot in the new operating theatre.'

f. *Az   orvosi   fakultáson   nemcsak   tanítanak,*
the   medical   faculty.SUP   not only   teach. INDEF.3PL

hanem   gyógyítanak   is   a   vendég professzorok.
but   treat.INDEF.3PL   also   the   guest.professors.NOM
'At the medical faculty the guest professors do not only teach [students], but also treat [patients].

g. *Ebben   a   kórházban   naponta   ezer   beteget*
this.INE   the   hospital.INE   a.day   thousand   patient.ACC

ápolnak   az   önkéntesek
care.for.INDEF.3PL   the   volunteers.NOM
'In this hospital the volunteers care for a thousand patients a day.'

h. *A   Mercedes   új   gyárában   régi   autókat   is*
the   Mercedes.NOM   new   factory.INE   old   cars.ACC   also

szerelnek   a   dieselautó-szerelők.
mend.INDEF.3PL   the   diesel.car.mechanics.NOM
'In the new Mercedes factory the diesel car mechanics also mend old cars.'

i. *Vasárnap   nem   kézbesítenek   az   egyetemisták   csomagot.*
Sunday   not   deliver.INDEF.3PL   the   students.NOM   package.ACC
'On Sunday the students do not deliver packages.'

j. *Egyetemünkön   több   száz   tárgyat   oktatnak*
our.university.SUP   several   hundred   subjects.ACC   teach.INDEF.3PL
a   bankárok.
the   bankers.NOM
'At our university bankers teach several hundred subjects.'

Since the subject arguments in (84a) and (84h) are specific tokens of a particular type and subject arguments in (84b–g) and (84i–j) are not of the type required by selection restrictions, they cannot be left lexically *unrealised* without specific contexts. In these utterances it is not only the activities denoted by the verbs of work which are the focus of attention, but their subject arguments as well, and thus they must be lexically expressed.

Let us turn back to the utterances in (81). It must be noted that these utterances differ from utterances which contain verbs conjugated for the indefinite form

3PL, which refer to lexically unrealised subject arguments and are considered indefinite or general subjects in the Hungarian grammatical tradition. Consider some examples from Kugler's chapter in *Magyar grammatika* (2000a: 410–411).

(85)   a.   *Csöngettek.*

rang.INDEF.3PL

'The doorbell rang.'

   b.   *Hogy   hívnak?*
how   call.INDEF.3PL
'What is your name?'

   c.   *Kirabolták   a   bankot.*
PVB.robbed.INDEF.3PL   the   bank.ACC
'The bank has been robbed.'

   d.   *Megválasztották   az   országgyűlés   új   elnökét.*
PVB.elected.INDEF.3PL   the   parliament.NOM   new   president.ACC
'The new president of the parliament has been elected.'

According to Kugler (2000a: 410–411), (85a) and (85d) involve an indefinite subject, while (85b) and (85c) a general subject. This grammar also emphasises that in the case of a third person subject it is not easy to decide whether it is an indefinite or a general subject. Both indefinite and general subjects are considered by Kugler (2000a: 410–411) to be underdetermined, more precisely unspecified. However, one can distinguish between (85a–b) and (85c–d) with regard to the determinacy or specificity, although there is no noun phrase with a definite article in it which can serve as a subject argument. In (85a–b) the identification of the subject argument is only possible if one takes into account the particular, specific physical environment c_{phys} or discourse context c_{disc}. In the absence of such a context the speaker does not intend to refer to an identifiable agent. But in (85c–d), without any specific context, one can know more about the intended reference of the implicit subject arguments than in (85a–b). The lexical-semantic representations of the verbs *rabol* 'rob' and *választ* 'elect' put selection restrictions on the type of their subject argument, which must be of the type RABLÓ 'burglar/robber' and VÁLASZTÁSRA JOGOSULT SZEMÉLY 'a person with a right to vote'. However, on the basis of the interaction between the verbs' lexical-semantic representations and the contexts involved, the subject arguments can be specified to a greater extent than is provided by the selection restrictions RABLÓ and VÁLASZTÁSRA JOGOSULT SZEMÉLY. The implicit subject arguments can be interpreted as *bankrabló(k)* 'bank robber(s)' in (85c) and *képviselők* 'parliamentarian' in (85d), respectively. In (85c–d), in addition to the verbs' selection restriction, the meanings of the other lexemes in the utterances play a crucial role in the identification of the implicit subject arguments, while in utterances in (81a–j) only the verbs' selection restrictions inducing typical, generic readings of utterances contribute to the construction of the meanings of the utterances.

There is a second, rival possible explanation of the occurrence of the verbs of work *vet* 'sow', *arat* 'harvest', *szánt* 'plough', *takarít* 'clean', *operál* 'operate on', *gyógyít* 'treat', *ápol* 'care for', *szerel* 'mend, repair', *kézbesít* 'deliver', and *oktat/tanít* 'teach' with implicit subject arguments in (81a–j). This can be based on the second (B) manner of the occurrence of Hungarian verbs with implicit arguments (see Section 3.2), in which the rest of the utterance, i.e. the immediate context in which they occur with its contextual (encyclopaedic) and grammatical requirements, provides a relevant, typical interpretation for implicit subject arguments. According to this analysis, the implicit subject arguments in (81a–j) are licensed by the interaction between the encyclopaedic information stored under the conceptual addresses of the verbs involved and the other lexemes in the utterances (Groefsema 1995). In this analysis, the encyclopaedic information concerning the type of subject arguments has not yet been built into the lexical-semantic representations as a selection restriction; instead, it is stored under the verb's conceptual address and becomes available in the course of interpretation. According to this explanation, the lexical-semantic representation of *vet* 'sow' and *takarít* 'clean' can be formed as (86) and (87), respectively.

(86)   *vet* 'sow':   'action of x causes that y which is seed goes into z which is field'

[[ACT x] CAUSE [[GO y] : [[SEED y] & [[FIN [LOC y] $\subset$ LOC z] : [FIELD z]]]]]

(87)   *takarít* 'clean':   'action of x causes y to become clean'

[[ACT x] CAUSE [BECOME [CLEAN y]]]

However, if we also consider the occurrences of verbs of work without any other lexemes in utterances, i.e. occurrences in one-word utterances such as [*az aratók*] *Aratnak* '[The harvesters] harvest [the grain]', [*a sebészek*] *Operálnak* '[The surgeons] operate [patients]', [*a tanárok*] *Oktatnak* 'The teachers teach [the students]', [*a kézbesítők*] *Kézbesítenek* '[The delivery men] deliver [packages]', we cannot explain the occurrences with implicit subject arguments in the second (B) manner in the absence of an immediate context. These occurrences in one-word utterances attest that verbs of work have encyclopaedically rich lexical-semantic representations, i.e. the encyclopaedic information concerning the subjects is included in them. Therefore, it is more plausible to assume the kind of lexical-semantic representations for the verbs *vet* 'sow' and *takarít* 'clean' that can be found in (82) and (83) than for those in (86) and (87). Of course, if verbs of work occur in immediate utterance contexts, the encyclopaedic information stored under the conceptual addresses of the other lexemes can support (or override) the interpretation according to the first (A) manner.

To conclude: in this section I have attempted to explain those occurrences of Hungarian verbs of work with implicit subject arguments which do not originate in the pro-drop characteristics of Hungarian, but in the interaction between their lexical-semantic representation and contextual information. I intended, firstly, to examine what kind of lexical-semantic representation can be assumed for Hungarian verbs of work and, secondly, how lexical-semantic and contextual factors license the occurrence of verbs of work with implicit subjects in Hungarian. I have proposed two rival accounts for the subjectless use of verbs of work relying on the (A) and (B) manners of occurrences of verbs with implicit arguments in Hungarian. The first explanation assumes an encyclopaedically rich lexical-semantic representation for verbs of work which licenses the occurrences of verbs of work with implicit subjects in interaction with the particular context. The second explanation suggests a poorer lexical-semantic representation for verbs of work as well as an interaction between the pieces of encyclopaedic information stored under the conceptual address of verbs of work and other lexemes in utterances. As to the first explanation, bearing in mind the above-mentioned two goals I have two final conclusions. Firstly, I have proposed a lexical-semantic representation of verbs of work which is encyclopaedically rich enough to serve as a basis for the use of these verbs with implicit subject arguments. The encyclopaedic information concerning the type of subject argument is built into the lexical-semantic representations of these verbs as selection restrictions which the implicit subject in the subjectless use can be identified with in a context where the communicator does not consider it important to express the subject argument lexically. Secondly, although the twofold interpretability of the lexical-semantic representations of verbs of work makes it possible to use them with or without explicit subjects, the particular occurrences are determined by the particular contexts, i.e. lexical-semantic representations and contexts interact.

As for the second explanation, the encyclopaedic information concerning the type of subject arguments has not yet been built into the lexical-semantic representations. In other words, the lexical-semantic representation of verbs of work does not contain a selection restriction constraining the type of subject arguments. Instead, the encyclopaedic information regarding the typical subject argument is stored under the verb's conceptual address, which also becomes available in the course of interpretation. In this case the lexical-semantic representation is poorer than the first explanation suggests. In a particular context, the verb's lexical-semantic representation, the general encyclopaedic information on the typical subject, and the encyclopaedic information stored under the conceptual address of other lexemes in immediate utterance contexts interact to identify the unlexicalised subject arguments.

In both kinds of explanation the lexical-semantic information and the contextual information interact in the meaning construction of utterances containing the verbs of work. The main difference between the two accounts is the extent to which the lexical-semantic representation and the context participate in the meaning construction of utterances. According to the first explanation, the lexical-semantic representation involves a kind of encyclopaedic information which belongs to contextual (encyclopaedic) information in the second account.

The proposed rival explanations are advantageous and novel on several counts. Firstly, they can both account for a subjectless use of verbs of work in Hungarian which cannot be explained only by the pro-drop characteristics of Hungarian. Secondly, they treat the occurrences of verbs of work with implicit subjects similarly to the uses of verbs of natural phenomena with implicit subjects and also to the uses of verbs with implicit direct objects (see Section 4.2). Thirdly, the suggested types of lexical-semantic representations reveal how and to what extent general encyclopaedic information can be built into utterances, and how particular contextual information influences the lexicalisation of the subject arguments in these utterances. Fourthly, the analysis based on the three manners of the occurrence of verbs with implicit arguments provides a new, more plausible analysis for the zero subject arguments which have been considered indefinite or general subjects in the Hungarian grammatical tradition.

However, comparing the two rival explanations suggested in this subsection, it can be established that the first account based on the first (A) manner of the occurrence of Hungarian verbs with implicit arguments has a greater explanatory power, since it can account for the subjectless one-word utterances including verbs of work, while the second explanation based on the second (B) manner of the occurrence of Hungarian verbs with lexically unrealised arguments cannot. To put it the other way round, while the plausible statement formed below in (88) which relies on occurrences of verbs of work with implicit subject arguments in one-word utterances is problematic for the second explanation, it is not for the first one, since the proposed rich lexical-semantic representation makes it possible to use verbs of work with implicit subject arguments without an immediate utterance context.

(88)   The verbs *vet* 'sow', *arat* 'harvest', *szánt* 'plough', *takarít* 'clean', *operál* 'operate on', *gyógyít* 'treat', *ápol* 'care for', *szerel* 'mend, repair', *kézbesít* 'deliver', and *oktat/tanít* 'teach' are verbs of work and they can be used in one-word utterances with a lexically unrealised subject argument.

Thus, (88) can be considered strong evidence against the second explanation, since it makes it implausible, but it serves as strong evidence for the first explanation, since it makes it plausible (see Section 4.1.1).

After the discussion of the role played by the lexical-semantic representation of Hungarian verbs of natural phenomena and its work in the licensing of occurrences with lexically unrealised subject arguments in the first (A) manner, let us examine in the next section how Hungarian verbs can be used with implicit direct object arguments.

4.2 Occurrence of verbs with implicit direct object arguments

4.2.1 Observations concerning the occurrence of verbs with direct object arguments

In the Hungarian grammatical tradition (Komlósy 1992; Keszler 2000; Pusztai 2003), there is an old observation that there are verbs which can occur with a direct object and verbs which can be used without any direct object. In the Hungarian grammatical tradition it is also well known that this observation grasps not only the difference between the transitive (e.g. *főz* 'cook', *eszik* 'eat', *iszik* 'drink', *olvas* 'read', *ír* 'write', *varr* 'sew', *arat* 'harvest', *vet* 'sow') and intransitive (e.g. *esik* 'fall', *szakad* 'tear', *törik* 'break', *csúszik* 'slip', *gurul* 'roll', *foszlik* 'fray', *hámlik* 'peel') verbs, but also refers to the fact that transitive verbs can occur without a direct object argument. For example, it is not necessary to add the object *étel* 'food' to the verb *főz* 'cook', because it is involved in the meaning of the verb as the object of the action denoted by the verb. However, if we want to use such a verb with a more specific direct object argument or a direct object argument of a different type then they must be explicitly realised, see (89).[18]

(89)   a.   *A   nagymama   főz   [ÉTEL].*
             the   grandmother.NOM   cooks.INDEF   food
             'The grandmother is cooking.'

        b.   *A   nagymama   vacsorát   főz.*
             the   grandmother.NOM   dinner.ACC   cooks.INDEF
             'The grandmother is cooking dinner.'

c.   *A   nagymama   szappant   főz.*

the   grandmother.NOM   soap.ACC   cooks.INDEF

'The grandmother is cooking soap.'

Transitive verbs in Hungarian can occur with and without a direct object argument in various ways. The utterances in (90)–(94) illustrate the variety of occurrences of transitive verbs regarding the definiteness of direct objects as well as the kind of conjugation. In Hungarian there are two types of conjugations, namely, what are traditionally called the indefinite[19] and definite conjugations. Transitive verbs can be conjugated for both indefinite and definite forms, but intransitive verbs only for indefinite forms. Intransitive verbs do not have a direct object argument position in their lexical-semantic representation; therefore, they cannot be used with a direct object and can only be conjugated for the indefinite forms. Transitive verbs have a direct object argument position in their lexical-semantic representation, and usually, if they are used with an indefinite direct object, they need to be conjugated for the indefinite forms. If they are used with a definite direct object, then they must be conjugated for the definite forms. The use of the indefinite/definite conjugations in case of transitive verbs is determined by mostly semantic/pragmatic and (morpho)syntactic criteria.[20]

Consider (90)–(94).

(90)   a.   *Mária   egy   kiflit   eszik.*

        Mária.NOM   a   croissant.ACC   eats.INDEF

        'Mária is eating a croissant.'

     b.   *Mária   eszi   a   kiflit.*

        Mária.NOM   eats.DEF   the   croissant.ACC

        'Mária is eating the croissant.'

     c.   *Mária   kiflit   eszik.*

        Mária.NOM   croissant.ACC   eats.INDEF

        'Mária is eating croissants.'

     d.   *Mária   eszik   [ÉTEL].*

        Mária.NOM   eats.INDEF   food

        'Mária is eating.'

     e.   *Mária   eszi   [Ø].*

        Mária.NOM   eats.DEF

        'Mária is eating [Ø].'

(91) a. *Gábor   egy sört   iszik.*
          Gábor.NOM   a   beer.ACC   drinks.INDEF
          'Gábor is drinking a beer.'

      b. *Gábor   issza   a   sört.*
          Gábor.NOM   drinks.DEF the beer.ACC
          'Gábor is drinking the beer.'

      c. *Gábor   sört   iszik.*
          Gábor.NOM   beer.ACC   drinks.INDEF
          'Gábor is drinking beer.'

      d. *Gábor   iszik   [FOLYADÉK].*
          Gábor.NOM   drinks.INDEF liquid.
          'Gábor is drinking.'

      e. *Gábor   issza   [Ø].*
          Gábor.NOM   drinks.DEF
          'Gábor is drinking [Ø]'

(92) a. *Eszter   egy újságot   olvas.*
          Eszter.NOM   a   newspaper.ACC   reads.INDEF
          'Eszter is reading a newspaper.'

      b. *Eszter   olvassa   az   újságot.*
          Eszter.NOM   reads.DEF   the newspaper.ACC
          'Eszter is reading the newspaper.'

      c. *Eszter   újságot   olvas.*
          Eszter.NOM   newspaper.ACC   reads.INDEF
          'Eszter is reading newspapers.'

      d. *Eszter   olvas   [SZIMBOLIKUS REPREZENTÁCIÓ].*
          Eszter.NOM   reads.INDEF   symbolic representation
          'Eszter is reading.'

      e. *Eszter   olvassa   [Ø].*
          Eszter.NOM   reads.DEF
          'Eszter is reading [Ø].'

(93) a. *Zsófia   egy könyvet   ír.*
          Zsófia.NOM   a   book.ACC   writes.INDEF
          'Zsófia is writing a book.'

    b.   *Zsófia*   *írja*   *a*   *könyvet.*
        Zsófia.NOM   writes.DEF   the   book.ACC
        'Zsófia is writing the book.'

    c.   *Zsófia*   *könyvet*   *ír.*
        Zsófia.NOM   book.ACC   writes.INDEF
        'Zsófia is writing books.'

    d.   *Zsófia*   *ír*   *[SZIMBOLIKUS REPREZENTÁCIÓ].*
        Zsófia.NOM   writes.INDEF   symbolic representation.
        'Zsófia is writing.'

    e.   *Zsófia*   *írja*   *[Ø].*
        Zsófia.NOM   writes.DEF
        'Zsófia is writing [Ø].'

(94) a.   *György*   *egy* *lakást*   *takarít.*
        György.NOM   a   flat.ACC   cleans.INDEF
        'György is cleaning a flat.'

    b.   *György*   *takarítja*   *a*   *lakást.*
        György.NOM   cleans.DEF   the   flat.ACC
        'György is cleaning the flat.'

    c.   *György*   *lakást*   *takarít.*
        György.NOM   flat.ACC   cleans.INDEF
        'György is cleaning flats.'

    d.   *György*   *takarít*   *[PISZKOS HELY].*
        György.NOM   clean.INDEF   dirty place.
        'György is cleaning.'

    e.   *György*   *takarítja*   *[Ø].*
        György.NOM   cleans.DEF
        'György is cleaning [Ø].'

The utterances in the (a)–(c) examples of (90)–(94) contain the verbs *eszik* 'eat', *iszik* 'drink', *olvas* 'read', *ír* 'write', *takarít* 'clean' with explicit, phonetically realised, syntactically present direct objects, but these verbs in the (d)–(e) examples occur without lexically realised direct objects. In the (a) examples the verbs have indefinite direct objects and are conjugated for the indefinite forms, while in the (b) examples the verbs have definite direct objects and are conjugated for the definite forms. In the (c) examples the verbal phrases are complex predicates: their verbs are inflected for the indefinite conjugation and the direct object arguments lack any article. Examining these verbs further, we should note that the act of eating necessarily involves the act of eating something,[21] the act of drinking the act of drinking something, the act of reading the act of reading something, the act of writing the act of writing something, and the act of cleaning the act of cleaning something. So the verbs *eszik* 'eat', *iszik* 'drink', *olvas* 'read', *ír* 'write', and *takarít* 'clean' have really two arguments in the (d) examples as well. Although in the (d) examples the direct object arguments are syntactically missing and are left lexically unrealised, in the course of the interpretation of these utterances the argument *something* is used. Moreover, it is to some extent specified semantically, similarly to the use of the verb *főz* 'cook' without a direct object in (89a). In the case of *eszik* the argument *something* must be some kind of food, in the case of *iszik* some kind of liquid, in the case of *olvas* some kind of symbolic representation, and so on. As I have indicated in Sections 2.3 and 3.1.2, many linguists are of the opinion that there are two verbs in these cases, one transitive and the other intransitive (e.g., Fodor and Fodor 1980; Dowty 1981; Komlósy 1994, 2001). But in my proposal there is no need to assume a transitive and an intransitive *eszik*, *iszik*, *olvas*, *ír*, and *takarít*. These and similar verbs are always transitive, but the object of eating, drinking, reading, writing, cleaning, etc. can be left lexically unrealised and unspecified if the speaker does not want to or does not consider it important to or cannot name the object of eating, drinking, writing, cleaning, etc. The assumption of one transitive lexical entry for *eszik*, *iszik*, *olvas*, *ír*, and *takarít*, instead of proposing two lexical entries, i.e. an intransitive and a transitive one, results in a more economical construction of the lexical component of grammar. However, such a proposal can be accepted if one assumes an interaction between pragmatic and grammatical factors (see Section 1.2.1). The proposal of a simple transitive entry is also supported by the natural interpretation of the following dialogue observed in a family context, where the members of a family were sitting at the dining table and eating soup when the husband suddenly arrived home. The wife asked her husband whether she should get some soup for him, while the husband refused his wife's offer.

(95)   Wife: *Merítsek*   *levest?*

get.IMP. INDEF 1SG.   soup.ACC

'Shall I get you some soup?'

Husband: *Nem, köszönöm,   már   ettem   [ÉTEL].*

no,   thank.DEF.1SG   already   ate.INDEF.1SG   food

'No, thanks, I have already eaten [food].'

In the husband's answer the verb *eszik* 'eat' occurs without a direct object, but the utterance is interpreted such that the husband has already eaten some kind of food, perhaps even a whole meal. What the meal was exactly is left indefinite and lexically unexpressed. The lexically unexpressed, syntactically missing direct object argument in the husband's response is considered preferably indefinite and is not considered coreferential with the *leves* 'soup' in the wife's question. However, the other interpretation would also be applicable in principle in the husband's answer. In this case the verb *eszik* 'eat' occurs with an indefinite implicit direct object argument which is coreferential with the soup in the wife's question as indicated in (96), i.e. the lexically unrealised direct object argument in the husband's response is a zero anaphor projected into the syntax of the utterance.

(96)   Wife: *Merítsek*   *leves$_i$?*

get.IMP.INDEF 1SG.   soup.ACC

'Shall I get you some soup?'

Husband: *Nem,   köszönöm,   már   ettem [Ø$_i$].*

no,   thank.DEF.1SG   already   ate.INDEF.1SG

'No, thanks, I have already eaten [soup].'

Such an interpretation can arise, for example, in a context in which the husband continues his response with an utterance like the one in (97).

(97)   Wife: *Merítsek*   *leves$_i$?*

get.IMP.INDEF 1SG.   soup.ACC

'Shall I get you some soup?'

Husband: *Nem,   köszönöm,   már   ettem [Ø$_i$].*

no,   thank.DEF.1SG   already   ate.INDEF.3SG

Csak   másodikat   kérek.

only   second.course.ACC   ask.INDEF.1SG

'No, thanks, I have already eaten [soup]. I would like only second course.'

The interpretation possibilities discussed in (95)–(97) have to be added with an observation in the Hungarian grammatical tradition according to which direct object arguments can be absent not only in cases in which transitive verbs are inflected for the indefinite conjugation, but also when transitive verbs are inflected for the definite conjugation; however, in the latter cases the lexically unrealised direct object arguments must be identifiable in the context. The (e) examples in (90–94) contain these kinds of implicit arguments.

The suitable form of the definite conjugation is used when the personal pronoun is not explicitly expressed but can be understood, and the utterance itself can be accounted for as elliptical, requiring a context (H. Molnár 1962: 158). Consider (98).

(98)   *Olvassa   Éva   a   Népszabadságot$_i$?*
     reads.DEF   Éva.NOM   the   Népszabadság.ACC
     'Does Éva read the Népszabadság?'

     Nem   olvassa   [Ø$_i$].
     not   reads.DEF
     'She does not read [Népszabadság].'

However, in (98) the answer should not be necessarily considered an elliptical utterance. The verb form inflected for the definite conjugation should have a direct object argument as it has a subject argument as well. The third person singular form of the direct object is a phonetically empty pronoun, i.e. *pro* (Bartos 2000: 740). Thus, the use of the lexically unrealised direct object argument comes from the pro-drop characteristics of Hungarian. If the direct object inflected for the third person singular form gets into the focus position, then it must be lexically realised, i.e. an overt pronoun must be used. Consider (99).

(99)   *Olvassa   Éva   a   Népszabadságot$_i$?*
     reads.DEF   Éva.NOM   the   Népszabadság.ACC
     'Does Éva read the Népszabadság?'

     Azt$_i$ nem   olvassa.
     it.ACC   not   reads.DEF
     'She does not read it.'

It is also worth examining the first person singular verb form with the *-lak/-lek* inflection. This form traditionally belongs to the definite conjugation, but recently it has been considered a form in the indefinite conjugation because of the parallelism between the phrases *várlak téged* 'I am waiting for you' and *vár téged* '(s)he is waiting for you' (Kiefer 1998: 218) as well as the functional difference between the forms *várok* 'I am waiting' and *várlak* 'I am waiting for you' (Kugler 2000b: 109). The two forms *várok* and *várlak* together indicate those types of direct object arguments which are indicated separately by the other first and second person inflections of the indefinite conjugation. For instance, while the first person plural form *várunk* 'we are waiting' can occur with both third and second person direct objects (cf. *várunk valakit* 'we are waiting for somebody' and *várunk téged* 'we are waiting for you'), the first person singular form *várok* 'I am waiting' can only be used with the third person direct object (cf. *várok valakit* 'I am waiting for somebody') and the first person singular form *várlak* 'I am waiting for you' can be used with the second person direct object argument (cf. *várlak téged* 'I am waiting for you'; Németh T. and Bibok 2001: 80). Thus, the specificity of the inflection *-lak/-lek* is that a verb conjugated for it can only occur with a second person singular direct object. In accordance with the previous observations, the second person singular direct objects can be omitted if a verb is conjugated for the *-lak/-lek* form. Consider (100).

(100) *Látlak*   *[téged]*   *és*   *irigyellek*   *[téged].*

see.INDEF.1SG.2OBJ you.SG.ACC and envy.INDEF.1SG.2OBJ you.SG.ACC

'I can see [you.SG] and envy [you.SG].'

The implicit object of the verbs *lát* 'see' and *irigyel* 'envy' has a second person singular interpretation, which refers to the communicative partner. The implicit direct object can be identified as a second person singular object with the help of the information stored in the meaning representation of the morpheme *-lak/-lek* without a context. Thus, the implicit object argument is interpreted in the first (A) manner, but not on the basis of the lexical-semantic representation of the verbs *lát* 'see' and *irigyel* 'envy', but rather by means of the information in the representation of the inflection morpheme *-lak/-lek*.

However, the direct object of the verbs conjugated for the *-lak/-lek* form can be the second person plural object as well. According to Kugler (2000b: 110), plural second person objects always have to be explicitly expressed with *-lak/-lek*. É. Kiss (2012) also shares the opinion that *-lak/-lek* cannot occur with zero second person plural object. H. Molnár (1962, 157) and Pete (1998: 140) also argue that second person plural direct object arguments occurring with the verbs conjugated for the *-lak/-lek* form cannot be left lexically unrealised. At the same time, consider the conversation in (101).

(101) (The children are shouting at their father in the playground.)

Apa,   *figyelj*   *csak* *ide!* *Látsz*   *minket?*

daddy.NOM look.IMP.INDEF.2SG just here see.INDEF.2SG us

'Daddy, look here. Can you see us?'

Látlak   *[titeket].*

see.1SG.2OBJ you.PL.ACC

'I can see [you.PL].'

In the father's answer the verb *látlak* has a second person plural implicit direct object. This second person plural implicit direct object can be identified with the help of the information from the physical environment c_{phys} and the preceding discourse c_{disc}: the shouting kids. Thus, it can be concluded that the verbs conjugated for the *-lak/-lek* form can occur with both singular and plural second person implicit direct objects. But while the singular second person direct object can be left implicit as a default case without any specific context, the plural second person direct object argument can be left implicit only in the third (C) manner. In Chapter 5, I will return to the questions raised by the examination of the occurrence of verbs conjugated for *-lak/-lek* form with implicit direct object arguments, when I discuss the object pro-drop phenomenon in Hungarian language use (see Section 5.1.2) as well as the role of indefinite/definite conjugations in the licensing and interpretation of the occurrence of transitive verbs with implicit direct object arguments in all three manners (see Section 5.4).

After this brief overview of the observations concerning the objectless use of Hungarian transitive verbs, let us turn to the question of what kind of lexical-semantic representation of verbs can be assumed to underlie the use of transitive verbs with and without a direct object argument.

4.2.2 The role of selection restrictions in the occurrence of verbs with implicit direct object arguments

Let us start with the meaning representations of the verb *iszik* 'drink' in (102a) and (102b) constructed on the basis of Jackendoff's (1990) conceptual-semantic analysis and Bibok's (2008, 2010) lexical-constructional approach, respectively (see Sections 2.3 and 2.4 as well as Németh T. 2001, 2008a, 2010; Bibok and Németh T. 2001).

(102) a. [Event CAUSE ([Thing]i, [Event GO ([Thing LIQUID]j, [Path TO ([Place IN ([MOUTH OF ([Thing]i)])])])])])

       b. 'action of x causes that y which is liquid moves into the mouth of x'
           [[ACT x] CAUSE [[move y] : [[LIQUID y] & [FIN [LOC y] ⊂ LOC x's MOUTH]]]]

As we have seen in Section 2.3, Jackendoff (1990) argues that verb meanings are decomposed conceptual-semantic representations consisting of constituents which belong to a small set of major ontological categories (THING, EVENT, STATE, PLACE, PATH, PROPERTY, etc.). Conceptual-semantic representations of verbs determine what categories of arguments verbs can occur with. One can see from (102a) that there are two arguments of the category THING in the conceptual representation of the verb *iszik* 'drink'. They are ordered, and the second THING argument must be LIQUID. If a verb with such a conceptual-semantic representation is included in an utterance, its first THING argument occupies the subject position, and its second argument the direct object position in the syntactic structure of the utterance. Conceptual-semantic representations of verbs also specify what selection restrictions are put on arguments. As we have seen in Sections 4.1.1 and 4.1.2, verbs may constrain their arguments by means of selection restrictions such that they must be of a particular type or an instance/token of a particular type or have a particular, unique property, etc. In (102a) the verb *iszik* imposes a selection restriction on its second THING argument to be of a type predicting that the second THING argument is LIQUID, i.e. it should belong to the type of THING which is LIQUID.[22]

Similarly, in Bibok's (2008, 2010; Section 2.4) lexical-constructional approach, the verb meanings can also be decomposed. In (102b) the verb *iszik* 'drink' has two arguments (*x* and *y*) on the semantic level, since the activity denoted by it is logically inconceivable without assuming a second argument, even in those occurrences where the second argument (*y*) is not projected into the syntax and the verb *iszik* is used without a direct object argument. In (102b) the type of the second argument (*y*) of *iszik* is constrained by a selection restriction: it must be the type LIQUID. Since the selection restriction to the type LIQUID constrains the information about the type of possible direct objects, in the case of typical liquids the second arguments of *iszik* can be syntactically omitted. This piece of information remains available as background information in the cases where the verb *iszik* occurs without a lexicalised direct object. According to Bibok's (2008, 2010) lexical-constructional framework, the lexical-semantic representation of the verb *iszik* is semantically underspecified. It has optional components for the one or the other constructional meaning: for the use with an explicit syntactic direct object argument and for the use without it. In other words, the under-specified lexical-semantic representation of *iszik* provides two interpretation pos-sibilities (see also García Velasco and Portero Muñoz 2002; Section 2.4). In the first case, only the activity of drinking itself is the focus of attention, but the infor-mation which is involved in the selection restriction – to be the type LIQUID – can also be accessed as background information, similarly to the interpretation mechanism of the utterances including verbs of natural phenomena and verbs of work with implicit subject arguments (see Sections 4.1.1 and 4.1.2). The verb *iszik* can occur without a syntactic direct object argument in (103) in this way, i.e. by means of the background information provided by the selection restriction in its lexical-semantic representation placed on the second argument.

(103)   *János*   *iszik*   *[FOLYADÉK]*.
         János.NOM   drinks.INDEF   liquid
         'János is drinking.'

In the second case the second argument is also the focus of attention, and the speaker wants to indicate the particular object of drinking as a specific instance/

token of the type of LIQUID, so it must be explicitly expressed, see (104).

(104)   *János   málnaszörpöt   iszik.*

        János.NOM   raspberry.juice.ACC   drinks.INDEF

        'János is drinking raspberry juice.'

If the object of drinking is not a typical liquid for living beings, then it must also be lexicalised in the absence of a specific context as in (105).

(105)   *János   fagyállót   iszik.*

        János.NOM   antifreeze.ACC   drinks.INDEF

        'János is drinking antifreeze liquid.'

The occurrences of the verb *iszik* with and without a direct object can be considered syntactic alternations in which the number of arguments decreases (Bibok 2008, 2010). Similarly, the verbs *eszik* 'eat', *lát* 'see', *hall* 'hear, listen', *olvas* 'read', and *főz* 'cook', etc. also have two arguments in their lexical-semantic representation, and they put a selection restriction on their second argument. The verb *eszik* predicts that its second argument must be the type FOOD, the verb *lát* predicts the type VISUALLY PERCEPTIBLE, the verb *hall* predicts the type AUDITORILY PERCEPTIBLE, and the verb *olvas* predicts the type SYMBOLIC REPRESENTATION for the second argument. The verb *főz* predicts that its second argument must be the type FOOD (see (89a–c) in Section 4.1.2)). These verbs can be used with implicit direct object arguments in the same manner as the verb *iszik*, i.e. by means of the selection restriction imposed on the type of their direct object arguments. In (106) there are Hungarian verbs which put a selection restriction – to be of a type, to be an instance/token of a type, to have a particular property or a unique selection – on their second argument:

(106)   *eszik* 'eat', *etet* 'make eat', *fal* 'devour', *zabál* 'devour/gobble', *rág* 'chew', *nyel* 'swallow', *iszik* 'drink', *itat* 'make drink', *vedel* 'swill', *bámul* 'gaze', *ír* 'write', *rajzol* 'draw', *fest* 'paint', *süt* 'bake', *mos* 'wash', *áztat* 'soak', *öblít* 'rinse', *vasal* 'iron', *mosogat* 'do dishes', *takarít* 'clean', *törölget* 'dry, dust', *varr* 'sew', *ás* 'dig', *gyomlál* 'weed', *permetez* 'spray', *kapál* 'hoe', *locsol* 'water', *szánt* 'plough', *vet* 'sow', *kaszál* 'scythe', *arat* 'harvest', *fej* 'milk', *épít* 'build', *fúr* 'drill', *farag* 'carve', *foltoz* 'patch', *stoppol* 'darn', *tereget* 'hang up [to dry]', *szárogat* 'dry', *fon* 'spin', *köt* 'knit', *sző* 'weave', *vásárol* 'shop', *kézbesít* 'deliver', *gyógyít* 'treat', *operál* 'operate on', *tanít* 'teach', *gyón* 'confess', etc.

The verbs in (106) always have a second, *y* argument in their lexical-semantic representation which can be realised as syntactic object. Therefore, these verbs are different from verbs such as *szuszog* 'pant', *bőg* 'cry', *elsápad* 'become pale', *leizzad* 'get sweaty', etc. which have only one *x* argument in their lexical-semantic representation, i.e. intransitive verbs which can take a syntactic object only in a marked, specific context and only in a highly constrained way. The lexical-semantic representation of verbs in (106) can be interpreted in two ways similarly to the lexical-semantic representation of verbs of natural phenomena and verbs of work (see Sections 4.1.1 and 4.1.2). Firstly, if the action denoted by the verbs alone is the focus of attention, then these verbs occur with implicit indefinite second arguments with the help of selection restrictions they put on their second argument. Secondly, if the second argument, i.e. argument *y*, which can be realised syntactically as an object, is also the focus of attention, then it must be explicitly expressed.

In the first case, the implicit direct object arguments can be identified with the information involved in the selection restriction concerning the type of argument *y* as in the case of the verb *eszik* 'eat', *etet* 'make eat', *fal* 'devour', *zabál* 'devour/gobble', and many others, or a unique selection, e.g. sin in the case of *gyón* 'confess'. In Section 4.1.1, when the notion of unique selection restriction was introduced into the analysis of occurrences of Hungarian verbs of natural phenomena with explicit and implicit subject arguments, I referred to a hypothesis formulated in the literature concerning implicit object arguments in various languages according to which if a verb can have only one specific object or a very limited number of specific objects, then the object(s) can be predicted on the basis of the particular verb meaning, and, therefore, be easily left lexically unrealised (Rice 1988; García Velasco and Portero Muñoz 2002). As we have seen, Goldberg (2005b) argues that in English the verbs of bodily emission such as *sneeze, blow, cry, spit, ejaculate, piss*, and *vomit*, and verbs of contribution such as *contribute, donate*, and *give* 'contribute' can occur with implicit direct object arguments in this manner. The pieces of information regarding these specific object(s) are included in the unique selection restrictions verbs impose on their direct object arguments. The lexically unrealised objects can be identified with the particular, unique kind of bodily emission or contribution involved in the selection restrictions. Lexical-functional grammar also applies unique selection restrictions to account for characterising idioms such as *to crane one's neck* (Komlósy 2001: 121). Hungarian verbs *gyón* 'confess', *meggyón* 'PVB.confess' also belong to the group of verbs with unique selection restriction, since the direct object must be sin.

In (106) one can also find various verbs of work such as *takarít* 'clean', *vet* 'sow', *arat* 'harvest', *épít* 'build', *kézbesít* 'deliver', *operál* 'operate on', *tanít* 'teach'. Recall that in Section 4.1.2, examining the behaviour of verbs of work with implicit subject arguments, I noted that several verbs of work can occur not only with implicit subjects, but also with implicit direct object arguments. Since in Section 4.1.2 I did not intend to analyse implicit direct object arguments, I did not indicate them in the Hungarian examples, but only provided implicit subject arguments in square brackets. Let us take the verb *vet* again and consider its occurrence with both implicit subject and direct object arguments. The utterance in (107) is a modified version of (81a) in Section 4.1.2.

(107)   *Ősszel   és   tavasszal   is   vetnek   [PARASZT]   [MAG].*
        in.autumn   and   in.spring   also   sow.INDEF.3PL   peasant   seed
        'In autumn and also in spring [the peasants] sow [seeds].

The lexical-semantic representation of the verb *vet* 'sow', which is repeated here as (108) for more convenience, contains selection restrictions on its subject and direct object arguments.

(108)   *vet* 'sow':   'action of x who is a peasant causes that y which is seed goes into z which is field'

        [[[ACT x] : [PEASANT x]] CAUSE [[GO y] : [[SEED y]] &
        [[FIN [LOC y] ⊂ LOC z] : [FIELD z]]]]]

The verb *vet* can occur with implicit subject and direct object arguments by means of the selection restrictions (x: PEASANT and y: SEED, respectively) in a context where only the act of sowing is in the focus of the speaker's attention and the subject and the direct object of sowing are not. In this context the pieces of information regarding the subject and object of the action of sowing are accessible as background information and are not projected into the syntactic structure of the utterance in (107). However, if the *x* and *y* arguments are also in the focus of the speaker's attention in a particular context, then they must be lexically realised and syntactically expressed in the utterance as in (109), where – without any further specific context – the speaker should explicitly express the subject and direct object arguments since they are particular tokens/instances of the type which the subject and direct object of the action of sowing belong to.

(109)   a.   *Ősszel   és   tavasszal   is   vetnek   az*
             in.autumn   and   in.spring   also   sow.INDEF.3PL   the

             alföldi   parasztok   búzát.
             plain   peasants.NOM   wheat.ACC
             'In autumn and also in spring the peasants of the plain sow wheat.'

It can also happen that two different selection restrictions on the second, direct object argument are involved in the lexical-semantic representation of a verb such as in the case of *itat* 'make drink' and *etet* 'feed'. The verbs *itat* and *etet* predict that their direct object argument must be the type ANIMAL or HUMAN. These verbs constrain their third argument as well. It must be the type LIQUID and the type FOOD, respectively. The formulae in (110) depict their lexical-semantic representations which are modified versions of (102b): (i) they contain LIQUID and FOOD, respectively, (ii) while a new causer is introduced, the original one which does not necessarily function as such disappears, and (iii), as a result of (ii), it should be indicated whom the mouth belongs to: to animals or humans. Consider (110a–b).

(110)   a.   *itat* 'make drink': 'action of x causes that y which is liquid moves into the mouth of z which is animal and/or human'

   [[ACT x] CAUSE [[MOVE y] : [[LIQUID y] & [[FIN [LOC z] ⊂ LOC z's MOUTH] : [ANIMAL z v HUMAN z]]]]]

   b.   *etet* 'feed': 'action of x causes that y which is food moves into the mouth of z which is animal and/or human'

   [[ACT x] CAUSE [[MOVE y] : [[FOOD y] & [[FIN [LOC z] ⊂ LOC z's MOUTH] : [ANIMAL z v HUMAN z]]]]]

Particular contexts in which the verbs *itat* and *etet* occur decide what selection restriction constrains the type of the direct object argument. Consider (111).

(111)   *Reggelente*   *először*   *itatok*   *[ÁLLAT/EMBER]/*
   in.the.morning   first   make.drink.INDEF.1SG   animal/human

   etetek   *[ÁLLAT/EMBER].*
   feed.INDEF.1SG   animal/human

   'In the morning first I make [animals/human beings] drink/feed [animals/human beings].'

If (111) is uttered in a conversation on farm life, the context makes the selection restriction ANIMAL active, thus, the lexically unrealised direct object argument cannot be human. The active ANIMAL selection restriction and the context provide a relevant interpretation: in the morning the speaker first makes the farm animals drink/feeds the farm animals. The implicit direct object argument of *itat* 'make drink' and *etet* 'feed' can be identified with the farm animals. Let us imagine now that the speaker works as a nurse at a day-care centre, an old people's home, or a hospital. There are people in these institutions who need feeding. In this context, the selection restriction HUMAN becomes active. Thus, the implicit direct object arguments of *itat* and *etet* in (111) can be identified with babies/children, old people, etc. who have to be helped to drink and to eat. In both cases one has to rely on the interaction between the verbs' lexical-semantic representations and context to construct the relevant utterance meanings.

It is worth mentioning that the verbs *itat* 'make drink', *etet* 'feed' and their perfective variants *megitat* 'pvb.make.drink' and *megetet* 'pvb.feed' can also be used with implicit adverbial arguments by means of the same selection restriction to be of the type LIQUID and FOOD, respectively, which is involved in the lexical-semantic representation of the verbs *iszik* 'drink' and *eszik* 'eat'. These selection restrictions were also involved in the lexical-semantic representations in (110), since they are inherited in the course of the derivation of the verb *itat* from the verb *iszik* as well as the verb *etet* from the verb *eszik* by the causative suffix *-at/-et*. If one examines the utterance in (111) more carefully, one can realise that both the second and third argument of the verbs *itat* and *etet* are left implicit, and both of them can be identified with the background information provided by the selection restrictions put on these arguments as is indicated in (112).[23]

(112) *Reggelente*   *először*   *itatok*   [ÁLLATOT/EMBERT]
       in.the.morning   first   make drink.INDEF.1SG   animal.ACC/human.ACC

       [FOLYADÉKKAL],   *etetek*   [ÁLLATOT/EMBERT]   [ÉTELLEL]
       liquid.INS   feed.INDEF.1SG   animal.ACC/human.ACC   food.INS

       'In the morning first I make [animals/human beings] drink [liquid]/feed [animals/human beings] [with food].'

Furthermore, if the direct object argument of *itat* is an adult person, the implicit adverbial argument of *itat* can refer to alcohol in the same way as the direct object argument of *iszik* does in a habitual reading in supporting contexts (see (125a–b),(126a), in Section 4.2.4). Consider (113).

(113) a. *Az*   *anya*   *itatja*   *a*   *kislányát*   [FOLYADÉK].
           the   mother.NOM   makes.drink.DEF   the   her.daughter.ACC   [LIQUID]
           'The mother makes her daughter drink [liquid].'

       b. *A*   *férj*   *itatja*   *a*   *sógorát*   [ALKOHOL].
           the   husband   makes.drink.DEF   the   his.brother.in.law.ACC   [ALCOHOL]
           'The husband makes his brother-in-law drink [alcohol].'

A further remark seems to be in order in connection with the verbs in (106). Alsina (1992: 524) assumes that verbs which denote an unbounded process, i.e. an event that takes place over time and is not inherently delimited, can be used without non-specific direct objects. However, this assumption cannot be applied to Hungarian in its entirety. In spite of the fact that the verbs *megitat* 'pvb.make. drink', *megetet* 'pvb.feed', and other verbs from (106) with preverbal suffixes (*megfőz* 'PVB.cook', *kimos* 'PVB.wash', *kivasal* 'PVB.iron', *elmosogat* 'PVB.do.dishes', *eltörölget* 'PVB.dry.dishes', *kitakarít* 'PVB.clean', *meglocsol* 'PVB.water', *learat* 'PVB. harvest', *elvet* 'PVB.sow', *kitereget* 'PVB.hang.up (to dry)') describe a bounded process, they can also occur with implicit unspecified direct object arguments relying on the background information involved in their lexical-semantic representations. Consider the utterances in (114).

(114) a. *Reggelente   először   megitatok   [ÁLLATOT/*
      in.the.morning   first   PVB.make.drink.INDEF.1SG   animal.ACC

      EMBERT]   [FOLYADÉKKAL]/   megetetek   [ÁLLATOT/
      human.ACC   liquid.INS   PVB.feed.INDEF.1SG   animal.ACC

      EMBERT]   [ÉTELLEL].
      human.ACC   food.INS

      'In the morning first I make [animals/human beings] drink [liquid]/feed [animals/human beings] [with food].'

    b. *Tegnap   délután   megfőztem   [ÉTEL],*
      yesterday   afternoon   PVB.cooked.INDEF.1SG   food

      kimostam   [SZENNYES RUHA],   kivasaltam
      PVB.washed.INDEF.1SG   dirty.textile   PVB.ironed.INDEF.1SG

      [GYŰRÖTT RUHA],   elmosogattam,   [KOSZOS EDÉNY],
      creased.textile   PVB.did.dishes.INDEF.1SG   dirty.dish

      eltörölgettem,   [NEDVES EDÉNY],   és   végül
      PVB.dried.dishes.INDEF.1SG   wet.dish,   and   finally

      kitakarítottam   [PISZKOS HELY].
      PVB.cleaned.INDEF.1SG   dirty.place

      'Yesterday afternoon, I cooked [food], washed [dirty textile], ironed [creased textile], did the [dirty] dishes, dried the [wet] dishes, and finally cleaned [dirty place].'

    c. *Nem   baj,   ha   nem   lesz   eső,   meglocsoltam*
      not   problem.NOM   if   not   will   rain.NOM   PVB.watered.INDEF.1SG
      [NÖVÉNY].
      [PLANT]

      'No problem, if there is no rain, I have watered [plants].'

    d.   *Augusztus   elejére   learatnak   a   parasztok*

        August   beginning.SUB   PVB.harvest.INDEF.3PL   the   peasants.NOM

        [GABONA].

        grain.

        'By the beginning of August, the peasants will have harvested [grain].'

    e.   *Késő októberben   elvetnek   a   parasztok   [MAG].*

        late   October.INE   PVB.SOW.INDEF.3PL   a   peasants.NOM   seed

        'In late October peasants sow [seeds].'

    f.   *A   férjem   minden   mosás   után*

        the   my.husband.NOM   every   washing.NOM   after

        kitereget   [NEDVES RUHA]

        PVB.hangs.up.(to.dry).INDEF   wet.textile

        'My husband hangs up [wet linen] to dry after every washing.'

At the same time, not all verbs which have an end point because of their preverbs can occur with implicit direct object arguments in a sentence environment without a specific context, in spite of the fact that they also have a selection restriction that their direct object argument be of a certain type. Consider (115).

(115)   **Az apa   megeszik/   megépít.*

        the   father.NOM   PVB.eats.INDEF   PVB.builds.INDEF

Therefore, the lexical-constructional approach (Bibok 2008: 63) emphasises that selection restrictions are only necessary but not sufficient conditions when using verbs without direct object arguments. This approach proposes that it must be marked in the lexical-semantic representation of verbs individually whether a participant can be syntactically unrealised (see also Fillmore's (1986), Saeboe's (1996), and Gillon's (2012) proposals in Section 2.3). Kiefer (2006: 46–47) also reminds us that not all transitive verbs with preverbal morphemes can occur without a direct object argument, e.g. *elénekel* 'PVB.sing', *megír* 'PVB.write', *eljátszik* 'PVB.play', *elolvas* 'PVB.read', *elbírál* 'PVB.judge', *kigombol* 'unbutton', *megszerel* 'PVB.mend'. In Kiefer's opinion, institutionalisation has an important role in the possibility to use these verbs with implicit direct object arguments, see *megetet* 'PVB.feed', *meggyón* 'PVB.confess', *megfej* 'PVB.milk', *megöntöz* 'PVB.water', *kimeszel* 'PVB.whitewash', but institutionalisation is also only a necessary but not a sufficient condition.

Scrutinising the verbs in (106), they can be classified into narrower semantic classes (cf. Pinker 1989: 126–127; Goldberg 2005b; Bibok 2008: 30): verbs of eating, drinking, work, housekeeping, agriculture, etc. The lexical-semantic representations of these verbs do not involve the same kind of selection restrictions.

While the verbs of eating and drinking constrain the general type of their direct object arguments, they must be of the type FOOD and LIQUID respectively, the verbs of work, housekeeping, and agriculture predict that their direct object argument must be of a more particular type connected to work, housekeeping, and agriculture or a token of these particular types. Finally, there are verbs such as *gyón* 'confess' which put a unique selection restriction on their direct object argument. The verb *gyón* 'confess' constrains its direct object argument to be sin.

The kind of selection restrictions in operation also influence the occurrences of the transitive preverbed verbs with and without direct object arguments. If we derive the perfective preverbed forms of the verbs in question, their direct object arguments also move into the focus of attention. If a transitive perfective preverbed verb constrains only the general type of its direct object argument by means of a selection restriction, the direct object argument must be lexicalised without a specific context. The perfective reading requires the identification of the direct object argument which cannot be provided by the selection restriction on a general type by itself, see *megeszik* 'PVB.eat', *megiszik* 'PVB.drink', *elolvas* 'PVB. read', *megír* 'PVB.write', *meglát* 'PVB.see', etc. However, if a particular, specific context provides the necessary information for the identification of the direct object arguments of the perfective preverbed verbs in the third (C) manner, the direct object arguments can be left lexically unrealised as in the case of the verb *elolvas* 'pvb.read' in (116).

(116)   (For homework the teacher asked the pupils to read a poem. In the next class nobody is putting up her/his hand.)

Senki	*nem*	*olvasott*	*el*	*mára*	*egy*	*verset?*
nobody.NOM	not	read.INDEF.3SG	PVB	today.SUB	a	poem.ACC

'Didn't anybody read a poem for today?'

Károly	*elolvasott.*		*Csak*	*nem*	*mer*	*jelentkezni.*
Károly.NOM	pvb.red.INDEF.3SG	but	not	dares.INDEF	to.put.up.his.hand

'Károly did. But doesn't dare to put up his hand.'

If a transitive perfective preverbed verb puts a selection restriction on a particular type or a token of a particular type or sets up a unique selection restriction, it can be used with an implicit direct object argument in the first (A) manner. The selection restrictions on a particular type or a token of a particular type, or the unique selection restrictions themselves, provide the information required to identify the direct object arguments, which are also the focus of attention because of perfectivisation, see, e.g., *learat* 'PVB.harvest', *kimos* 'PVB.wash', *meggyón* 'PVB.confess', *megszoptat* 'PVB.breastfeed', and other verbs in (114). The interaction between the different kinds of selection restrictions and the aspectual properties of perfective preverb forms of transitive verbs make a prediction as to whether a transitive perfective preverbed verb can occur with an implicit direct object argument in a sentence environment without any specific context, i.e. in the first (A) manner.[24]

4.2.3 The characteristic manner of action

Several verbs in (106) can occur with implicit arguments not only with the help of a selection restriction, but also through information on the characteristic manner (or goal) of the action. Let us examine the verbs *eszik* 'eat', *zabál* 'devour, gobble', *iszik* 'drink', and *vedel* 'swill' from this perspective. It is not sufficient that the lexical-semantic representations of these verbs contain selection restrictions on the direct object argument to be of the type FOOD or LIQUID, respectively, for at least two reasons (Bibok and Németh T. 2001: 295–296; Németh T. 2001: 138–143; 2010: 329–330). On the one hand, there is a sharp difference in the characteristic manner of the denoted activities between the verbs *eszik*, *zabál* and the verbs *iszik*, *vedel*. On the other hand, the verbs *eszik* and *zabál*, as well as *iszik* and *vedel* also differ from each other in the characteristic manner of the actions expressed. Consider Bibok and Németh T.'s (2001: 295) examples.

(117) a. *Péter   eszi   a   levest/   joghurtot/*
Péter.NOM   eats.DEF   the   soup.ACC   yogurt.ACC

kakaót/   bólét.
cocoa.ACC   punch.ACC

'Péter is eating the soup/yogurt/cocoa/punch.'

b. *Péter   zabálja   a   levest/   joghurtot/*
Péter.NOM   devours.DEF   the   soup.ACC   yogurt.ACC

kakaót/   bólét.
cocoa.ACC   punch.ACC

'Péter is devouring the soup/yogurt/cocoa/punch.'

c. *Péter   issza   a   levest/   joghurtot/*
Péter.NOM   drinks.DEF   the   soup.ACC   yogurt.ACC

kakaót/   bólét.
cocoa.ACC   punch.ACC

'Péter is drinking the soup/yogurt/cocoa/punch.'

d. *Péter   vedeli   a   levest/   joghurtot/*
Péter.NOM   swills.DEF   the   soup.ACC   yogurt.ACC

kakaót/   bólét.
cocoa.ACC   punch.ACC

'Péter is swilling the soup / yogurt / cocoa/ punch.'

Soup, yogurt, cocoa, and punch can be both eaten/devoured and drunk/swilled, since they are FOOD and LIQUID at the same time. However, there is a difference, on the one hand, between eating and drinking, as well as between devouring and swilling, and on the other hand, there is also a difference between eating and devouring, and drinking and swilling. The differences between these verbs concern not only the quantity of FOOD and LIQUID but also the characteristic manner of the actions expressed, i.e. eating, devouring, drinking, and swilling. Bibok and Németh T. (2001: 296) highlights that the status of the latter information relating to the lexical-semantic representation is not uniquely conceived in the literature. There are various rival solutions to this problem depending on whether the linguistic knowledge and the encyclopaedic knowledge are distinguished or not. But it is indisputable that the lexical-semantic representation must be extended by this information or this information somehow must be added to it. Jackendoff (1990) does not distinguish between the linguistic and encyclopaedic information in conceptual semantic representations, so the information on the manner of action must be built into them. Similarly, Pustejovsky (1995, 1998) does not differentiate these two types of information, so they must be involved in the lexical-semantic representations of words. Gergely and Bever (1986) make a distinction between the two types of knowledge, and the characteristic manner of eating and drinking is captured by the so-called lexical stereotype.[25] Two-level conceptual semantics (e.g. Bierwisch 1983, 1996) also differentiates these two types of knowledge. Thus, the characteristic manner of eating, devouring, drinking, and swilling is captured by the lexical stereotype belonging to the encyclopaedic knowledge. Although Sperber and Wilson (1986/1995: 86) make a distinction between linguistic and encyclopaedic information, they treat them in the same way. When a verb is processed in an utterance, its conceptual address becomes accessible in the course of processing. According to relevance theory, at a certain conceptual address three types of information are stored, namely, logical, lexical, and encyclopaedic information (Sperber and Wilson 1986/1995: 86). The logical information of a conceptual address involves a set of deductive rules which can be applied to the logical forms of which that concept is a constituent. The encyclopaedic entry for a conceptual address includes encyclopaedic information concerning the extension and/or denotation of the concept, i.e. the objects, events, and properties which instantiate it. And the lexical entry for a conceptual address contains information about what natural language expression can lexicalise the concept involved or, in other words, what the natural language counterpart of the concept is. All these three kinds of information can be accessed simultaneously if the conceptual address of a verb becomes active. According to relevance theory-based thinking, the encyclopaedic information about the manner of eating and drinking is processed together with the lexical information of *eszik* 'eat'/*iszik* 'drink' in the course of its use or interpretation.

García Velasco and Portero Muñoz (2002) also assume an intensive interaction between the verbs' lexical-semantic representations and the cognitive level which involves the encyclopaedic kind of information (see Section 2.4). When any of these rival solutions is selected by a researcher, information on the characteristic manner of eating, devouring, drinking, and swilling should be taken into account in addition to the selection restriction involved in the lexical-semantic representations of these verbs in the course of their use and interpretation. It is worth mentioning that verbs with manner components resist *wh*-extraction of a constituent from the direct object position precisely because the manner of the action focalises the verbs and it is difficult to focalise the *wh*-element at the same time (Németh T. 2010). This can be explained by Grice's (1975) maxim of relation or by Sperber and Wilson's (1986/1995) cognitive principle of relevance. If a speaker uses a manner of action verb, it is expected that (s)he wishes to direct her/his addressee's attention to the verbal action itself, rather than to the object or *wh*-element.

4.2.4 The prototypical structure of implicit arguments

In addition to selection restrictions and information on the characteristic manner of action, the typical properties of the direct object types also influence the occurrence of verbs with implicit direct object arguments (Bibok and Németh T. 2001; García Velasco and Portero Muñoz 2002; Goldberg 2005b; Bibok 2008; Németh T. 2010). In the case of *eszik* 'eat'/*zabál* 'devour' and *iszik* 'drink'/*vedel* 'swill', it must also be taken into account what prototypical structure the categories FOOD and LIQUID have. Consider (118), which answers the question *Mit csinál Sándor?* 'What is Sándor doing?' (Németh T. 2001: 139, 2010: 331).

(118) a. *Sándor   eszi/   zabálja   az   akácvirágot.*
           Sándor.NOM   eats.DEF   devours.DEF   the   acacia.flowers.ACC
           'Sándor is eating/devouring acacia flowers.'

       b. *A   kicsi   Sándor   eszi   a   szappant.*
           the   little   Sándor.NOM   eats.DEF   the   soap.ACC
           'Little Sándor is eating the soap.'

Although people do not usually consider the flower of an acacia tree in (118a) FOOD, one can conceptualise it as such. The flowers of the acacia trees have several characteristic properties of the category FOOD: they are solid, chewable, and fragrant, and have an excellent taste. On the basis of these characteristic properties of FOOD, the flowers of the acacia trees can be categorised as FOOD. Children, and people who like the edible flowers, tend to eat acacia flowers because of their excellent sweet taste. However, it must be admitted that acacia flowers can be categorised as non-typical instances of the category FOOD. Similarly to acacia flowers, traditional soap is not something which normally belongs to the category FOOD, i.e. it is not a typical FOOD. Comparing acacia flowers and soap, the latter is a more atypical FOOD. However, it can also be conceptualised as FOOD in at least two distinct ways. Firstly, for some living beings other than humans – say, for Martians or some other fictive living beings – soap can serve as food. Secondly, soap shares some characteristic properties of food, i.e. it is also solid and chewable as well as having a good smell; therefore one can categorise it as food (Groefsema 1995: 152), as little Sándor does in (118b). Naturally, in both cases soap can be spoken of as an atypical instance of food. FOOD is a category which has a prototypical structure including typical (e.g. bread, meat, vegetable, fruits) and other, non-typical members. While most typical members of the category FOOD seem to be universal in various cultures, the atypical members of the category FOOD are culturally determined. For instance, while some insects are typical food for eastern cultures, they are categorised as highly atypical food in western cultures. Acacia flowers can be included in the category of FOOD in this way, but in spite of the fact that soap has similar properties to acacia flowers, it can be categorised as (atypical) food only for fictive living beings or for a child – e.g. little Sándor – who has not yet acquired the typical categorisation of the world. Also, considering liquid soap, we have the same problem as in the case of soup/yogurt/milk. Liquid soap can be categorised as LIQUID, and although it is not a typical FOOD, similarly to traditional soap, it can be categorised as FOOD as well. Although liquid soap is not a typical food, and is not a typical liquid either, it can be used both with *eszik* 'eat' and *iszik* 'drink' depending on the manner of action, if one describes little Sándor's action. Cf. (119).

(119) *A   kicsi   Sándor   eszi/   issza   a   folyékony   szappant.*
       the   little   Sándor.NOM   eats.DEF   drinks.DEF   the   liquid   soap.ACC
       'Little Sándor is eating/drinking the liquid soap.'

Now consider (120).

(120) a.   *Sándor   eszi/   zabálja   a   kovászos*
             Sándor.NOM   eats.DEF   devours.DEF   the   pickled

             uborka   levét.
             cucumber.NOM   juice.ACC
             'Sándor is eating/devouring pickle juice.'

b. *Sándor*   *issza/*   *vedeli*   *a*   *kovászos*

   Sándor.NOM   drinks.DEF   swills.DEF   the   pickled

   uborka   *levét.*

   cucumber.NOM   fluid.ACC

   'Sándor is drinking/swilling pickle juice.'

Pickle juice can also be categorised as an atypical FOOD, and since it is liquid, also as a LIQUID. If a direct object argument can be categorised as FOOD and LIQUID at the same time (see (117)), it can be used with the verbs *eszik* 'eat', *zabál* 'devour', *iszik* 'drink', and *vedel* 'swill' as well. The use of these verbs with the *kovászos uborka leve* 'pickle juice' is determined by the characteristic manner of action in the course of which pickle juice gets into one's mouth.

However, the question *Mit csinál Sándor?* 'What is Sándor doing?' can be answered with utterances which include implicit direct object arguments. Consider (121).

(121)   *Sándor*   *eszik/*   *zabál/*   *iszik/*   *vedel.*

   Sándor.NOM   eats.INDEF   devours.INDEF   drinks.INDEF   swills.INDEF

   'Sándor is eating/devouring/drinking/swilling.'

Selection restrictions in the lexical-semantic representations of the verbs *eszik/zabál* and *iszik/vedel*, as well as information on the characteristic manner of actions, make it possible to reach relevant interpretations: Sándor is eating/devouring some FOOD and is drinking/swilling some LIQUID. The verbs in (121) mean only the physical activity of eating/devouring some FOOD and drinking/swilling some LIQUID, but they do not designate exactly what the particular objects of eating/devouring and drinking/swilling are; i.e. in (121) only the activities with their characteristic manners themselves are the focus of attention. To obtain a relevant interpretation one also has to take into account the prototypical structure of the categories FOOD and LIQUID predicted by the selection restrictions. The speaker communicates by means of (121) that the lexically unrealised direct object is specific in some sense. It is not an atypical food or potable liquid or, in other words, the object refers to something that the hearer would not think abnormal for Sándor to eat/devour and drink/swill. Cote (1996: 150–151) comes to the same conclusion about the English verb *bake* used with an implicit direct object argument in an utterance like (122).

(122)   Joe baked today.

By using the utterance in (122), the speaker does not only express that the action of baking is in the focus of her/his attention, but also that the object of baking is typical. If the object of baking is atypical in a culture, for instance, the speaker is baking locusts in a Hungarian restaurant, then (s)he cannot leave it lexically unrealised (see also note 18 in Section 4.2.1). Similarly, if Sándor is eating acacia flowers or he is drinking pickle juice or other atypical members of the categories FOOD and LIQUID, the speaker cannot communicate this by using the utterance in (121) without a specific discourse or physical context, i.e. c_{disc} or c_{phys}. Atypical members of categories cannot be left implicit without an adequate context because accessing them requires more processing effort which contradicts the relevance considerations. As Bibok and Németh T. (2001: 298) emphasise, in these cases the speaker produces utterances with corresponding explicit arguments in the same way as (s)he would if (s)he meant the particular (typical) stuff being eaten/devoured or drunk/swilled.

In addition, two further remarks seem to be necessary relating to *eszik* 'eat' and *iszik* 'drink'. Firstly, there is an interesting relation between the possibility of leaving an argument implicit and noun incorporation in Hungarian. Any imperfective transitive activity verb can incorporate its (bare) direct object argument, but the semantic representation of the emerging lexical entry has to be supplemented by a conceptual constraint which accounts for the 'institutionalised' or conventionalised character of the complex activity in question (Kiefer 1990). While (123a) denotes an institutionalised activity, a conventionalised form of suicide, (123b) does not.

(123)   a.   *János*   *sósavat*   *ivott.*

           János.NOM   hydrochloric acid.ACC   drank.INDEF.3SG

           'János drank hydrochloric acid (to commit suicide).'

    b.   *?János*   *szappant*   *evett.*

           János.NOM   soap.ACC   ate.INDEF.3SG

           'János ate soap.'

Therefore, on the one hand, no typical argument which cannot be incorporated can be left lexically unrealised, i.e. the non-typical objects (see (123b)) for *eszik* 'eat' and *iszik* 'drink' cannot be left implicit or be incorporated. On the other hand, not every argument which can be incorporated can be left implicit. In (123a) the object *sósav* 'hydrochloric acid' has been incorporated by *iszik* 'drink', but it cannot be left implicit because it is an atypical member of the category LIQUID.

Secondly, it is worth noting that the verb *iszik* denoting a habitual or long-lasting activity has a further specification of 'drink alcoholic beverages', as was indicated above when the occurrences of the verb *itat* 'make drink' with implicit second and third arguments were examined (see (113) and their analyses in Section 4.2.2). The specification 'drink alcoholic beverages' must be added to the lexical-semantic representation of *iszik* or can even be included within it. Let us specify the lexical-semantic representation of *iszik* in (102b) – repeated here as (124) for convenience – in this respect and as a result, consider (125).

(124)   'action of x causes that y which is liquid moves into the mouth of x'
[[ACT x] CAUSE [[MOVE y] : [[LIQUID y] & [FIN [LOC y] $\subset$ LOC x's MOUTH]]]]

(125)   'action of x causes that y which is (alcoholic) liquid moves into the mouth of x'
[[ACT x] CAUSE [[MOVE y] : [[[LIQUID: y (ALCOHOL y)]] & [FIN [LOC y] $\subset$ LOC x's MOUTH]]]]

If we do not want to add the information 'drink alcoholic beverages' to the lexical-semantic representation of the verb *iszik* at the lexical-semantic level or to involve this information in it, then we do not need any specific discourse context c_{disc} necessarily to reach this interpretation. There is a rival solution. Relying on a pragmatic division of labour, one can say that the meaning 'to drink alcohol' is a typical extension of the meaning of the verb *iszik* by an informativity implicature at the pragmatic level (Horn 1984; Levinson 2000: 138). Informativity implicatures (henceforth I-implicatures) belonging to the group of generalised conversational implicatures are pragmatic inferences induced by typical pieces of background information, more precisely typical information in the shared encyclopaedic context c_{enc}. With the help of I-implicatures, speakers can achieve their communicative goals producing minimal linguistic information without any specific particular discourse context c_{disc}, and hearers can enrich the informational content of utterances by achieving the most specific interpretation relying on common world knowledge included in the shared encyclopaedic context c_{enc}. A thorough analysis of I-implicatures can shed light on an interesting and important opposition between implicit and explicit forms (Levinson 2000: 146–149). Implicit forms are open to induce I-implicatures, enriching the interpretation with typical situations, related events, and participants. However, the typical interpretation can be deleted if the utterances in the discourse context c_{disc} involve explicit forms instead of implicit ones or contain information which overwrites the I-implicature. For example, while in (126a) the interpretation 'drink alcoholic beverages' is available, in (126b) it is not, since, although the verb *iszik* can also induce the I-implicature 'drink alcoholic beverages' in (126b), the explicit realisation of the object of *iszik* by the noun *tej* 'milk' deletes the I-implicature 'drink alcoholic beverages'.

(126) a. *János*   *iszik*   *[FOLYADÉK] & [I-implicature: alkoholos italok].*
           János.NOM   drinks.INDEF   liquid & I-implicature: alcoholic.beverages
           'John drinks [alcoholic beverages].'

    b. *János*   *tejet*   *iszik.*
           János.NOM   milk.ACC   drinks.INDEF
           'John drinks milk.'

The informativity principle as the principle of the typical interpretation provides rich, relevant interpretations of utterances by combining the underspecified linguistic meanings originating in the minimal linguistic forms and the communicative partners' shared knowledge about regularities in the world. The two rival hypotheses agree that there is a division of labour between lexical-semantic and pragmatic pieces of information, but at the same time they differ as to what kind of pragmatic information interacts with the lexical-semantic representation. When the information 'drink alcoholic beverages' is built into the lexical-semantic representation of the verb *iszik* as an optional selection restriction on the type of direct object argument, the verb *iszik* can occur with an implicit direct object argument with this meaning in a context in which the optional selection restriction can also become active as background information. Consider the utterances in (127).

(127) a. *A*   *férjem*   *iszik*   *[FOLYADÉK (ALKOHOL)].*
           the   my.husband.NOM   drinks.INDEF   liquid (alcohol)
           'My husband drinks [alcohol].'

    b. *A*   *baba*   *iszik*   *[FOLYADÉK (ALKOHOL)].*
           the   baby.NOM   drinks.INDEF   liquid (alcohol)
           'The baby is drinking [liquid].'

In (127a) the long-established habitual reading of drinking alcoholic beverages can be available since *iszik* occurs in an utterance where the using and processing of the noun phrase *a férjem* 'my husband' make accessible the encyclopaedic information that there are husbands who have the habit of drinking alcohol. This encyclopaedic piece of information can activate the optional selection restriction ALCOHOL in the lexical-semantic representation of the verb *iszik*. The interaction between the encyclopaedic information stored under the conceptual address of the noun *férj* 'husband' and the activated optional selection restriction in the lexical-semantic representation of the verb *iszik* results in a relevant interpretation: 'My husband drinks alcohol habitually'. But in (127b) the reading 'drink alcoholic beverages' is not available since in the lexical-semantic representation of the verb *iszik* the optional selection restriction ALCOHOL cannot become active in the context of the noun phrase *a baba* 'the baby' since there is no encyclopaedic information stored under the conceptual address of the noun *baba* 'baby' which can activate it. In both cases adequate use and interpretation are accessed by the interaction between the underspecified lexical-semantic representation of the verb *iszik* 'drink' and the particular utterance context in which *iszik* 'drink' occurs. To put it the other way round, the lexical-semantic representation and the particular pragmatic (contextual) information interact.

At the same time, when the information 'drink alcoholic beverages' is not involved in the lexical-semantic representation of the verb *iszik* as an optional selection restriction, but is available as an I-implicature, the lexical-semantic representation of the verb *iszik*, the general pragmatic knowledge, and the particular pragmatic (contextual) information interact. Consider (128) which reflects the analysis by I-implicature.

(128)   a.   *A   férjem   iszik   [FOLYADÉK] & [I-implicature:*
the   my husband.NOM   drinks.INDEF   [LIQUID] & [I-implicature:
alkoholos italok].
alcoholic beverages]
'My husband drinks [I-implicature: alcoholic beverages].'

b.   *A   baba   iszik   [FOLYADÉK].*
the   baby.NOM   drinks.INDEF   [LIQUID]
'The baby is drinking [liquid].'

In (128a) the verb *iszik* occurs with an implicit direct object argument by means of the selection restriction [LIQUID] and the I-implicature 'drink alcoholic beverages' which is induced by the verb *iszik* and is supported by the encyclopaedic information stored under the conceptual address of the noun *férj* 'husband' in the utterance context. The appropriate interpretation 'My husband drinks alcoholic beverages' is available through the interaction between the lexical-semantic representation, general pragmatic knowledge including I-implicature, and particular pragmatic (contextual) information. But in (128b) an interpretation such as 'The baby drinks alcoholic beverages' is not accessible. Although in (128b) the verb *iszik* also induces the I-implicature 'drink alcoholic beverages', there is no encyclopaedic information stored under the conceptual address of the noun *baba* 'baby' which can support the I-implicature; moreover, it contradicts the I-implicature according to our shared world knowledge. Therefore, the interaction between the lexical-semantic representation of the verb *iszik*, the I-implicature 'drink alcoholic beverages', and the particular pragmatic (contextual) information yields the deletion of the I-implicature and results in the interpretation based on the selection restriction LIQUID put on the direct object argument of *iszik* as we have seen above in (103) in Section 4.2.2.

The main difference between the two rival explanations is the evaluation of the status of the encyclopaedic piece of information 'drink alcohol'. While in the first explanation it is lexicalised, and therefore involved in the lexical-semantic representation of the verb *iszik* 'drink' as an optional selection restriction, in the second account it is not lexicalised and belongs to the general pragmatic (encyclopaedic) knowledge as an I-implicature. When the particular discourse context c_{disc} does not support the I-implicature, then it is deleted. Comparing these two rival hypotheses, it can be established that the first explanation is more plausible than the second on the basis of economy considerations. According to the first hypothesis, it is enough to consider the lexical-semantic representation of the verb *iszik* including the optional selection restriction ALCOHOL placed on the direct object argument and the minimal discourse context c_{disc}, i.e. the immediate utterance context. When the utterance context is supporting, the optional selection restriction becomes active, while when the utterance context is non-supporting, then only the selection restriction LIQUID is active and the optional selection restriction ALCOHOL is not. According to the second hypothesis, not two, but three kinds of information should be taken into account: the lexical-semantic representation of the verb *iszik* with the selection restriction LIQUID placed on the direct object argument, the I-implicature 'drink alcoholic beverages' involved in general pragmatic knowledge, and the particular immediate utterance context. Taking into account these three kinds of information needs more processing effort, but it does not result in more contextual effects (cf. Sperber and Wilson 1986/1995). Sperber and Wilson assume three kinds of contextual effects. The first is contextual implication, which results from the interaction between the pieces of new and old information in a synthetic implication (1986/1995: 107–112). The second type is contextual strengthening, when a piece of information processed in the course of interpretation affects the strength of any assumption already present in the context (1986/1995: 120). It must be noted that contextual implication can be considered a special case of contextual strengthening, namely dependent contextual strengthening (1986/1995: 112–113). The third kind of contextual effect is the elimination of contradictions (1986/1995: 114–115, 120–121). According to Sperber and Wilson's (1986/1995: 49) relevance theory, human information processing automatically aims to be most efficient. To maximise the efficiency of information processing, it is not enough to take into account the contextual effects achieved in communication; one has to consider the processing effort as well. Comparing the efficiency of two interperation procedures, the more effective is the one which applies less processing effort, i.e. where the same contextual effects can be achieved by less effort. Thus, on the basis of this relevance-theoretic economy consideration about information processing in the interpretation procedures, the second account above is less plausible and the first is more plausible.

There is a further argument for the first hypothesis. It is not plausible to assume that the I-implicature 'drink alcoholic beverages' is induced in every context where the verb *iszik* occurs without a lexicalised direct object argument. The utterances in (126b) and (128b) attest that the I-implicature 'drink alcoholic beverages' is not involved in their interpretation. The theory of generalised conversational implicatures assumes that generalised conversational implicatures as default inferences can be deleted if particular contexts do not support them (Levinson 2000). Thus, as we have seen above, according to the second hypothesis, I-implicatures are also induced in (126b) and (128b), but they are deleted in the particular non-supporting utterance contexts. However, this contradicts the economy considerations: why suppose the inducing of an I-implicature if it should be deleted? The inducing of an I-implicature when it should be deleted requires unnecessary processing efforts without extra contextual effects. Moreover, in (126b) and (128b) the non-supporting parts (*tej* 'milk' and *a baba* 'the baby', respectively) of the immediate utterance context precede the occurrence of the verb *iszik* with an implicit direct object argument. Thus, it is rather counterintuitive that the I-implicature 'drink alcoholic beverages' is induced by the verb *iszik* 'drink' at all. Consequently, the second hypothesis can be conceived of as less plausible than the first. On the basis of the occurrences in (126), (127), and (128), the structure of data with the verb *iszik* can be reconstructed as the following statements, to which a high plausibility value can be assigned:

> The verb *iszik* 'drink' can occur with an implicit direct object argument which can be identified with the optional selection restriction ALCOHOL which is put on the direct object argument and available as background information in the lexical-semantic representation of the verb *iszik* 'drink' in the particular supporting contexts.

> The verb *iszik* 'drink' can occur with an implicit direct object argument which can be identified with the selection restriction LIQUID which is put on the direct object argument and available as background information in the lexical-semantic representation of the verb *iszik* 'drink' in the contexts which do not support the activation of the optional selection restriction ALCOHOL put on the direct object argument.

These statements can be considered strong evidence against the second, I-implicature hypothesis (see Kertész and Rákosi 2012: 178–185 as well as Section 4.1.1).

Relying on the data structures reconstructed in the previous paragraph as well as the argumentation about how to select from the two rival hypotheses concerning the use and interpretation of the verb *iszik* 'drink' with an implicit direct object argument with the reading 'drink alcohol', it can also be proposed that the lexical-semantic representation of the verb *iszik* always contains the optional selection restriction ALCOHOL and not only when *iszik* refers to a long-lasting, habitual activity. If one assumes that the selection restriction ALCOHOL is involved in the lexical-semantic representation of *iszik* only in cases when *iszik* denotes a long-lasting, habitual activity of drinking alcoholic beverages, then a latent background assumption can be recovered according to which one assumes two lexical entries for the verb *iszik*: one for the occurrence where the reading 'drink alcoholic beverages' cannot be available when the verb *iszik* occurs with an implicit direct object argument, and the other one where it can be available. From this line of thinking it follows that one should suggest two lexical-semantic representations similar to those in (129a–b).[26]

(129)   a.   *iszik₁* 'drink': 'action of x causes that y which is liquid moves into the mouth of x'

[[ACT x] CAUSE [[MOVE y] : [[LIQUID y] & [FIN [LOC y] ⊂ LOC x's MOUTH]]]]

   b.   *iszik₂* 'drink': 'action of x causes that y which is alcohol moves into the mouth of x'

[[ACT x] CAUSE [[GO y] : [[ALCOHOL y] & [FIN [LOC y] ⊂ LOC x's MOUTH]]]]

In accordance with the recent trends in lexical-semantics which attempt to exceed the enumerative conception of the lexicon (cf. Bibok 2010), it is not reasonable to assume two lexical entries with two different lexical-semantic representations to obtain the two interpretation possibilities in question. It is more plausible to build both possibilities into one lexical-semantic representation in such a way that if the verb *iszik* occurs with an implicit direct object argument in a context which supports the reading 'drink alcohol', the lexical-semantic representation could provide this interpretation when interacting with the context. The lexical-semantic representation with the optional selection restriction ALCOHOL put on the direct object argument in (125b) which, for convenience, is repeated here as (130), can fulfil this aim.

(130)   *iszik* 'drink':   action of x causes that y which is (alcoholic) liquid moves into the mouth of x'

[[ACT x] CAUSE [[MOVE y] : [[[LIQUID: y (ALCOHOL y)]] & [FIN [LOC y] ⊂ LOC x's MOUTH]]]]

It is worth noting that from the previous argumentation it can be concluded that the long-lasting, habitual interpretation of the occurrence of the verb *iszik* with an implicit direct object argument emerges from the interaction of the lexical-semantic representation of *iszik* and the particular context. If the particular context does not support this interpretation, this interpretation cannot emerge.

Let us take another verb from (106), namely, *épít* 'build' and consider (131).

(131)   *Mit   csinál   Gergő?*
what.ACC   does.INDEF   Gergő.NOM
'What does Gergő do?'

Gergő   épít   [ÉPÍTMÉNY].
Gergő.NOM   builds.INDEF   building
'Gergő builds [building].'

The verb *épít* 'build' puts a selection restriction on the implicit direct object argument such that it is of the type BUILDING. The category BUILDING includes all things that can be built: house, castle, bridge, channel, as well as theory, plan, future. If the question in (131) inquires about Gergő's occupation, then the reply names Gergő's usual activity. In other words: in the answer the verb *épít* occurs without a lexicalised direct object argument because the activity determined by the particular job is the focus of attention. It is unimportant what Gergő actually builds since it is not the focus of attention. At the same time, in the lexical-semantic representation of *épít*, the selection restriction on the direct object argument of BUILDING type is also accessible as background information. It is worth mentioning that the present tense and the indefinite conjugation are also relevant here, since they are associated with a regular, habitual activity. The information according to which the lexical-semantic representation of the verb *épít* includes the selection restriction to be the type of BUILDING put on the direct object argument, the particular grammatical form of the verb *épít* and the particular context in which the focus of attention is only on the activity denoted by the verb *épít* together license the verb *épít* to occur with an implicit direct object argument with the reading indicated in (131).

Similarly to the categories FOOD and LIQUID, the category BUILDING has a prototypical structure. Since in our culture a house can be considered as the prototype of BUILDING – or at least a very typical member of the category BUILDING – the reply *Gergő épít* may be equivalent, for example, to the utterance *Gergő házakat épít* 'Gergő builds houses'. In the case of *épít* the direct object argument can be incorporated into the verb and it can also be omitted (cf. Kiefer 1990). Given that under the conceptual address of *épít* the selection restriction BUILDING placed on the type of the direct object argument is accessible in the lexical information and, furthermore, that the grammatical form of the utterance as well as the particular context are such that they do not demand that an instance (or instances) of the type BUILDING be named, the direct object argument should indeed be left implicit, taking into account the cognitive principle of relevance (see Section 3.1.1 and Chapter 6). This implicitness saves the speaker and the hearer considerable processing effort, e.g. that of lexicalising the direct object argument and uttering sounds or going through the process of recovering the phonological, morphological, and lexical forms of the direct object argument.

If the question in (131) refers to the actual present, then again the activity is the focus of attention and the direct object argument is accessible as background information involved in the selection restriction. However, in this reading there is no possibility for the verb *épít* to incorporate its direct object argument because of the lack of the condition of conventionalisation or institutionalisation, although it can be omitted because the speaker does not want to name what particular object Gergő is building.

Making the analysis more precise, it can be established that the category BUILDING can have two prototypical structures. If the subject of the action is an adult, BUILDING has the same prototypical structure as above. But if the subject of the action is a child, the prototype of BUILDING may be a block, Lego structure, or sand castle. Two kinds of analysis can be made on the basis of the two prototypical structures, but this, of course, does not mean that the lexicon should contain two lexical entries for the verb *épít*. The verb *épít* has an under-specified lexical-semantic representation which contains the selection restriction put on the direct object argument to be the type of BUILDING, and the category of BUILDING has two prototypical structures according to our encyclopaedic knowledge. If Gergő is an adult, the same explanation can be given as in the case of the usual action related to the profession or actual present action. If Gergő is a child, then the other prototypical structure of BUILDING becomes active and the implicit direct object argument in the utterance *Gergő épít* 'Gergő is building [something]' may refer to a block, Lego structure, or sand castle, i.e. to the thing Gergő is playing with.

Even if one does not accept that the type BUILDING of the direct object argument of the verb *épít* has two kinds of prototypical structure, then this interpretation can still be assigned to the reply. In terms of relevance theory (Groefsema 1995), the proper name Gergő when it refers to a child and the verb *épít* together make immediately accessible an assumption that children build houses or castles for fun. Thus, the implicit direct object argument can be identified with these houses or castles. When the proper name Gergő refers to an adult, in the context of the verb *épít* the encyclopaedic piece of information that adults build houses for a living becomes active, i.e. the implicit direct object argument of the verb *épít* can be identified with this type of house. What kind of reading takes place is determined by the interaction between the lexical-semantic representation of the verb *épít*, the general encyclopaedic knowledge included in the encyclopaedic context c_{enc} connected to the concept of building and Gergő as an adult or a child, as well as the particular discourse context c_{disc} and/or physical context c_{phys} on the basis of which one can decide whether Gergő is an adult or a child.[27]

Taking into account the considerations discussed so far, the underspecified lexical-semantic representation of the verb *épít* can be formulated as (132).

(132)   'action of x causes that y which is building comes into existence'
         [[ACT x] CAUSE [[EXIST y] : [BUILDING y]]]

If it is important what particular type or what particular entity within the type of building is being built by Gergő, then this particular type or entity should be lexically realised in the answer to the above mentioned question *Mit csinál Gergő?* 'What does Gergő do?' as in (133).

(133)   a.   *Gergő   hidat/   csatornát/   tornyot   épít.*
              Gergő.NOM   bridge.ACC   channel.ACC   tower.ACC   builds.INDEF
              'Gergő builds bridges/channels/towers'

         b.   *Gergő   a   Kormányos   utcai   házat   építi.*
              Gergő.NOM   the   Kormányos.NOM   in.street   house.ACC   builds.DEF
              'Gergő is building the house in Kormányos street.'

It is worth highlighting that in (133a) the verb *épít* is conjugated for the indefinite form and the interpretation of the utterance follows the same line as in the case of the reply in (131) above. But in (133b) the verb *épít* is conjugated for the definite form, which together with the present tense excludes the reading of a usual, habitual activity; (133b) refers to a particular activity in a particular context.

Finally, a further remark on the verb *épít* seems to be in order. In Section 4.2.2, analysing the verbs perfectivised with the help of a preverbal morpheme, the verb *megépít* 'PVB.build' was mentioned in addition to the verb *megeszik* 'PVB. eat', which cannot occur without a direct object argument in a sentential environment. This behaviour cannot be considered an idiosyncratic feature of the verb *megépít* 'PVB.build'; instead, it can be derived from the property of the base verb – *épít* – that it constrains the type of its direct object argument by means of a selection restriction. The perfectivised version of the base verb inherits this selection restriction. In the case of the perfectivised version of *épít*, i.e. *megépít* 'PVB.build', the direct object argument is also the focus of attention because of the perfectivisation. Since the selection restriction on the type of the direct object argument cannot provide the necessary information to identify the direct object argument in the focus of attention, the perfective verb *megépít* 'PVB.build' requires that its direct object argument be lexicalised. If a verb which has an endpoint and can be perfectivised with the help of a preverbal morpheme such as *gyón* 'confess' vs *meggyón* 'PVB.confess' places a unique selection restriction on its direct object argument (*y*: sin), then the perfectivised version of the base verb (*meggyón* 'PVB.

confess') also inherits the unique selection restriction. In accordance with the perfectivisation, the direct object argument also comes into the focus of attention, and since it can be identified exactly with the help of information provided by the unique selection restriction (*y*: sin), there is no need to lexicalise it.

4.3 Internal summary

The verbs studied in Chapter 4 have rich lexical-semantic representations. They constrain their subject and/or direct object arguments very strongly, by means of selection restrictions, lexical stereotypes, and the prototypical structures of their categories. Their lexical-semantic representations can be interpreted in two ways. This twofold interpretability makes it possible for them to occur with implicit arguments in the first (A) manner. If it is only the actions or events designated by the verbs which are the focus of attention, the subject and/or direct object arguments can be left lexically unrealised. The information concerning whether the arguments in question are of a particular type or a token of a type or a unique token involved in the selection restrictions can also be accessed as background information. In the case of verbs whose lexical-semantic representation involves a unique selection restriction put on the subject or direct object arguments, these arguments can be left implicit; indeed, they must be (see, e.g., *havazik* 'snow', *villámlik* '[for lightning to] strike' in Section 4.1.1 as well as *gyón* 'confess', *meg-gyón* 'PVB.confess' above).

Although what particular constraint a verb imposes on its arguments can be considered an idiosyncratic lexical-semantic property of the verb, the fact that a verb puts a selection restriction on its arguments predicts that the verb can be used with implicit arguments in the first (A) manner without a larger context. However, as we have seen in several cases, information stored in the lexical-semantic representations of verbs is not by itself sufficient to license the occurrence of verbs with implicit subject and/or direct object arguments. One has to take into consideration morphosyntactic (indefinite/definite conjugations) and pragmatic (general pragmatic and particular contextual) factors to the appropriate extent. Thus, it is necessary to assume an interaction between the lexical-semantic representations of verbs, grammatical factors, and contexts. On the basis of these results, two further conclusions can be formulated. Firstly, the particular detailed analyses provided in this chapter have supported the plausibility of the hypothesis formulated in Sections 1.2.1 and 3.1.1 that the use and identification of implicit subject and direct object arguments should be conceived of as a phenomenon at the grammar-pragmatics interface. Secondly, the division of labour between lexical-semantics, grammatical factors, and pragmatics in the use and interpretation of implicit arguments is under the control of an economy balance, i.e. they are guided by the cognitive principle of relevance (see Sperber and Wilson 1986/1995: 260 as well as Chapter 6).

As to the methodological aim of my research, in this chapter I have relied on several sources of data which attest to the fact that relationships and overlaps can be assumed between them without any inconsistency. The use of data from various direct sources has eliminated the disadvantages of the particular sources. And finally, it can also be concluded in this chapter that the relationship between the theory and data has proven to be cyclic and prismatic as was supposed in Section 1.2.3 on the basis of Kertész and Rákosi's (2012) metatheoretical framework. It is always the actual aims, problems, and argumentation processes of the research or the presentation of the research that determine what can serve as data in what functions in a particular phase of the research and its presentation. The data selected this way and newly introduced into the context of the research can yield new insights and help to select from the rival explanations as we have seen in the case of Hungarian verbs of natural phenomena in Section 4.1.1.

After discussing how Hungarian verbs can occur with implicit subject and direct object arguments in the first (A) manner, let us turn to the second (B) and third (C) manners and examine how the immediate utterance context and extended context with its grammatical and encyclopaedic properties license the use of Hungarian verbs with implicit subject and direct object arguments and guide their identification mechanisms.

CHAPTER 5

Second (B) and third (C) manners: grammatical constraints and the role of the immediate utterance context and the extended context

5.1 Zero anaphors in utterance and discourse contexts and extralinguistically motivated pro-drop phenomena

5.1.1 Zero subject anaphors and extralinguistically motivated subject pro-drop[1]

In Section 3.1.1 I referred to the fact that in Hungarian there are various types of implicit arguments, and their presence in utterances can be demonstrated by various kinds of evidence which point to the presence of an implicit argument and attest that the particular utterance does not have any performance error. Zero anaphors are types of implicit arguments which have their own position in the syntactic structure of utterances and antecedents with which they are coreferential and coindexed (see Németh T. 2007; Németh T. and Bibok 2010; Section 4.1.1). Thus they differ from the implicit arguments occurring in the first (A) manner, which are not projected into the syntactic structure of utterances but are available through the lexical-semantic representations of verbs as background information (see Chapter 4).

Zero anaphors are lexically unexpressed types of anaphor. The vast majority of the literature on anaphors, e.g. in textlinguistics, discourse analysis, pragmatics, and computational linguistics, agrees that anaphors refer back to explicitly expressed words or word phrases (see, e.g., Huang 2000; Tolcsvai Nagy 2001b; Lejtovicz and Kardkovács 2007), and these words or word phrases serve as antecedents for the anaphors. From this it follows that the antecedents of zero anaphors should also occur in the previous parts of the utterances in which the zero anaphors are used, or in places in the previous discourse outside the scope of the utterances containing the zero anaphors, i.e. they must be identifiable in the preceding discourse context c_{disc}. This characterisation of zero anaphors shows that they are not considered purely sentential phenomena in this book, but as phenomena that should be analysed in utterance contexts and the discourse contexts of language use. Consider (134) and (135).

(134)   (The father arrives home late evening, looks around and cannot see his son. The mother says:)

András$_i$ fáradt   volt,   [Ø$_i$]   lefeküdt   aludni.

András.NOM   tired   was.3SG   PVB.lay.INDEF.3SG   to.sleep

'András was tired, he went to sleep.'

(135)   (At a party two friends are chatting.)

Új   szomszédunk$_i$ van.   Tegnap   átjött   [Ø$_i$]

new   our.neighbour.NOM   is   yesterday   PVB.came.INDEF.3SG

bemutatkozni,   kedves   embernek   látszik   [Ø$_i$].

PVB.to introduce   kind   man.DAT   seems.INDEF

'We have a new neighbour, he came over yesterday, and he seems to be a kind man.'

Megkínáltad [Ø$_i$]?

PVB.offered.DEF.2SG

'Did you offer him something?'

Igen,   de   [Ø$_i$]   nem   fogadta   el.

yes   but   not   accepted.DEF.3SG   PVB

'Yes, but he did not accept my offer.'

In (134) the subject argument of the verb *lefeküdt* 'PVB.lay' in the second part of the utterance is left implicit as a zero anaphor [Ø$_i$] which is coreferential with *András$_i$*, the subject argument of the predicate phrase *fáradt volt* 'was tired' in the first part of the utterance. In (135) the zero subject argument [Ø$_i$] of the verbs *átjött* 'PVB.came' and *látszik* 'seems' in the second utterance, the zero object argument [Ø$_i$] of the verb *megkínáltad* 'PVB.offered' in the third utterance, and the zero subject argument of the verb *elfogadta* 'PVB.accepted' in the fourth utterance are coreferential with the explicitly expressed subject argument *szomszédunk$_i$* 'our neighbour' in the first utterance. In (135) zero anaphors operate at the discourse level across utterance boundaries. In both (134) and (135) the zero anaphors have an antecedent in the previous part of the utterance or in previous utterances in the discourse.

However, it must be noted that it can happen that the antecedent of a zero anaphor is not explicitly expressed in the utterance or discourse context c_{disc} but is itself an implicit argument which can be identified with the help of a piece of information from the observable physical context c_{phys} or encyclopaedic knowledge c_{enc}. Consider (136) and (137).

(136) (Péter, András, and Jakab are distributing bread to children.)

Péter: *Mindenki   kapott   [kenyeret$_i$ PHYS]?*
everybody.NOM got.INDEF.3SG bread.ACC
'Has everybody got bread?'

András: *Nem. Pálnak   nincsen [Ø$_i$.DISC]*
no   Pál.DAT not.is.INDEF
'No. Pál does not have any.'

Jakab: *Péter   adott   Pálnak$_j$ [Ø$_i$. DISC]*
Péter.NOM give.PAST.INDEF.3SG Pál.DAT

Biztosan már   megette [Ø$_j$ DISC] [Ø$_i$. DISC]
certainly already PVB.ate.INDEF.3SG
'Péter gave [bread] to Pál. He must have eaten [it] already.'

(137) (A customer would like to pay with a bank card in a supermarket. The shop-assistant turns the card reader to the customer and asks her/him:)

Legyen   szíves, üsse   be [a Pin-kódját$_i$ ENC]!
be.IMP.INDEF.3SG please punch.IMP.DEF.3SG in your.Pin-code.ACC
'Please, punch [your Pin-code] in!'

Jaj, nem jut   eszembe   [Ø$_i$]
ouch not gets.INDEF my.mind.ILL
'Oh no, [it] doesn't come to mind.'

In the interlinear rendering, the abbreviation DISC marks the fact that the identification of implicit arguments is possible by means of pieces of information coming from the preceding discourse, including the previous parts of the same utterance in which the implicit argument in question is included. The abbreviation PHYS marks pieces of information originating in the observable physical environment, and the abbreviation ENC signals that the assumption by means of which the implicit argument is identified is encyclopaedic. In (136) the direct object argument of the verb *kapott* 'got' is left lexically unrealised. It is easily identifiable by extending the utterance context with the information from the physical context c_{phys}: [kenyeret$_i$ PHYS] 'bread'. Although the direct object argument of the verb *kapott* 'got' has a zero form, it cannot be categorised as a zero anaphor, since it does not have any antecedent in the utterance or previous discourse with which it can be coreferential and coindexed. The implicit arguments indicated as

[Øi] in the subsequent part of the conversation are coreferential with the lexically unrealised direct object argument in the first utterance *[kenyereti PHYS]*, thus these implicit arguments can be considered zero anaphors with their antecedent in the first utterance.

A similar analysis can be suggested in the case of (137), with the difference that the implicit direct object argument *[Øi]* in the second utterance as a zero anaphor has its antecedent in the first utterance identifiable not from the observable physical environment as in (136) but from encyclopaedic knowledge. In a situation where a shopping event takes place in a supermarket, a customer who would like to pay with a bank card is expected to know that her/his Pin-code is required to use the card reader. Since this piece of encyclopaedic information is assumed to be highly available to card-owning customers, the shop assistant can leave the direct object argument *[a Pin-kódjáti ENC]* 'your Pin-code' of the verb *üsse be* 'punch in' lexically unrealised. Similarly to the lexically unrealised direct object argument in the first utterance *[kenyereti PHYS]* in (136), the encyclopaedically licensed implicit occurrence of the direct object argument of the verb *üsse be* 'punch in' in (137) cannot be categorised as a zero anaphor either. At the same time, it can serve as an antecedent of the *[Øi]* zero subject anaphor of the second utterance.

In Section 4.1.1, when the use of verbs of natural phenomena with explicit and implicit subject arguments was discussed, it was argued that the implicit subject argument of verbs of natural phenomena can serve as an antecedent for zero anaphors or, to put it the other way round, the zero anaphors occurring in the same or subsequent utterances attest that verbs of natural phenomena are used with implicit subject arguments with which the zero anaphors are coreferential. In (74) and (80), repeated here as (138) and (139) for convenience with a slight modification to indicate implicit arguments, the verbs *hull* 'fall' and *esik* 'fall' occur with implicit subject arguments which can be considered zero anaphors, the antecedents of which are not expressed explicitly in the utterance or the previous discourse context. Consider (138) and (139).

(138)   (The weather forecast predicts snow.)

       Szállingózik   *már*   *[a   hói]?*
       softly.snows.INDEF   already   the   snow.NOM
       'Is it [= the snow] snowing softly yet?'

       Már   *hull*   *[Øi]*.
       Already   falls.INDEF   the snow.NOM
       'It [= the snow] is falling already.'

(139)   *Havazik*   *[a   hó_i].*   *Nagyon   szépen   esik*   *[Ø_i].*

snows.INDEF   the   snow.NOM   very   nicely   falls.INDEF

'[Snow] is snowing. [The snow] is falling very nicely.'

In the question posed in (138), the verb *szállingózik* 'snow softly' occurs with an implicit subject argument in the first (A) manner by means of the selection restriction. As was suggested in Section 4.1.1, the lexical-semantic representation of *szállingózik* puts a selection restriction on its subject argument: it must be *hó* 'snow', i.e. x: *hó*. This unique selection restriction makes it possible to use the verb *szállingózik* without an explicit subject argument. This implicit subject argument available as background information by means of the unique selection restriction in the lexical-semantic representation of *szállingózik* can serve as an antecedent for the lexically unrealised subject argument of the verb *hull* 'fall' in the answer. In the answer, the verb *hull* occurs with the implicit subject argument *[Ø_i]* in the third (C) manner as a zero discourse anaphor. In (139) the verb *esik* 'fall' in the second utterance can occur with implicit subject argument *[Ø_i]* since it has an antecedent in the first utterance which is the implicit subject argument *[a hó_i]* 'the snow' of the verb *havazik* 'snow'. In other words, the lexically unrealised subject argument of the verb *esik* is a zero discourse anaphor.

When an implicit argument has a postcedent, it is called a zero cataphor. In other terms, the expression with which the cataphor is coreferential follows the cataphor later in the subsequent utterance or discourse. Consider (140), where the zero subject in the first part of the utterance gets its interpretation from the second part of the utterance, since *[Ø_i]* is coreferential with the subject of the second clause *András_i*. Thus *[Ø_i]* can be considered a cataphor.

(140)   (The father arrives home late evening, looks around and does not see his son. The mother says:)

Mivel   [Ø_i]   fáradt   volt,   *András_i*   *lefeküdt*   *aludni.*

since   tired   was.INDEF.3SG   András.NOM   PVB.lay.INDEF.3SG   to.sleep

'Because he was tired, András went to sleep.'

In the literature one can also find a wide definition of anaphors, according to which anaphors are uses of expressions the identification of which is dependent upon other expressions in context, either their antecedents in the previous discourse or postcedents in the subsequent discourse. Thus, zero forms categorised as cataphors elsewhere are also covered by the term *anaphor* in a wider sense (Lyons 1979: 659; Ehlich 1982; Huang 2012). Cataphors are sometimes called backward anaphors in the generative linguistics tradition as well (see, e.g., Mittwoch 1983; Reinhart 1985).[2] However, the term *anaphor* is only applied in the present book to expressions which have antecedents. Expressions with post-cedents are called cataphors in accordance with the majority of the literature (see, e.g., Tolcsvai Nagy 2001a, b; Renkema 2004; Huang 2009) and will not be discussed in more detail in the subsequent part of this book, since they have similar coindexing identification principles to those which govern anaphors. Both anaphors and cataphors are endophors, since they obtain their antecedents and postcedents, respectively, from the previous or subsequent part of the utterance or discourse (Gillon 2012 as well as Section 2.3).

When an implicit argument obtains its interpretation extralinguistically, for instance from the physical context c_{phys}, it is a manifestation of exophoric reference. Exophoric implicit arguments do not have any antecedents or postcedents in the utterance or discourse context they occur in; instead, they refer to items in the external world (see Peral and Fernández 2000; Gillon 2012 as well as Section 2.3). Such implicit arguments include zero personal pronouns which refer to the discourse participants, i.e. the speaker and the hearer, and can be classified as zero exophoric pronouns or zero deictic referential pronouns (Laczkó 2003; Kim et al. 2010; Mitkov 2013). Consider (141).

(141)　(Two students are discussing how to solve a problem. Both of them have their own idea. Finally, one of them suggests a solution which seems to be plausible and asks the other:)

　　　Megtaláltam　　　*a*　　*megoldást.*　　*Egyetértesz?*

　　　PVB.found.DEF.1SG　the　solution.ACC　agree.INDEF.2SG

　　　'I have found the solution. Do you agree with me?'

In (141) the verb *megtaláltam* 'found' occurs with a lexically unrealised first person subject argument which refers extralinguistically to the speaker, as is indicated by the inflectional morpheme *-m*. The verb *egyetértesz* 'agree' also occurs with zero subject exophorically; it refers to the hearer, as is indicated by the inflectional morpheme *-sz*. Zero exophoric implicit arguments including zero exophoric pronouns are not considered zero anaphors in the present study. The Hungarian verbs can occur with them in the third (C) manner by taking into account the inflectional morphemes of the definite conjugation paradigm on the verbs and extending the immediate utterance context in which the verbs in question are used with the information from the observable physical environment or with encyclopaedic knowledge. (The licensing and identification of implicit arguments in Hungarian language use in the third (C) manner by extending the immediate utterance context with information from the observable physical context or encyclopaedic knowledge will be discussed in more detail in Section 5.3)

It must be noted that an implicit argument can obtain its interpretation extralinguistically not only from the physical context c_{phys} through exophoric reference as is widely assumed in the literature, but also from the encyclopaedic context c_{enc} as we have seen above in (137), where the implicit direct object argument of the verb *üsse be* 'punch in' can be identified with the Pin-code from encyclopaedic knowledge (see also the implicit indirect object argument *a gólyával* 'by the stork' of the verb *hozat* 'to have somebody/something brought' in (6) in Section 1.1). This type of implicit argument cannot be categorised as a zero anaphor either; it can be identified by extending the immediate utterance context in which the verb occurs with the information from the encyclopaedic knowledge in the third (C) manner (see Section 5.3).

It is also worth mentioning that the term *anaphor* applied in the present book differs from the conception of anaphors in the generative grammatical tradition. In the Chomskyan types of generative grammar, anaphors have a narrower scope and are defined as expressions which have dependent reference which is taken from an antecedent within the same phrase or sentence (Radford 1997b: 492). Anaphors include reflexives (e.g. the English reflexive pronouns *myself/yourself/ herself/themselves*, etc.) and reciprocals (e.g. English reciprocal pronoun *each other*) which must be bound by an antecedent in the same phrase or sentence (Chomsky 1981; Radford 1997b: 114–116). The same analysis can be provided for the behaviour of Hungarian reflexive pronouns (*magam* 'myself', *magad* 'yourself', *maga* 'herself/himself', etc.) as well as the reciprocal pronoun *egymás* 'each other' (É. Kiss 1985, 1998). Unlike the generative grammatical tradition, in the present study I apply the term *anaphor* in harmony with the line of thinking presented previously in this Section similarly to textlinguistics, discourse analysis, pragmatics, and computational linguistics, as was referred to above.

After discussing how the term *anaphor* is interpreted in various rival approaches and clarifying what I mean by *zero anaphors*, let us start to examine zero subject anaphors in Hungarian language use.

Since Hungarian is a pro-drop language, there is a wide range of lexically unrealised subjects in Hungarian language use.[3] However, not all kinds of subject pro-drop phenomena can be considered zero subject anaphors. Zero subject anaphors are only those subject pro-drop phenomena which have an antecedent in the previous part of the utterances or discourses in which they occur. As we have seen above, zero anaphors in utterances and discourses which act similarly to overt anaphoric pronouns refer to referents that have already been introduced into the utterance or discourse, i.e. they have an antecedent which they are coreferential with. Those subject pro-drop phenomena which do not have an antecedent in the previous part of the utterance or discourse, however, obtain their interpretation extralinguistically from the speech situation in the physical context c_{phys}, and cannot be categorised as zero subject anaphors. They have been termed exophoric zero pronouns, as we have seen above. Thus, zero first and second personal subject pronouns which refer to discourse participants such as the speaker and hearer are also manifestations of subject pro-drop. Dropped subjects are indicated by the first and second personal inflectional morphemes on the verbs, but they are not zero anaphors (see (141) above). Third personal subject pronoun can also be dropped on the basis of extralinguistical information, when they can be identified from the physical context c_{phys} or encyclopaedic context c_{enc}.

Third person zero subject anaphors which can be considered manifestations of subject pro-drop are also indicated by means of the inflection morphemes on the verbs. Previous research into zero subject anaphors in Hungarian has demonstrated that the licensing and interpretation of zero subject anaphors are influenced not only by grammatical requirements, but by pragmatic factors as well (see, e.g., Pléh 1994, 1998; Tolcsvai Nagy 2001a; Dankovics 2001, 2005; Németh T. 2007, and also Section 3.1.1). The results of Pléh's (1994, 1998: 164–194) psycholinguistics experiments have also supported the hypothesis that, on the one hand, the grammar cannot account for all pro-form relations, and, on the other hand, encyclopaedic information and particular contextual factors can override the use or interpretation predicted by grammar. Testing the influence of constituency constraints on interpretations of coreference in Spanish, Blackwell (2001) also concludes that anaphor interpretations are constrained not only by grammatical (syntactic) factors. Instead, they are strongly constrained by semantic entailments, general semantic predictions, background knowledge, antecedent salience and choice of linguistic alternates. Similarly, studying null appositives, Capone (2008) comes to the conclusion that often the semantics of sentences does not by itself result in a complete and adequate interpretation, and, instead, pragmatics must contribute to the identification of implicit constituents.

Pléh (1994) also emphasises that when the antecedent of an anaphor is highly accessible in the context, this means that it can be identified straightforwardly, and consequently the anaphor can have a zero form. A similar claim is made by Ariel (1991), when she places referring expressions on an accessibility scale on the basis of their cognitive accessibility and linguistic cues. Relevance theory also takes this view (Sperber and Wilson 1986/1995). Thus, on the basis of these economy (relevance) considerations, we can state that when the referent of an anaphor can be easily and unambiguously identified in the context, there is no need to use an explicit lexical form in Hungarian language use (Pléh 1998: 167; Németh T. and Bibok 2010). The distribution of the forms of anaphors *az/azok* 'that/those', *ő/ők* '(s)he/they', and [Ø] supports this relevance consideration (see also above in this section as well as Pléh 1998: 164–194).

Tolcsvai Nagy (2001a: 289–290; 2001b: 205–222) has come to similar conclusions. He overviews the possible realisations of third person subject anaphors in Hungarian and emphasises that when there is one potential antecedent in the position of subject, topic, and agent or experiencer, and the anaphor itself is in an unstressed subject and topic position, the anaphor is manifested by the zero form and inflectional morpheme on the verb. If the anaphor in a stressed subject or focus position is human, it is manifested as a third person personal pronoun *ő* '(s)he' or *ők* 'they'. If the antecedent is inanimate and the anaphor is in a stressed subject position, it is realised by the third person demonstrative pronoun *az* 'that' or *azok* 'those' (Tolcsvai Nagy 2001a: 289–290). Since the aim of the present study is to investigate implicit arguments including zero subject anaphors in Hungarian language use, I do not intend to deal with *ő/ők* '(s)he/they' and *az/azok* 'that/those' anaphors here. The choice between the various possible forms of anaphors in Hungarian language use is motivated by the accessibility of their referents. Zero realisations of subject anaphors are supported by the high accessibility of the referents of anaphors.

Consider (142) and (143).

(142) *Péter$_i$*   *hazament.*   *Már*   *[Ø$_i$]*   *befejezte*   *a*
       Péter.NOM   home.went.INDEF.3SG   already   PVB.finished.DEF.3SG   the

       munkáját.
       his.work.ACC

       'Péter went home. He had already finished his work.'

(Tolcsvai Nagy 2001a: 288)

(143) *Az   euró$_i$*   *árfolyama*   *tovább   emelkedik.*   *[Ø$_i$]*
       the   euro.NOM   its.exchange.rate.NOM   further   rises.INDEF

       Elérheti   *a*   *310*   *forintot.*
       may.reach.DEF.3SG   the   310   forint.ACC

       'The exchange rate of the euro is still rising. It may reach 310 HUF.'

In (142) the antecedent of *[Ø$_i$]* is human (*Péter$_i$*) while in (143) it is inanimate (*Euro$_i$*), i.e. the zero anaphor can be used in both animate and inanimate cases when the anaphor itself is not stressed. The zero subjects of the second utterance in (142) and (143) refer to the subject of the first utterance. This is what has been called in the generative grammatical tradition the subject continuation principle originating in the pro-drop property of Hungarian. According to this principle, the subject of the second clause in utterances with complex and compound sentence structures can be realised as a zero anaphor if it is coreferential with the subject of the first clause (Pléh 1994, 1998; Németh T. and Bibok 2010; Németh T. 2014b). The zero anaphor in the second clause has its own position in the syntactic structure of the utterance as in all cases of overt anaphors. Thus, they differ from the kind of implicit subject arguments, occurrences of which are licensed in the first (A) manner, i.e. by the lexical-semantic representation of verbs (see the analysis of the occurrence of verbs of natural phenomena as well as verbs of work with implicit subject arguments in Sections 4.1.1 and 4.1.2, respectively).

In other words, the basic syntactic rule is that when subjects are repeated, they can be dropped. However, if a noun in the previous clause is selected as an antecedent of the subject in the second clause which was not a subject in that previous clause, then the subject in the second clause must be pronominalised by the demonstrative pronoun *az* 'that' (Pléh and Radics 1978; Pléh and McWhinney 1987; Németh T. 2012).

Pléh's (1998: 164–194) and Dankovics's (2001, 2005) psycholinguistic experiments have shown that, when there is more than one potential antecedent in a previous clause of the same utterance or discourse, the interpretation of sentential and discourse anaphors in Hungarian language use are constrained not only by the syntactic rule of subject continuation, but also by various other grammatical factors, such as sentence-grammatical typicality effects, thematic roles of verbs, types of conjugation, word order, and pragmatic considerations. However, not all these factors do in fact influence the occurrence of zero subject anaphors. For instance, the word order of the previous clause does not have an impact on the antecedent selection in the case of a zero subject anaphor (Pléh 1998: 177). Tolcsvai Nagy (2001a: 293) criticises these psycholinguistic approaches since they do not reveal the underlying cognitive basis of the difference between the use of zero pronouns and the additive pronouns *ő/ők* '(s)he/they' and *az/azok* 'that/ those' as anaphors. He proposes to take into consideration the notion of perspective treated in cognitive linguistics (cf. Sanders and Spooren 1997: 85–112) in order to arrive at an explanation. The use of zero pronouns and additive pronouns *ő/ők* and *az/azok* indicates different perspectives (viewpoints) or changes in perspectives. When the speaker uses a zero subject pronoun, this indicates that there is no change in the perspective of the two clauses. The clause in which the anaphor occurs should be interpreted from the same perspective as the previous clause of the utterance in which the full nouns occur. Thus, the syntactic rule of subject continuation formulated in the generative grammatical tradition and applied in Pléh and colleagues' psycholinguistic experiments can be considered a syntactic manifestation of the identity of the perspectives of the two clauses.

According to the results of the sentence-oriented psycholinguistic experiments mentioned above, when there is more than one potential antecedent in a previous clause of the same utterance or discourse, the subject continuation rule of grammar strongly predicts that the zero anaphor must be coreferential with the subject of the previous clause, although there are other factors to be taken into account. However, it must be highlighted that these results are valid only in a default case, i.e. in the absence of specific, particular contextual information.

If we consider utterances in particular contexts of language use, it can be argued that grammar and pragmatics interact intensively in multiple ways in the licensing and interpretation of zero subject anaphors (Németh T. and Bibok 2010; Németh T. 2012).[4] Pragmatic factors can support, modify, or change the reading predicted by grammar. Consider the case of the zero subject anaphor in the utterance environment in (144) (see Németh T. and Bibok 2010: 510; Németh T. 2014b: 687).

(144) A   *férj$_i$*   *elkísérte*   *a*   *feleségét$_j$*
the   husband.NOM   accompanied.DEF.3SG   the   his.wife.ACC

az   *orvoshoz$_z$,*   *mert*   *[Ø$_{i/j/z}$]*   *nagyon*   *izgult.*
the   doctor.ALL   because   very.much   was.nervous.INDEF.3SG

'The husband accompanied his wife to the doctor, because [(s)he] was very nervous.'

Following from the syntactic rule of subject continuation, the zero subject of the second clause in (144), i.e. *[Ø$_i$]* has to be coreferential with the subject phrase *a férj$_i$* 'the husband.NOM' in the first clause. According to the generalisations made by Pléh (1994, 1998), Dankovics (2001, 2005), and Tolcsvai Nagy (2001a), if a speaker wants to refer to the noun phrase *a feleségét* 'his wife.ACC' or *az orvoshoz* 'the doctor.ALL' in the second clause, then (s)he must use the demonstrative pronoun *az* 'that' as in (145).

(145) A   *férj$_i$*   *elkísérte*   *a*   *feleségét$_j$*
the   husband.NOM   accompanied.DEF.3SG   the   his.wife.ACC

az   *orvoshoz$_z$,*   *mert*   *az$_{j/z}$*   *nagyon*
the   doctor.ALL   because   she$_j$/he$_z$ very.much

izgult.
was.nervous.INDEF.3SG

'The husband accompanied his wife$_j$ to the doctor$_z$, because she$_j$/he$_z$ was very nervous.'

Pragmatic factors, namely the background knowledge and particular speech situation, can support the interpretation of the zero anaphor in (144) predicted by grammar. If, however, the husband is nervous and his wife is not, the pragmatic factors support the interpretation constrained by grammar, i.e. the antecedent of the zero anaphor *[Ø$_i$]* is the noun phrase *a férj$_i$* 'the husband.NOM'.

However, pragmatic factors can override the interpretation of the zero anaphor predicted by grammar. The speaker can refer to the noun phrase *a feleségét$_j$* 'his.

wife.ACC' in the first clause with a zero pronoun *[Øⱼ]* in the second clause. If there is a speech situation in which it is known from the background knowledge that the wife is nervous and her husband is not, the antecedent of the zero anaphor *[Øⱼ]* is the direct object phrase *a feleségét*ⱼ 'his wife.ACC' in contrast to the interpretation forced by the grammatical rule of subject continuation and the explanation by Tolcsvai Nagy (2001a) based on the identity of underlying perspectives.

If both the husband and the wife are usually nervous, even the pragmatic factors, more precisely the background knowledge, cannot identify the antecedent. In such a case, to resolve the zero anaphor, one needs to consider the particular speech situation to find out who is (more) nervous, otherwise the interpretation cannot be unambiguous.

Finally, there is a fourth interpretation possibility. The doctor also can be nervous. For example, in a situation where the doctor has diagnosed the wife with a serious disease and does not know how to tell her the diagnosis, (s)he can ask the husband to accompany his wife in order for the doctor to tell the diagnosis to the wife in her husband's presence, in supporting circumstances. In this situation the zero anaphor *[Øᵤ]* is coreferential with the adverbial phrase *az orvoshoz*ᵤ 'the doctor.ALL' and not with the subject phrase *a fér*ⱼ 'the husband.NOM' in the first clause predicted by the grammar itself. However, it must be noted that there are Hungarian native speakers who evaluate this fourth interpretation possibility as rather strange, while other Hungarian native speakers – including myself – can accept it easily without any difficulty. To put it the other way round, while the first three interpretation possibilities of the utterance containing a zero subject anaphor in (144) are undoubtedly acceptable according to the intuition of Hungarian native speakers, the fourth interpretation possibility is less available for some Hungarian native speakers, thus it can be considered less plausible for these native speakers.

Let us take another occurrence of zero subject anaphor where, in addition to the background world knowledge and particular contextual information, another kind of pragmatic information, namely general pragmatic knowledge, should be taken into account to identify the antecedent of the zero subject anaphor. Consider Pléh's (1998: 178) example analysed by Németh T. and Bibok (2010) in detail.

(146) a. *A*   *bácsi*ᵢ   *emlékezett*   *a*   *fiúra*ⱼ,

the   old.man.NOM   remembered.INDEF.3SG   the   boy.SUB

[Øᵢ/ⱼ]   *tanácsot*   *adott*   *neki*ⱼ/ᵢ.

advice.ACC   gave.INDEF.3SG   him.DAT

'The old manᵢ remembered the boyⱼ, [heᵢ/ⱼ] had given himⱼ/ᵢ advice.'

b. *A   fiú*ᵢ   *emlékezett*   *a   bácsira*ⱼ,
    the boy.NOM   remembered.INDEF.3SG   the   old.man.SUB

*[Øⱼ/ᵢ] tanácsot   adott   neki*ᵢ/ⱼ.
    advice.ACC   gave. INDEF.3SG   him.DAT

'The boyᵢ remembered the old manⱼ, [heⱼ/ᵢ] had given himᵢ/ⱼ advice.'

The utterances in (146a) and (146b) have the same structure. In (146a) the zero subject anaphor *[Øᵢ]* can be co-indexed with the subject phrase *a bácsi*ᵢ 'the old.man.NOM' according to the grammatical requirement, i.e. the subject continuation principle. In spite of the structural coincidence between (146a) and (146b), in (146b) the zero subject cannot be identified typically with the referent of the subject phrase *a fiú* 'the boy.NOM'. The preferred reading is that the zero subject anaphor *[Øⱼ]* is coreferential with the sublative noun phrase *a bácsira*ⱼ 'the old.man.SUB'. Giving advice is a socially governed speech act. Searle (1969: 67) adds a comment to the conditions for achieving success in giving advice that advice is not a form of requesting. Advising is more likely to involve telling another person what is best for her/him. Therefore, the preparatory conditions of the speech act of advising can be extended with the condition that the adviser can only be a person with a considerable advantage in knowledge, experience, age, or social status; otherwise (s)he cannot tell what is the best for another person. This piece of information is involved in the general pragmatic knowledge concerning the speech act of giving advice, and it can override the reading predicted by grammar in (146b). In (146b) the grammatical principle of subject continuation predicts that the zero subject anaphor in the second clause is coreferential with the subject phrase *a fiú* 'the boy.NOM' in the first clause, but the general pragmatic knowledge regarding advising requires that the antecedent of the zero subject anaphor in the second clause is the sublative noun phrase *a bácsira* 'the old.man.SUB' in the first clause. Since in a typical situation an old man can be assumed to have more experience and knowledge than a boy has, the old man fulfils the requirement placed by general pragmatic knowledge on the successful performance of the speech act of advising. Therefore, general pragmatic knowledge can override the interpretation predicted by grammar and selects the sublative noun phrase *a bácsira*ⱼ 'the old.man.SUB' as an antecedent of the zero subject anaphor *[Øⱼ]* in (146b).

However, a particular speech situation in which the boy is better informed than the old man (for instance, in how to use the Internet) overrides the reading provided by general pragmatic knowledge and supports the grammatical reading. It is worth noting that, similarly to the analysis of (146b), in (146a) pragmatic factors, namely, the particular speech situation according to which the boy is better informed than the old man, can also override the interpretation predicted by grammar. In this latter situation the antecedent of the zero anaphor in (146a) must be identified with the referent of the phrase *a fiúra* 'the boy.SUB'.

In Hungarian language use, zero subject anaphors can also occur in such a way that their antecedents are not posited in the same utterance. In these cases the immediate utterance context of zero subject anaphors must be extended with the information from the preceding discourse to identify the referent of the implicit argument, i.e. the antecedents of zero subject anaphors are found in the previous utterances in discourse. Thus, while zero subject anaphors in utterance contexts are used and interpreted in the second (B) manner of the occurrence of implicit arguments, zero subject anaphors in discourses are licensed and identified in the third C manner (see Section 3.2). Consider (147a–b).

(147) a. A   *Mikulás$_i$*   *odament*   *a*   *kisfiúhoz$_j$.*

        the   Santa.Claus.NOM   there.went.INDEF.3SG   the   little.boy.ALL

        Cukrot   *adott*   *[Ø$_{i/j}$]* *neki$_{j/i}$.*

        candy.ACC   gave.INDEF.3SG   him.DAT

        'Santa Claus went up to the little boy. [He$_{i/j}$] gave him$_{j/i}$ candy.'

    b. *A*   *kisfiú$_i$*   *odament*   *a*   *Mikulráshoz$_j$.*

        the   little.boy.NOM   went.INDEF.3SG   the   Santa.Claus.ALL

        Cukrot   *adott*   *[Ø$_{j/i}$]* *neki$_{i/j}$.*

        candy.ACC   gave.INDEF.3SG   him.DAT

        'The little boy went up to Santa Claus. [He$_{j/i}$] gave him$_{i/j}$ candy.'

In (147) one can find zero discourse anaphors whose antecedents are not posited in the same utterances. Resolving these types of zero anaphors is also governed by the interaction between grammatical and pragmatic constraints, including background encyclopaedic knowledge, general pragmatic knowledge, and pieces of information from the particular speech situation. According to the grammatical requirements, in (147a) the zero subject of the second utterance *[Ø$_i$]* is coreferential with the subject of the first utterance, i.e. with *Mikulás$_i$* 'Santa. Claus.NOM'. The interpretation predicted by grammar is supported by the encyclopaedic expectation that Santa Claus be a person who distributes candy to children. However, in (147b) this encyclopaedic assumption and the reading forced by grammar are not in harmony with each other. According to the requirement of the subject continuation, the zero subject in the second utterance *[Ø$_i$]* must be coreferential with the subject of the first utterance, i.e. with *a kisfiú$_i$* 'the little. boy.NOM'. Instead, in (147b) due to the encyclopaedic knowledge concerning the typical behaviour of Santa Claus, the zero subject of the second utterance *[Ø$_j$]* is coreferential with the allative noun phrase *a Mikulàshoz$_j$* 'Santa.Claus.ALL' in the first utterance.[5] Furthermore, a particular speech situation in which Santa Claus had no more candy to distribute but realised that he had given more candy to the little boy can override the reading predicted by grammar in (147a) and the reading predicted by the encyclopaedic assumption in (147b). Thus, in both cases the referent of the zero subject anaphor in the second utterance can be identified as the little boy, and grammar and pragmatics interact in multiple ways.

On the basis of the analysis of zero subject anaphors in (144), (146), and (147), it can be seen, on the one hand, that the use or interpretation predicted by grammar can be considered only a typical, default interpretation that emerges due to the lack of any specific context, and, on the other hand, that grammar (e.g. syntactic, morphosyntactic, and semantic constraints) and pragmatics (general pragmatic knowledge and particular contextual information from the observable physical context c_{phys}, from the encyclopaedic knowledge c_{enc}, and previous parts of discourse c_{disc}) interact intensively (perhaps, in multiple ways) in the licensing and recovering of zero subject anaphors, i.e. a kind of implicit argument with its own syntactic position in the structure of utterances. After discussing zero subject anaphors and exophoric subjects in Hungarian language use, let us turn to the analyses of zero anaphoric and exophoric objects.

5.1.2 Zero object anaphors in utterance and extralinguistically motivated object pro-drop

In Hungarian language use it is not only pronominal subjects which can be dropped but pronominal direct objects as well, i.e. in Hungarian language use object pro-drop also occurs. If it is expressed by the verbal inflection on the transitive verbs and/or can straightforwardly be identified in the context, the pronominal direct object can also be dropped. An implicit direct object argument can be considered a result of anaphoric pro-drop if it has an antecedent in the previous part of the utterance in which it occurs or in a previous utterance of the discourse as is exemplified in (148) by the occurrence of the implicit direct object arguments *[Ø$_i$]* of the verbs *kapott* 'got.INDEF.3SG', *adsz* 'give.INDEF.2SG', and *ad* 'gives.INDEF'. These implicit direct object arguments have an antecedent in the previous discourse; they are coreferential with the subject *cukor$_i$* 'candy.NOM' of the first utterance.[6]

(148)   (Santa Claus is distributing candy among the children.)

        Santa Claus: *[mindenkinek]*   *Jutott*   *cukor$_i$?*

                everybody.DAT   got.INDEF.3SG   candy.NOM

                'Did [everybody] get candy$_i$?'

A child: *Az   öcsém*   *nem   kapott*   *[Ø*$_i$*]*.
            the   my.younger.brother.NOM   not   got.INDEF.3SG

            [Ø$_j$*]   Adsz*   *[Ø*$_i$*]   neki*   *is?*
                        give.INDEF.2SG   him.DAT   too

            'My younger brother did not get [any$_i$]. Will [you$_j$] give [some$_i$]
            to him, too?'

The mother: *Ne   izgulj,*   *neki*   *is*   *ad*   *[Ø*$_i$*]*
             not   worry.IMP.2SG   him.DAT   too   gives.INDEF

             a   Mikulás,   *mielőtt*   *[Ø*$_j$*]*   *visszamegy*
             the   Santa.Claus.NOM   before   back.goes.INDEF

             a   szánnal   *[az   Északi   sarkra]*.
             the   sledge.INS   the   North   Pole.SUBL

             'Don't worry, Santa Claus will give [some$_i$] to him, too, before
             [he] leaves in his sledge [for the North Pole].'

Similarly to the zero subject arguments, not all kinds of zero object arguments
can be considered zero object anaphors. Those object pro-drop phenomena which
do not have an antecedent in the previous part of the utterances or discourse, and
instead obtain their interpretation extralinguistically from the speech situation
in the physical context c_{phys}, cannot be categorised as zero object anaphors, similarly to the extralinguistically identifiable zero subjects. Thus, they can be considered zero exophoric, or deictic, object pronouns. Thus, zero first and second
person personal object pronouns, which refer to discourse participants such as
the speaker(s) and the hearer(s), are manifestations of object pro-drop, but they
are not anaphoric. The third person object can also be dropped without having
an antecedent in the previous utterance or discourse if it can be identified extralinguistically.

The first and second person dropped objects are indicated by the inflectional
morphemes on the transitive verbs conjugated for the indefinite form; they do
not occur with definite conjugations (É. Kiss 2012: 194). In (149a) the verb *szeret*
'love' is conjugated for the indefinite form, it agrees with the singular or plural
second person subject, and the inflectional morpheme can refer to both the singular and plural first person dropped object indicating the actual speaker(s). In
(149b) the verb *szeret* is also conjugated for the indefinite form, but it has a singular or plural third person subject, and its inflectional morphemes can indicate
both a singular and plural first or second person dropped object identifiable with
the actual speaker(s) and hearer(s). If the subject is first person singular, the verbal suffix *-lak/-lek* can indicate both a singular and plural second person dropped

object which refer(s) to the actual hearer(s), see (149c).

(149)   a.   *Szeretsz/*   *szerettek*   *[engem/minket].*
        love.INDEF.2SG   love.INDEF.2PL   me.ACC/us.ACC
        'Do you.SG.NOM/PL.NOM love me/us?'

    b.   *A*   *nagypapa*   *szeret*   *[engem/minket/*
        the   grandfather.NOM   loves.INDEF   me.ACC/us.ACC/
        téged/titeket].
        you.SING.ACC/you.PL.ACC
        'The grandfather loves [me/us/you.SG.ACC/you.PL.ACC].'

    c.   *Szeretlek*   *[téged/titeket].*
        love.1SG.2OBJ.   you.SG.ACC/you.PL.ACC
        'I love [you.SG.ACC/you.PL.ACC].'

It has to be noted that É. Kiss (2012: 193–195) assumes that Hungarian allows only singular null pronominal objects. If a transitive verb is conjugated for the indefinite form and occurs without an explicitly expressed first or second person object, then a zero singular first or second person object is supposed. So, according to É. Kiss's (2012: 193) claim, utterances in (149a–b) are only grammatical if they contain a null singular first or second person object. However, in (149a) if the null first person pronominal object refers to the speaker and some other people (e.g. inclusive *we*), it has a plural reading. Similarly, in (149b) if the null first and second person objects refer to the speaker and some other people (e.g. inclusive *we*) and to the hearer and some other people, respectively, they have a plural reading. The singular first and second readings are a default interpretation due to the lack of specific context.

    É. Kiss (2012: 195) especially highlights that the plural second person object pronoun cannot be dropped with verbs conjugated for the *-lak/-lek* form. Therefore, (149c) and the second utterance in (150) are ungrammatical according to her intuition. Overviewing the previous approaches to the objectless use of Hungarian transitive verbs, I have indicated in Section 4.2.1 that Kugler (2000b: 110) has the same opinion, i.e. it assumes, similarly to É. Kiss (2012), that plural second person objects always have to be explicitly expressed with verbs conjugated for the *-lak/-lek* form.

(150)   *Ne*   *búj-ja-tok*   *el!*   *Lát-lak*   *titeket/*pro.*
        not   hide-IMPL-2PL   PRT   see-2OBJ.1SG   [you$_{PL}$-ACC]
        'Don't hide! I see you$_{pl}$.'[7]

As has been mentioned in Section 4.2.1, H. Molnár (1962: 157) and Pete (1998: 140) also argue that the verbs conjugated for the *-lak/-lek* form cannot be used with lexically unrealised plural second person direct object arguments. However, my intuition and other native speakers' intuition contradict H. Molnár's (1962: 157) and Pete's (1998: 140) opinion as they differ from Kugler's (2000b: 110) and É. Kiss's (2012) intuition. Thus, according to my intuition as well as that of other Hungarian native speakers, (149c) and the second utterance in (150) are also grammatical and acceptable when *szeretlek* 'I love you' and *látlak* 'I can see you' occur with an implicit plural second person personal object pronoun [*titeket* 'you. PL.ACC'] (see also (101) in Section 4.2.1). However, it must be noted that there are Hungarian native speakers whose intuition considers (149c) and the second utterance (150) questionable, i.e. these native speakers evaluate these occurrences as neither absolutely acceptable nor totally unacceptable. However, if we perform a thought experiment and situate *szeretlek [titeket]* 'I love [you.PL.ACC]' and *látlak [titeket]* 'I can see [you.PL.ACC]' in a particular context, the native speakers in question change their acceptability evaluations from questionable to acceptable; see (151) and (152), respectively.

(151)   (Children are playing hide-and-seek. The children, whose turn it is to hide, are hesitating where to hide, and so they are running out of time. The boy who finishes the counting, says:)

Ne	*bújjatok*		*el!*	*Látlak*		*[titeket].*
not	hide.IMPL.INDEF.2PL	PVB	see.1SG.2OBJ	you.PL.ACC		

'Don't hide! I can see [you.PL.ACC].'

(152)   (Grandchildren are behaving terribly; they are shouting and quarrelling with each other. The grandfather punishes them. The grandchildren become frightened and grow sad. After a while the grandfather says:)

Gyertek	*ide*	*gyorsan!*	*Szeretlek*	*ám*	*[titeket],*
come.IMPL.INDEF.2PL	here	quickly	love.1SG.2OBJ	really	you.PL.ACC

nincs	*semmi*	*probléma.*
not.is.INDEF	nothing	problem.NOM

'Come here quickly. I do love [you.PL.ACC], there is no problem.'

In (151) and (152) the contexts support the interpretation that *látlak* 'I can see you' and *szeretlek* 'I love you' occur with zero plural second person pronouns [*titeket* 'you.PL.ACC']. The implicit plural second person subject indicated by the verbal inflection of the verbs can serve as an antecedent for the zero objects of *látlak* and *szeretlek* in the discourse context c_{disc}. However, it is worth emphasising that if we imagine the contexts described above without the first utterances, *Látlak [titeket]* 'I can see you.PL.ACC' and *Szeretlek ám [titeket]* 'I really love you.PL.ACC' remain grammatical and acceptable with a zero plural second object reading. Thus, the physical context c_{phys} and the encyclopaedic context c_{enc} with information about the rules of the game *hide-and-seek* are strong enough to license the occurrence of the zero plural second person object with the *-lak/-lek* inflection.

If we take the verbs *megkeres* 'PVB.seek' and *megtalál* 'PVB.find' which are semantically related to the verb *elbújik* 'PVB.hide' into consideration and replace the verb *lát* 'see' with them in the second utterance in (150), the resulting utterances are quite acceptable without a larger context, e.g. without the situation of the game *hide-and-seek*. Consider (153) and (154).

(153) *Ne* *bújjatok*   *el!*   *Megkereslek*   *[titeket]*.
       not   hide.IMPL.INDEF.2PL   PVB   PVB.seek.1SG.2OBJ   you.PL.ACC
       'Don't hide! I'll look for [you.PL.ACC].'

(154) *Ne* *bújjatok*   *el!*   *Megtalállak*   *[titeket]*.
       not   hide.IMPL.INDEF.2PL   PVB   PVB.find.1SG.2OBJ   you.PL.ACC
       'Don't hide! I'll find [you.PL.ACC].'

The semantic relations between *elbújik* 'PVB.hide', *megkeres* 'PVB.seek', and *megtalál* 'PVB.find' can also support the plural second person object reading of the implicit direct object argument in (153) and (154). The verb *elbújik* 'PVB.hide' is used without a lexically realised plural second person subject argument which is indicated by the verbal inflection. This implicit plural second person subject argument can serve as an antecedent for the zero object argument of the verbs *megkereslek* 'PVB.seek.1SG.2OBJ' and *megtalállak* 'PVB.find.1SG.2OBJ' in (153) and (154). The semantic relation between these verbs can strengthen this reading, i.e. *megkereslek* and *megtalállak* occur with implicit plural second person object pronoun [*titeket* 'you.PL.ACC']. The implicit plural second person object in (153) and (154) can be treated as a manifestation of the anaphoric object pro-drop. However, from another point of view, it can also be considered an exophoric, or, in other words, deictic, zero object pronoun whose referent can be identified extralinguistically with the actual hearers. In (153) and (154) we can see that the occurrence of the *-lak/-lek* form with an implicit direct object argument is influenced by the anaphoric relations in subsequent utterances, and the anaphoric reading is supported by the lexical-semantic properties of the verbs which are conjugated for the *-lak/-lek* form.

Let us return to the situations in (151) and (152) and modify them using the verbs *lát* 'see' and *szeret* 'love' with third person subjects. Consider (155) and (156).

(155) (Children are playing hide-and-seek. The children, whose turn it is to hide, are hesitating where to hide, and so they are running out of time. The boy, who finishes the counting, begins looking and can see other children not hiding. A girl realises that the boy who has begun looking can see them:)

Ne bújjatok   el! Lát   [titeket].

not hide.IMPL.INDEF.2PL PVB sees.INDEF you.PL.ACC

'Don't hide! He can see [you.PL.ACC].'

(156) (Children are behaving terribly; they are shouting at their mother. The grandfather punishes them. The children become frightened and grow sad. After a while the mother says:)

Szaladjatok   oda gyorsan nagypapához! Szeret   ám

run.IMPL.INDEF.2PL there quickly grandfather.ALL loves.INDEF really

[titeket], nincs   semmi probléma.

[you.PL.ACC] not.is.INDEF nothing problem.NOM

'Run there to the grandfather quickly. He does love [you.PL.ACC], there is no problem.'

The occurrence of the verbs *lát* 'see' and *szeret* 'love' with an implicit plural second person object pronoun in (155) and (156) also attest that in Hungarian language use it is not only the singular second person object pronoun which can be dropped but the plural one as well. Furthermore, similar analysis can be provided in the other forms of indefinite conjugation, which can be used with second person objects, i.e. in plural first person and third person forms.

Let us modify the situations again. Consider (157) and (158), where the implicit direct object arguments of the verbs *látnak* 'see.INDEF.3PL' and *szeretnek* 'love.INDEF.3PL' are coreferential with the implicit plural second person pronominal subjects in the first utterances. Thus, they can be considered zero second person anaphoric pronominal objects.

(157) (Children are playing hide-and-seek. The children, whose turn it is to hide, are hesitating where to hide, and so they are running out of time. The boys, who finish the counting, begin to look and can see other children not hiding. A girl realises that the boys who have begun looking can see them:)

Ne bújjatok   el! Látnak   [titeket].

not hide.IMPL.INDEF.2PL PVB see.INDEF.3PL [you.PL.ACC]

'Don't hide! They can see [you.PL.ACC].'

(158) (Children are behaving terribly; they are shouting at their mother and grandmother. The grandfather punishes them. The children become frightened and grow sad. After a while the grandfather says:)

> *Szaladjatok*   *oda*   *gyorsan*   *anyához*   *és*   *nagymamához!*
> run.IMPL.INDEF.2PL   there   quickly   mother.ALL   and   grandmother.ALL
>
> *Szeretnek*   *ám*   *[titeket],*   *nincs*   *semmi*   *probléma*
> love.INDEF.3PL   really   you.PL.ACC   not.is.INDEF   nothing   problem.NOM
>
> 'Run there to mum and grandma quickly. They do love [you.PL.ACC], there is no problem.'

And finally, let us modify the situations once more and use the verbs *lát* 'see' and *szeret* 'love' with plural first person subjects and plural zero second person anaphoric pronominal objects which are coreferential with the implicit plural second person pronominal subjects in the first utterances. Consider (159) and (160).

(159)   (Children are playing hide-and-seek. The children, whose turn it is to hide, are hesitating where to hide, and so they are running out of time. The boys, who finish the counting, begin to look and can see other children not hiding. They say:)

> *Ne*   *bújjatok*   *el!*   *Látunk*   *[titeket].*
> not   hide.IMPL.INDEF.2PL   PVB   see.INDEF.1PL   you.PL.ACC
>
> 'Don't hide! We can see [you.PL.ACC].'

(160)   (Children are behaving terribly; they are shouting at their mother. The grandfather punishes them. The children become frightened and grow sad. After a while the mother says:)

> *Szaladjatok*   *ide*   *gyorsan!*   *Szeretünk*   *ám*   *[titeket],*
> run.IMPL.INDEF.2PL   here   quickly   love.INDEF.1PL   really   you.PL.ACC
>
> *nincs*   *semmi*   *probléma.*
> not.is.INDEF   nothing   problem.NOM
>
> 'Run here, quickly. We do love [you.PL.ACC], there is no problem.'

To summarise: the analyses of the utterances in (151)–(160), based on my own and other native speakers' intuition, as well as thought experiments in which the situations were systematically modified, attest that plural second person pronominal objects can also be dropped in Hungarian language use if the contextual factors and/or anaphoric relations in subsequent utterances license it. If a verb conjugated for the *-lak/-lek* form occurs without an overt second person object, the interpretation of the zero object as a singular second person pronominal object can only be considered a default reading predicted by grammar in the absence of a specific context, similarly to the case of the singular and plural first and third person forms of the indefinite conjugation. However, in particular contexts verbs conjugated for the indefinite form in the first and third person can also occur with plural second person pronominal objects as in (155)–(160). Thus, in particular contexts the singular second person pronominal object interpretation of the implicit direct object argument of the verbs conjugated for the *-lak/-lek* (i.e. first person subject with second person object) form and indefinite forms (singular and plural third person subject as well as singular and plural first subject with second person object) predicted by the sentence grammatical constraint assumed by H. Molnár (1962: 157), Pete (1998: 140), Kugler (2000b: 110), and É. Kiss (2012) can be overridden by contextual factors.

One can see that, on the basis of the analyses of *-lak/-lek* cited and presented above, two inconsistent hypotheses can be formulated at this stage of research: (i) transitive verbs inflected for *-lak/-lek* cannot occur with null plural second person object pronouns, and (ii) transitive verbs inflected for *-lak/-lek* can occur with null plural second person object pronouns. The first hypothesis is supported by H. Molnár's (1962: 157), Pete's (1998: 140), Kugler's (2000b: 110), and É. Kiss's (2012) intuitions and analyses as direct sources. The second hypothesis is supported by the following direct sources: my intuition and that of some other native speakers; furthermore, my systematic analyses through thought experiments.

Let us introduce a new direct data source into the research, namely, the Hungarian National Corpus (corpus.nytud.hu/mnsz), and check whether there are occurrences of verbs conjugated for the *-lak/-lek* form with zero plural second person objects. If the search is successful, the corpus data can help to eliminate the above-mentioned inconsistency and strengthen the plausibility of the second hypothesis. In the Hungarian National Corpus we do indeed find occurrences of verbs conjugated for the *-lak/-lek* form with zero plural second person object pronouns. Consider, e.g., *látlak* 'I can see you.PL' in (161), *szeretlek* 'I love you.PL' in (162), *utolérlek* 'I catch up on you.PL' in (163), and *megpofozlak* 'I slap you.PL' in (164).

(161)   *Eltévedt   madaraim$_i$,   látlak   [titeket$_i$],   látlak*
        PVB.lost   my birds.NOM   see.1SG.2OBJ   you.PL.ACC   see.1SG.2OBJ
        [titeket$_i$].
        you.PL.ACC
        'My lost birds, I can see [you.PL.ACC], I can see [you.PL.ACC].'

(162)   a. *ha   a   szüleidnek   mondod: Anya$_i$,   Apa$_i$,*
            if   the   your.parents.DAT   say.DEF.2SG   Mum.NOM   Dad.NOM

            szeretlek   [titeket$_i$],   amögött   az   van,   hogy   szeretd,
            love.1SG.2OBJ   you.PL.ACC   behind.it   that   is   that   love.DEF.2SG

> *ha   gondoskodnak   rólad.*
> if   take.care.INDEF.3SG   about.you
> 'if you say to your parents: Mum, Dad, I love [you.PL.ACC], you really mean that you like it when they take care of you.'

   b. *Ági,   Margit,   Kati,   hol   vagytok   [Ø_{subj i}]?*
       Ági.NOM   Margit.NOM   Kati.NOM   where   are.INDEF.2.SG

   Szeretlek   [titeket_i]!
   love.1SG.2OBJ   you.PL.ACC
   'Ági, Margit, Kati, where are [you.PL.NOM]? I love [you.PL.ACC].'

(163) *Megálljatok   [Ø_{subj i}] gyalog   is   utolérlek*
       PVB.stop.IMP.INDEF.2PL   on foot   also   catch.up.on.1SG.2OBJ

   [titeket_i]   és   lesz   nemulass!,
   you.PL.ACC   and   will   hell.to.pay
   'Stop, I will catch [you.PL.ACC] up on foot, too, and there will be hell to pay.'

(164) *Na   most   már   elég   legyen,   hagyjátok*
       so   now   already   enough   be.IMP.INDEF3.SG   stop.IMP.DEF.2SG

   [Ø_{subj i}] abba,   mert   megpofozlak   [titeket_i].
               PVB   because   PVB.slap.1SG.2OBJ   you.PL.ACC
   'Now that's enough already; stop, otherwise I will slap [you.PL.ACC].'

The occurrence of the verbs *látlak* 'see.1SG.2OBJ', *szeretlek* 'love.1SG.2OBJ', *utolérlek* 'catch.up.on.1SG.2OBJ', and *megpofozlak* 'PVB.slap.1SG.2OBJ' with zero plural second person objects in the cited extracts from the Hungarian National Corpus can also be analysed as anaphoric null plural second person pronominal objects which are coreferential with their coindexed antecedents in the first part of the utterance or in the previous utterance. While in (161)–(162) the antecedents are lexicalised forms, in (163)–(164) they are left implicit and indicated by the verbal inflections. However, the zero plural second person objects in (161)–(164) can also be analysed as zero exophoric objects since they also refer extralinguistically to the partners of the communicators.

These corpus occurrences also support the second hypothesis according to which transitive verbs inflected for *-lak/-lek* can occur with null plural second person object pronouns. So, in addition to the above enumerated direct sources, the second hypothesis is also supported by the newly introduced direct source, the Hungarian National Corpus. Therefore a higher plausibility value can be assigned to it.

On the basis of corpus occurrences, the following plausible statement can be formulated, which can serve as strong evidence for the second hypothesis and against the first one (for strong evidence, see Kertész and Rákosi 2012: 178–185 as well as Section 4.1.1):

> The verbs *lát* 'see', *szeret* 'love', *utolér* 'catch up on', and *megpofoz* 'slap' conjugated for *-lak/-lek* form occur with zero plural second person objects in the Hungarian National Corpus.

Thus, on the metatheoretical level it can be concluded that the second hypothesis can be considered more plausible than the first one, and the inconsistency can be eliminated at this stage of research by deleting the first less plausible hypothesis.

The conclusion of the study at the object-theoretical level concerning the occurrence of transitive verbs conjugated for *-lak/-lek* form with second person objects is that their plural second person pronominal objects can also be left lexically unrealised if contextual factors and/or anaphoric relations license it (see also Németh T. and Bibok 2001). In Section 5.4, when I discuss the role of indefinite/definite conjugations in the licensing and interpretation of the occurrence of Hungarian verbs with implicit direct object arguments, I will return to some questions raised by the functioning of the inflectional morpheme *-lak/-lek*.

Finally, let us examine the use and interpretation of the verbs with implicit third person pronominal objects in Hungarian language use. É. Kiss (2012: 193) claims that, if in a Hungarian sentence there is no overt object and the verb is conjugated for the definite form, a singular third person pronominal object is assumed. Consider É. Kiss's (2012: 194) example with glosses used in the present book.

(165)   *Ismerem* pro_{subj} =*[én]* pro_{obj} =*[őt/azt]*.
    know.DEF.1SG I   her.ACC/him.ACC/it.ACC
    'I know [her.ACC/him.ACC/it.ACC]'.

In the case of animate objects, the singular third person object pronoun *őt* 'her/him' and, in the case of inanimate objects, the demonstrative object pronoun in the singular form *azt* 'it.ACC' can be dropped if their referents can be identified anaphorically in the preceding utterance and discourse context c_{disc} or extralinguistically from the physical context c_{phys}. Consider (166) and (167).

(166)   a.   *A*   *rendőr$_i$*   *elfeledkezett*   *a*   *tanúról$_j$,*
     the   policeman.NOM   PVB.forgot.INDEF.3SG   the   witness.DEL

bezárta		*pro~subj~ =[ő~i~]*	*pro~obj~ =[őt~j~]*	*az*	*irodába.*
PVB.locked.DEF.3SG		he	him.ACC	the	office.ILL

'The policeman forgot about the witness, he locked [him.ACC] in the office.'

b.

A	*férjemnek*	*tetszett*	*a*	*cipő~i~.*
the	my.husband.DAT	liked.INDEF.3SG	the	shoe.NOM

Megvettem	*pro~subj~ =[én]*	*pro~obj~ =[azt~i~]*
PVB.bought.DEF.1SG	I	it.ACC

'My husband liked the shoes. [lit. I bought [it.ACC]]'

(167) a. (The six-year-old child wants to go to his friend alone. The mother is worrying. The father says:)

Elkísérem	*pro~obj~ =[őt]*
PVB.accompany.DEF.1SG	her.ACC/him.ACC

'I will accompany [her.ACC/him.ACC].'

b. (The mother enters the room and realises that her daughter is reading in the half-light.)

Kapcsold	*fel*	*pro~subj~ =[te]*	*pro~obj~ =[azt]*,	*így*	*nem*
switch.IMP.DEF.2SG	PVB	you.SG	it.ACC	so	not

látsz	*pro~subj~ =[te]*	*[olvasni].*
see.INDEF.2SG	you.SG	to.read

'Switch [it.ACC] on, because you cannot see (to read).'

In (166a) the transitive verb *bezárta* 'locked.DEF.3SG' occurs with the singular zero third person animate pronominal object *[őt~j~]* 'her.ACC/him.ACC' which can be identified anaphorically. It is coreferential with *a tanúról~j~* 'witness.DEL' in the first clause. In (166b) the singular zero third person pronominal object *[azt~i~]* of the verb *megvettem* 'bought.DEF.1SG' is inanimate and its antecedent is the *cipő~i~* 'shoe' in the first utterance. In (167) the zero singular third person pronominal objects of the verb *elkísérem* 'accompany.DEF.1SG' and *kapcsold fel* 'switch.IMP. DEF.2SG' can be identified extralinguistically from the physical context. In (167a) the animate object *pro [őt]* '(s)he' can be identified with the six-year-old child. In (167b) the inanimate object *pro [azt]* can be identified with the light. The dropped pronominal objects in these latter cases are exophoric.

According to É. Kiss (2012: 194), the plural pronominal object cannot be dropped, since the plural feature cannot be reconstructed from the verbal suffix. However, she admits that there are plural zero third person pronominal objects in Hungarian in the second conjuncts of coordinated sentences and in responses to yes–no questions. They are licensed when their antecedent is an object in the previous clause, but they are not anaphoric object *pro*; instead, their use involves VP-deletion. Consider É. Kiss's (2012: 194) example with the glosses used in the present book.[8]

(168)   *Az   ismerőseimet   keresem,   de   nem   találom*   *[vp 0]*
          the   my.acquaintances.ACC   seek.DEF.1SG   but   not   find.DEF.1SG
          'I am looking for my acquaintances but I cannot find [them.ACC].'

However, we can find occurrences of zero plural third person pronominal objects when their antecedent in the previous clause or utterance is not an object, and so VP-deletion cannot take place. Let us examine the occurrences of zero plural third person pronominal objects in (169)–(174) which can be identified anaphorically, i.e. which are manifestations of the plural anaphoric object pro-drop.

(169)   *Kihűltek   a   sütemények$_i$.   Megettük   pro$_{subj}$ =[mi]*
          PVB.got.cool.INDEF.3SG   the   cookies.NOM   PVB.ate.DEF.1PL   we
          pro$_{obj}$ =[azokat$_i$].
          them.ACC
          'The cookies got cool. We ate [them.ACC].'

(170)   *Kérdeztél   pro$_{subj}$ =[te]   a   süteményekről$_i$.   Hát*
          asked.INDEF.2SG   you   the   cookies.DEL   well

          szétosztottuk   pro$_{subj}$ =[mi]   pro$_{obj}$ =[azokat$_i$].
          PVB.distributed.DEF.1PL   we   them.ACC
          'You asked about the cookies. Well, we shared [them.ACC] round.'

(171)   *Kész   vannak   a   fényképek$_i$.   Nézzük   pro$_{subj}$ =[mi]*
          ready   are.INDEF.3PL   the   photos.NOM   see.IMP.INDEF.1PL   we

          meg   pro$_{obj}$ =[azokat$_i$]!
          PVB   them.ACC
          'The photos are ready. Let's see [them.ACC].'

(172)   *A   hallgatók   felkészültek   a   vizsgákra$_i$.   Le   is*
          the   students.NOM   PVB.prepared.PL.3SG   the   exams.SUBL   PVB   really

          tették   pro$_{subj}$ =[ők]   pro$_{obj}$ =[azokat$_i$].
          passed.DEF.3PL   they   them.ACC
          'The students prepared for the exams. They really passed [them.ACC].'

(173) *Professzor*   *úr*   *beszélt*   *a*   *ppt-kről$_i$.*
       professor.NOM   mister.NOM   talked.INDEF.3SG   the   ppt-s.DEL

      Feltöltötte $pro_{subj}=[ön]$ *a*   *CooSpace-re* $pro_{obj}=[azokat_i]?$
      PVB.uploaded.DEF.3SG   you.SG   the   CooSpace.SUB   them.ACC
      'Professor, you talked about the ppt-s. Did you upload [them.ACC] to CooSpace?'

(174) *A*   *lottószámokkal$_i$*   *álmodtam.* $pro_{subj}=[én].$ *Sajnos,*
       the   lottery.numbers.INS   dreamed.DEF.1SG   I   unfortunately

      nem   *írtam* $pro_{subj}=[én]$ *fel* $pro_{obj}=[azokat_i].$
      not   wrote.DEF.1SG   I   PVB   them.ACC
      'I dreamed about the lottery numbers. Unfortunately, I didn't write [them.ACC] down.'

      Én   *viszont*   *olvastam* $pro_{obj}=[azokat_i]$ *az*   *újságban.*
      I   but   read.DEF.1SG   them.ACC   the   newspaper.INE
      'But I read [them.ACC] in the newspaper.'

Although the verbal suffixes in (169)–(174) do not mark the plural feature either, as É. Kiss (2012: 194) claims, the verbs *megettük* 'PVB.ate.DEF.1PL', *szétosztottuk* 'PVB.shared round.DEF.1PL', *nézzük meg* 'see.IMP.INDEF.1PL PVB', *letették* 'PVB.passed.DEF.3SG', *feltöltötte* 'PVB.uploaded.DEF.3SG', *felírtam* 'wrote.DEF.1SG.PVB', and *olvastam* 'read.DEF.1SG', conjugated for the definite forms, occur with plural zero third person pronominal objects which do not have object antecedents in the previous utterances, i.e. they cannot be analysed as cases of VP-deletion. The particular contexts override the evaluation predicted by grammar, i.e. these anaphoric occurrences are acceptable, since they are licensed by particular contextual information. It is worth mentioning that not only anaphoric plural zero third person pronominal objects can be licensed by contextual factors, but exophoric ones as well. Exophoric plural zero third person pronominal objects can be identified with the help of information from the physical context c_{phys} as in (175)–(178).

(175) (The teacher writes a lot of four-digit numbers on the blackboard. Then she says:)
      Adjátok $pro_{subj}=[ti]$ *össze* $pro_{obj}=[azokat]!$
      add.IMP.DEF.2PL   you   PVB   them.ACC
      'Add [them.ACC] up.'

(176) (The doctor distributes the written instructions to the patients. After a while he says:)

> *Megértették* pro_{subj} =[önök] pro_{obj} =[azokat]?
> PVB.understood.DEF.3PL   you.PL   them.ACC
> 'Did you understand [them.ACC]?'

(177)   (The mother baked various kinds of cookies for the birthday of her son who was living in another city. When she returned to the kitchen, she didn't find them. Her daughter realised her mother's surprise and said:)

> *Elcsomagoltuk* pro_{subj} =[mi] pro_{obj} =[azokat].
> PVB.packed.DEF.1PL   we   them.ACC
> 'We packed [them.ACC] up.'

(178)   (The husband receives his wife's ashes. He says:)

> *Szétszórom* pro_{subj} =[én]   a   hegyekben pro_{obj} =[azokat].
> PVB.scatter.DEF.1SG   I   the   mountains.INE   them.ACC
> 'I am going to scatter [them.ACC] in the mountains.'

In (175)–(178) the verbal forms *adjátok össze* 'add.IMP.DEF.2PL PVB', *megértették* 'PVB.understood.DEF.3SG', *elcsomagoltuk* 'PVB.packed up.DEF.1PL', and *szétszórom* 'PVB.scatter.DEF.1SG' conjugated for the definite form occur with plural zero third person pronominal objects which do not have object antecedents in the previous utterances, either. In other words, they cannot be analysed as cases of VP-deletion; instead, they have exophoric identification in the physical context. The deictic interpretation of plural zero third person pronominal objects in (175)–(178) occurs similarly to the interpretation of the zero first and second person pronominal objects discussed above, although the verbs they occur with are conjugated for the definite forms, while the verbs with which zero first and second person pronominal objects occur are conjugated for the indefinite forms.

Summarising the results of the analyses and theoretical considerations in this section, it can be concluded that in Hungarian language use transitive verbs can occur not only with zero singular pronominal objects, but with plural ones, as well, both anaphorically and exophorically. On the basis of a thorough examination of various kinds of examples, in Hungarian language use we can assume the existence of zero plural object pro-forms in all persons. Their use and interpretation are guided mainly by pragmatic factors, in addition to grammatical and semantic constraints. In many cases grammar cannot explain their occurrence; moreover, according to sentence grammar, they should not occur. However, particular contexts can override the grammatical constraints and license the use and guide the interpretation of zero plural pronominal objects. Thus, the investigation of zero objects in this section yielded the same conclusion as the research into zero pronominal subjects in Section 5.1.1. In other words, the use or interpretation predicted by grammar at sentence level can be considered only a typical, default one which emerges due to the absence of any specific context. In particular contexts this use or interpretation can be modified or even overridden.[9]

From the methodological point of view, we have seen that introducing new data sources into research resulted in strong evidence for the hypothesis that verbs can be used with zero plural pronominal objects in Hungarian language use, as well as against the hypothesis that they cannot. Thus, the integration of data from various direct data sources has strengthened the plausibility of the hypothesis that transitive verbs can also occur with plural zero pronominal objects in Hungarian language use.

After discussing zero anaphoric and exophoric objects in Hungarian language use, let us examine how the encyclopaedic properties of the immediate utterance context influence the use and interpretation of Hungarian verbs with implicit subject and direct object arguments.

5.2 Encyclopaedic properties of the immediate utterance context

Investigating understood arguments in English, Groefsema (1995: 152–160) claims that if a verb does not put any selection restriction on its arguments, the arguments can be left lexically unexpressed only if the rest of the utterance makes immediately accessible an assumption that yields an interpretation in accordance with the cognitive principle of relevance. As we have seen in Section 2.4, an assumption defined as a conceptual representation is immediately accessible (i.e. it is retrievable in one step) during extensions of the context if it is accessible from more than one conceptual address currently accessed, i.e. from conceptual addresses already present in the context and in the logical form of the utterance being processed (Groefsema 1995: 150). Sperber and Wilson (1986/1995: 72) define logical form as logical properties of conceptual representations. Logical form includes the logical properties that conceptual representations are both capable of implying or contradicting one another, and also of undergoing deductive rules. A logical form is propositional if it is semantically complete and a truth value can be assigned to it. Otherwise it is non-propositional, i.e. it contains free variables. These non-complete logical forms can be stored in conceptual memory as various schemas which can be enriched on the basis of particular contextual information (Sperber and Wilson 1986/1995: 73). Fully fledged logical forms of utterances, i.e. propositional forms, are composed from smaller constituents called concepts. In other words, they are a structured set of concepts (Sperber and Wilson 1986/1995: 85). Each concept has a label or address under which three types of information are stored, namely logical, lexical, and encyclopaedic. The logical entry of a concept refers to a set of deductive rules which applies to logical forms in which the concept at issue occurs. The lexical entry concerns the natural-language realisation of concepts, i.e. words or phrases which express them in languages. And finally, under the encyclopaedic entry the information about the extension of the concept is stored, or more precisely, various objects, events, and/or properties which contribute to the determination of the denotation of the concept (Sperber and Wilson 1986/1995: 86).

The immediate accessibility suggested by Groefsema (1995: 152–160) is also valid for concepts and is fully in harmony with Jackendoff's (1990) proposal according to which a lexically realised verb gives access to its conceptual representation during interpretation (see Section 2.3). However, Groefsema's proposal can only be applied with a slight modification. Let us set out from (179).

(179)   *Ági   [pénzt]   adott   a   koldusnak.*
        Ági.NOM   money.ACC   gave.INDEF.3SG   the   beggar.DAT
        'Ági gave [money] to the beggar.'

In Hungarian the verb *ad* 'give' places no selection restriction requiring that the direct object argument be of a particular type, or an instance of a particular type. However, the conceptual address of the verb *ad* 'give' and the conceptual address of the noun *koldus* 'beggar' make immediately accessible, for instance, the assumption that well-meaning, charitable people give money or some other donation to a beggar. Accessing this assumption results in an interpretation that is in accordance with the cognitive principle of relevance: 'Ági gave some money (or some other donation) to the beggar'. Ági's good character can also be inferred from this. A similar interpretation can be assigned to the lexically unrealised direct object argument of *ad* 'give' in (180) in a corpus occurrence which is cited from a Hungarian newspaper *Népszabadság* (24 December 1998, p. 3).

(180)   *Időnként   adunk   a   koldusnak,   még   akkor   is,   ha   ma*
        sometimes   give.INDEF.1PL   the   beggar.DAT   even   then   too   if   today

        már   legtöbbjük   piacgazdasági   profi.
        already   most.of.them   market.economical   professional.NOM
        'Sometimes we give to the beggar, even if nowdays most of them are already professionals in the market economy.'

It is worth noting that if in (179) Ági had given the beggar an atypical donation,[10] the speaker could not communicate this event by means of (179), as it can only be denoted by the utterance in which the thing given is expressed explicitly. So, because of the non-typicality of the 'donation', the direct object argument of *ad* in (181) cannot be left implicit.

(181) *Ági   egy   kifestőkönyvet   adott   a   koldusnak.*
Ági.NOM a   painting.book.ACC   gave.INDEF.3SG the   beggar.DAT
'Ági gave a painting book to the beggar.'

Taking (181) into account, Groefsema's (1995: 152–160) proposal requires a slight modification: an argument can be left implicit in Hungarian language use if the rest of the utterance in which the argument occurs makes immediately accessible an assumption whose typical interpretation is in accordance with the cognitive principle of relevance. To illustrate this second (B) manner of the occurrence of verbs with implicit arguments in Hungarian language use, consider some further examples:

(182) *A   Máltaiak   [pénzt/adományt]   gyűjtenek   a*
the   Maltese.NOM   money/donation.ACC   collect.INDEF.3PL   the
szegényeknek.
poor.DAT
'The Maltese (a charity organisation) collect [money/donations] for the poor.'

(183) *A   ferencesek   [pénzt/adományt]   osztanak   a*
the   Franciscans.NOM   money/donation.ACC   distribute.INDEF.3PL   the
népnek.
people.DAT
'The Franciscans distribute [money/donations] among the people.'

(184) *A   Vöröskereszt   [pénzt/adományt]   juttat   a*
the   Red Cross.NOM   money/donation.ACC   distributes.INDEF   the
rászorulóknak.
those.in.need.DAT
'The Red Cross distributes [money/donations] among those in need.'

(185) *Születésnapomra   mindig   könyveket   kapok   [a*
my.birthday.SUB   always   books.ACC   get.INDEF.1SG   the

rokonaimtól/   barátaimtól/   közeli ismerőseimtől].
my.relatives.ABL/   my.friends.ABL/   my.close.acquaintances.ABL
'I always get books on my birthday [from my relatives, friends, and acquaintances].'

(186)   A   nagymama   hétvégeken   mindig   [süteményt]   süt
      the   grandmother.NOM   weekends.SUP   always   cake.ACC   bakes.INDEF
      'The grandmother always bakes [cakes] at the weekends.'

In (182) the verb *gyűjt* 'collect' has no selection restriction in Hungarian on the direct object argument requiring it to be of a particular type, or to be an instance of a particular type. Furthermore, the other elements of its lexical-semantic representation do not restrict the set of possible referents for this argument either. However, the conceptual addresses of the verb *gyűjt* 'collect' and nouns *Máltaiak* 'the Maltese' and *szegény* 'the poor' make immediately accessible an assumption that, for example, the members of the Maltese order are well-meaning, charitable people who collect money or some other donations for poor people. Accessing this assumption results in an interpretation which is in accordance with the cognitive principle of relevance: 'The Maltese collect money/donations for poor people'. The relevant interpretation processed in the way presented here is the typical interpretation. If the Maltese collect something other than what is expected on the basis of the encyclopaedic information which the conceptual address contains about them, the direct object argument cannot be left implicit. Consider (187).

(187)   A   Máltaiak   képeslapot   gyűjtenek   a   szegényeknek.
      the   Maltese.NOM   postcard.ACC   collect.INDEF.3PL   the   poor.DAT
      'The Maltese (a charity organisation) collect postcards for the poor.'

In (187) the direct object argument *képeslap* 'postcard' of the verb *gyűjt* 'collect' is lexically realised. But if the direct object argument were left implicit, one could not recover it without extending the immediate context, i.e. the utterance context in which the argument occurs.

Utterances in (183) and (184) can be analysed similarly to (182). The lexical-semantic representations of the verbs *oszt* 'distribute' and *juttat* 'distribute' do not contain the kind of information concerning their direct object arguments that would restrict the range of the possible entities which these arguments can refer to. Therefore, accessing the lexical-semantic representations of these verbs alone does not yield interpretations in accordance with the cognitive principle of relevance, and the implicit arguments cannot be identified. So, the rest of the utterance has to be taken into account. The verb *oszt* 'distribute', the nouns *ferencesek* 'Franciscans' and *nép* 'people' in (183) as well as the verb *juttat* 'distribute', the nouns *Vöröskereszt* 'Red Cross' and *rászorulók* 'those in need' in (184) make immediately accessible assumptions that are very similar to the assumptions processed in (182). Thus, the implicit arguments in these examples can also be identified. If the speaker wishes to refer to something other than money or other donations, i.e. (s)he deviates from the default value, (s)he has to express the direct object arguments explicitly, because the atypical kinds of donations are less accessible, if they are accessible at all.

In (185) the direct object argument of the verb *kap* 'get' is explicitly expressed with the noun *könyv* 'book', but the adverbial argument is left lexically unrealised. The interpretation mechanism and the identification process of the adverbial implicit argument are the same as in the case of the implicit direct object arguments in (182)–(184).[11] The verb *kap* 'get', together with the noun *születésnap* 'birthday', makes immediately accessible the assumption that people get presents from other people on their birthdays, especially from their relatives, friends, and close acquaintances. This assumption leads one to the relevant typical interpretation: 'the speaker always gets books on her/his birthdays from the people who usually give presents to the speaker on her/his birthdays'. If the speaker gets books from a person that usually does not belong to the group of people one gets presents from on birthdays, then the argument referring to this person has to be lexically realised as in (188): it is not typical for most people to get presents from the Pope on their birthdays.

(188) *A   születésnapomra   mindig   könyveket   kapok   a   pápától.*
      the   my.birthday.SUB   always   books.ACC   get.INDEF.1SG   the   Pope.ABL
      'I always get books from the Pope on my birthday.'

When, in Section 4.2.4, we dealt with the prototypical structure of categories involved in selection restrictions, we saw that the object of the English verb *bake* has a prototypical structure. The Hungarian *süt* 'bake' can be used with an implicit direct object argument in the same way as its English equivalent. In the utterance *Mihály tegnap sütött* 'Mihály baked [something] yesterday' the zero object cannot refer to an atypical thing. In (186) the implicit object of baking has some further specification. The conceptual addresses of *nagymama* 'grandmother' and *süt* 'bake' make immediately accessible the encyclopaedic information that grandmothers usually bake cakes at weekends. It should be noted that the noun *nagymama* has a componential lexical-semantic representation, its meaning can be given by necessary and sufficient conditions: it can be decomposed as a female person who has at least one child who has also at least one child.[12] On the basis of this definition, one cannot identify the referent of the implicit argument in (186). However, the concept of *nagymama* has some prototypical properties. In other words, *nagymama* has a prototype: a kind, elderly lady with grey hair who can bake good cakes, cook chicken soup, tell beautiful tales, etc. In the context of the verb *süt* 'bake', cake-baking becomes active from among the prototypical properties of *nagymama*, and the implicit argument of *süt* can be identified with the cake.

Let us consider some other cases where the encyclopaedic information stored and immediately accessible under the conceptual address of lexical entries in utterances licenses the occurrence of implicit arguments.

(189) *Karácsonyra   általában   könyveket   veszek   [a   szeretteimnek].*
Christmas.SUB usually   books.ACC   buy.INDEF.1SG   the   my.loved.ones.DAT
'I usually buy books for Christmas [for my loved ones].'

(190) *A   szenvedélyes   bélyeggyűjtők   gyakran   cserélnek*
the   passionate   stamp-collectors.NOM   often   trade.INDEF.3PL
[bélyeget].
stamp.ACC
'Passionate stamp-collectors often trade [stamps].'

(191) *A   fegyőrök   szigorúan   büntetnek   [rabokat].*
the   prison.guards.NOM   strictly   punish.INDEF.3PL   prisoners.ACC
'The prison guards punish [prisoners] strictly.'

In (189) the direct object argument of the verb *vesz* 'buy' is lexically expressed by the noun *könyveket* 'books.ACC', but its syntactic dative argument is left lexically unrealised. The conceptual addresses of the verb *vesz* 'buy' and the noun *Karácsony* 'Christmas' make immediately accessible an assumption that people usually buy Christmas presents for other people, their relatives, friends, and close acquaintances, i.e. their loved ones. This assumption leads one to the relevant interpretation: 'the speaker usually buys books at Christmas for the people who get Christmas presents from him/her'. Thus, the implicit dative argument can be identified with the speaker's loved ones. If the speaker buys books at Christmas for a person who usually (or typically) does not belong to the group of people one buys presents for at Christmas, then the dative argument referring to this person has to be lexically expressed as in (192). Similarly, if the speaker thinks of a particular loved one, (s)he has to refer to this person explicitly, and this person must be lexically realised in the utterance. Consider (193).

(192) *Karácsonyra   általában   könyveket   veszek   az   elítélteknek.*
Christmas.SUB usually   books.ACC   buy.INDEF.1SG   the   prisoners.DAT
'I usually buy books for the prisoners for Christmas.'

(193) *Karácsonyra   általában   könyveket   veszek   az   unokaöcséimnek.*
Christmas.SUB usually   books.ACC   buy.INDEF.1SG   the   my.nephews.DAT
'I usually buy books for my nephews for Christmas.'

Let us return to the examples in (190)–(191). In (190) the direct object argument of the verb *cserél* 'trade' is left lexically unexpressed, i.e. it is syntactically missing. The lexical-semantic representation of *cserél* does not contain information concerning the direct object argument that would restrict the range of the possible entities which this argument can refer to. Thus, accessing the lexical-semantic representation of *cserél* with its argument structure does not yield an adequate interpretation by itself; the reference of the implicit direct object argument cannot be recovered. So, the rest of the utterance has to be taken into account. Encyclopaedic information retrievable from the conceptual addresses of the noun *bélyeggyűjtő* 'stamp-collector' and the verb *cserél* provides the assumption that stamp-collectors trade stamps. Therefore, the implicit direct object argument in (190) can be identified with stamps.

The implicit argument in (191) can be identified similarly. The conceptual addresses of the noun *fegyőr* 'prison guard' and the verb *büntet* 'punish' make immediately accessible the assumption that prison guards usually punish prisoners. So the syntactically missing direct object argument refers to prisoners.

My previous work (e.g. Bibok and Németh T. 2001; Németh T. 2001) concerning the second (B) manner in which Hungarian verbs can occur with implicit arguments mainly concentrated on the role of the encyclopaedic information immediately accessible under the conceptual addresses of the words included in the utterances in which the verbs themselves were involved. However, Németh T. and Bibok (2010: 509–510) also analysed the morphosyntactic properties of utterances which involve implicit arguments in the second (B) manner. If we examine the morphosyntactic properties of utterances in (179)–(193), we can realise that the verbs in these utterances are conjugated for the indefinite form as in the first (A) manner (see Chapter 4). What is the focus of attention is the pure activity reading of transitive verbs as in the first manner. Implicit arguments in these utterances do not have their own positions in the syntactic structures of the sentences uttered; they are not pro-forms. In other words, they are not zero anaphors or exophoric zero pronouns, so they do not have any antecedent or extralinguistic (deictic) identification in the physical context, respectively. Compare the utterances in (194).

(194) a. *Az   edző*   *[játékost]*   *cserél.*
           the   coach.NOM   player.ACC   substitute.INDEF
           'The coach is substituting [players]'.

       b. **Az   edző*   *cseréli*   *[Ø].*
           the   coach.NOM   is substituting.DEF

In (194) the verb *cserél* 'substitute' conjugated for the indefinite conjugation occurs with an implicit direct object argument. The encyclopaedic information under the conceptual address of the lexeme *edző* 'coach', according to which coaches typically change players during a game, as well as the indefinite conjugation, pro-vide the possibility of identifying the implicit direct object argument: players.

The utterance in (194a) can be handled in terms of a neo-Gricean pragmatic analysis by applying I(nformativeness)-implicatures as well (cf. Huang 2000: 163–173; Levinson 2000; Németh T. 2006: 251; Németh T. 2008a: 122; Németh T. and Bibok 2010: 509–510). As we have seen in Section 4.2.4, I-implicatures as a kind of generalised conversational implicature are systematic pragmatic inferences based on the typical background information. Relying on this typical background information, speakers can achieve their aims by using a minimal linguistic form without any special context, and the audience can complete the informational content of the utterance. The I-principle, as the principle of typical interpretation, yields an adequate interpretation combining the underspecified linguistic meanings of utterances and shared background information concern-ing regularities and stereotypes existing in the world. The implicit argument in (194a) can be identified by means of this kind of I-implicature. The minimal lin-guistic form of the utterance in (194a), i.e. the occurrence of an implicit direct object argument, induces a pragmatic inference that the situation must be typical; otherwise, the direct object argument cannot be left lexically unrealised. Since coaches typically change players during a game, the implicit direct object argu-ment in (194a) can be identified with players.

However, if the verb *cserél* 'substitute is conjugated for the definite form as in (194b), then the encyclopaedic pieces of information under the conceptual address of the lexeme *edző* 'coach' or the I-implicature that coaches change play-ers cannot license an implicit occurrence of the direct object argument of *cserél*. The definite conjugation requires a salient entity in the context (see Section 5.4). Since (194b) has no context with such a salient entity, it is unacceptable. Never-theless, if (194b) occurs in a particular situation with a salient entity in the dis-course context c_{disc} or physical context c_{phys} required by the definite conjugation, the utterance in (194b) becomes acceptable as in (195).

(195)   a.   (A father and his little son are watching a football match on TV. The son asks:)

        Miért   jön   le   az   a   játékos$_i$ a   pályáról?
        why   comes.INDEF   PVB   that   the   player.NOM   the   pitch.DEL
        'Why is that player coming off the pitch?'

        Az   edző   cseréli [Ø$_i$].
        the   coach.NOM   substitutes.DEF
        'The coach is substituting [him].'

b.   (A father and his little son are watching a football match on TV. They see that player number 7 is coming off the pitch. The father says:)

Az   edző   cseréli   [Ø].

the   coach.NOM   substitutes.DEF

'The coach is substituting [him].'

In (195a), in the father's response the verb *cserél* 'substitute' conjugated for the definite form occurs with a zero anaphoric pronominal direct object which is coreferential with its antecedent *a játékos* 'the player' in the son's question in the previous part of the discourse. In (195b) there is no discourse context present, the implicit direct object argument of *cserél* is an exophoric pronominal object licensed by the physical context. It can easily and straightforwardly be identified extralinguistically, since the player which the zero exophoric pronominal object refers to is saliently present in the physical context.

Summarising the interpretation mechanisms of (179)–(195), one can generally establish that the identification of implicit arguments appearing in this second (B) manner relies to a large extent on the encyclopaedic information stored under the conceptual addresses of lexemes used in the utterances in which the implicit argument in question occurs. According to the alternative analysis based on generalised conversational implicatures, the encyclopaedic information which licenses the use of implicit arguments with a typical interpretation is not yet built into the lexical-semantic representation of verbs but is induced as an I-implicature. Both explanations highlight the role of encyclopaedic information, but they differ as to the extent to which they consider it conventionalised. If we consider implicit direct object arguments used in this manner, the interaction between grammatical constraints required by the indefinite/definite conjugations and typical encyclopaedic information must be emphasised in the meaning construction of the utterances which contain them. This interaction has a crucial role in both alternative accounts, namely both in the explanation in which the encyclopaedic information is supposed to be stored under the conceptual address of lexemes in utterances, and in the proposal in which an I-implicature is assumed, since in both cases the verb should be conjugated for the indefinite form.

5.3 Extending the immediate utterance context

In Hungarian language use there are many occurrences where implicit arguments cannot be identified either by the first (A) or the second (B) manners. In Section 5.1 and 5.2, we have seen that there are cases where the immediate utterance context has to be extended with information from the previous discourse or the observable physical environment in order to identify zero pronominal subjects and direct objects. It is worth highlighting that, while a zero anaphoric pronominal subject or object can be identified without a context extension if its antecedent is involved in the same utterance, i.e. the immediate utterance context, a zero exophoric pronominal subject or object cannot be identified without a context extension. The immediate utterance context of a zero exophoric pronominal subject or object has to be extended with information from the physical context c_{phys}. These kinds of context extension belong to the third (C) manner, according to which an argument can be lexically unrealised if extending its immediate utterance context results in an interpretation consistent with the cognitive principle of relevance. In the third (C) manner the immediate utterance context of implicit arguments can also be extended with information from further encyclopaedic knowledge in addition to the extensions with information from the previous discourse and physical environment (for the methods of context extension, see Sperber and Wilson 1986/1995; Németh T. 2001; and also Sections 5.1 and 5.2). Now consider the conversation in (148) again, repeated here as (196) for convenience. In (196) implicit arguments can be identified in various ways by means of various context extensions.

(196)   (Santa Claus is distributing candy among the children.)

Santa Claus: *[mindenkinek]   Jutott   cukor$_i$?*
everybody.DAT   got.INDEF.3SG   candy.NOM
'Did [everybody] get candy$_i$?'

A child: *Az   öcsém   nem   kapott   [Ø$_i$].*
the   my.younger.brother.NOM   not   got.INDEF.3SG

[Ø$_j$]   Adsz   [Ø$_i$]   neki   is?
give.INDEF.2SG   him.DAT   too

'My younger brother did not get [any$_i$]. Will [you$_j$] give [some$_i$] to him, too?'

The mother: *Ne   izgulj,   neki   is   ad   [Ø$_i$]*
not   worry.IMP.2SG   him.DAT   too   gives.INDEF

a   Mikulás,   mielőtt   [Ø$_j$]   visszamegy
the   Santa.Claus.NOM   before   back.goes.INDEF

a   szánnal   [az   Északi   sarkra].
the   sledge.INS   the   North   Pole.SUBL

'Don't worry, Santa Claus will give [some$_i$] to him, too, before [he] leaves in his sledge [for the North Pole].'

In (196) one needs all three kinds of context extension to determine the referents of the implicit arguments. We have to extend the utterance contexts with information from the observable physical environment in order to identify the referents of the implicit recipient argument of the verb *jutott* 'got.INDEF.3SG' in Santa Claus's question, as well as the implicit subject argument of the verb *adsz* 'give.INDEF.2SG' in the child's question: 'everybody (around Santa Claus)' and 'you, i.e. Santa Claus', respectively. In both cases the identification of implicit arguments is performed extralinguistically, i.e. these implicit arguments can be considered exophoric zero arguments and not zero anaphors. However, in the case of the implicit subject argument of the verb *adsz* 'give INDEF.2SG' the verbal inflection *-sz,* which belongs to the indefinite conjugation paradigm, also indicates that the subject is a second person subject. Thus, it must be identical with the particular addressee in the speech situation, i.e. with Santa Claus. The implicit direct object arguments of the verbs *kapott* 'got. INDEF.3SG' and *ad* 'gives.INDEF' in the child's and mother's utterances can be recovered by extending the context with information from the previous discourse, specifically from Santa Claus's question. The noun *cukor$_i$* 'candy' in Santa Claus's question provides the necessary antecedent for the zero object anaphors [Ø$_i$] in the child's and mother's utterances. And, finally, to identify the implicit locative argument of the verb *visszamegy* 'goes back.INDEF' in the mother's utterance we have to take into account the encyclopaedic information concerning the location of Santa Claus's home.

Consider also the conversations in (197) and (198) from the spoken corpus referred to in Section 1.2.3.

(197)   (The subject is speaking about her relationship with her younger brother in their childhood.)

Nem	*voltál*		[Ø$_{subj}$]	*rá$_i$*	*mérges*	*néha,*	*hogy*
not	were.INDEF.2SG			on.him	angry	sometimes	that

te		*most*	*nem*	*mehetsz*		*oda,*	*ahova*	*akarsz,*
you.SG.NOM		now	not	can.go.INDEF.2SG		there	where	want.INDEF.2SG

[Ø$_{subj}$]	*mert*	*az*	*öcsédre*		*kell*		*vigyáznod?*
	because	the	younger.brother.SUB		has.to.INDEF		take.care.IN/DEF.2SG

'Were you not angry with him sometimes because you weren't able to go where you wanted to, because you had to take care of your younger brother?'

Dehogynem.	*Dehogynem.*	*Sokszor*		*előfordult [ ]^{13}*
of course	of course	many.times		occured.PAST.INDEF.3SG

és	*meg*	*is*	*szoktam*	*verni*	[Ø$_{obj\,i}$]	*érte.*
and	PVB	also	used.DEF.1SG	to.beat		for.this

Azon   töltöttem   ki   [Ø_{subj}]   a   bosszúmat.
that.SUP   took.DEF.1SG   PVB   the   my.vengeance.ACC
'Yes, of course. Of course. It happened many times and I used to beat him for this. I took it out on him.'

(198)   (The conversation is about the subject's unexpected pregnancy.)

És   sok   gond   van   egy   ilyen   gyerekkel,   egy   ilyen
and   much   trouble.NOM   is   a   such   child.INS   a   such

pici   gyerekkel,   ugye?
little   child.INS   right
'And, there is a lot of trouble with such a child, such a little child, isn't there?'

Hát   [Ø_{subj}]   mondom   én   már   majdnem   elfelejtettem   [ ].
well   say.DEF.1SG   I   already   nearly   forgot.DEF.1SG

Olyan   régen   volt   '77.   Hát   bizony   hogy   sok   [ ].
so   long.ago   was.INDEF.3SG   '77   well   really   that   many

Nagyon   sok   törődés   meg   hát   csak   övele
very   much   care.NOM   and   well   just   with.her/him

övele   kell   tényleg   lenni   pár   hónapos
with.her/him   has.to.INDEF   really   to.be   few   month.old

korában   csak   nem   [ ].
age.INE   just   no
'Well, as I say, I have already nearly forgotten about this. '77 was so long ago. Well, you really have to give a child a lot of care. (S)he needs so much care, and, well, you have to really be just with her/him, a few-months-old child cannot be left alone.'

Nem   lehet   otthagyni   [ ].
no   can   to.leave
'(S)he cannot be left alone.'

Csak   övele.   Csak   arra   kell   fordítani   mindent.
just   with.her/him   just   that.SUB   has.to.INDEF   to.devote   all.ACC
'You have to care just for her/him. You have to devote all your attention just to her/him.'

Hát   most   majd   [Ø_{subj}]   beletanulsz   újból   [ ].
well   now   will   PVB.learn.INDEF.2SG   again
'Well, you will learn it again now.'

In (197) and (198) to identify implicit arguments, the immediate contexts of utterances have to be extended. In (197) and (198) implicit arguments become accessible by extending the context with assumptions from the preceding discourse and by extending the context with encyclopaedic information. In (199) and (200) I put implicit arguments into brackets and use both the bold and italic font type. In the interlinear rendering, the abbreviation DISC marks those assumptions which make it possible to identify implicit arguments coming from the preceding discourse, and the abbreviation ENC signals that the assumption by means of which the implicit argument is identified is encyclopaedic (see also (136) and (137) in Section 5.1.1). For better transparency and clarity, I do not repeat glosses here, since they would be the same as in (197) and (198); I provide only translations for expressions in parentheses.

(199)   (The subject is speaking about her relationship with her younger brother in their childhood.)

Nem voltál rá mérges néha, hogy te most nem mehetsz oda, ahova akarsz, mert az öcsédre kell vigyázni?

'Were you not angry with him sometimes because you weren't able to go where you wanted to, because you had to take care of your younger brother?

*Dehogynem. Dehogynem. Sokszor előfordult [az, hogy mérges voltam rá*DISC*]* és
                                                    [that I was angry with him]

*meg is szoktam verni [őt*DISC*] érte. Azon töltöttem ki a bosszúmat.*
                    [him]

'Yes, of course. Of course. It happened many times [that I was angry with him] and I used to beat [him] for this. I took it out on him.'

(200)   (The conversation is about the unexpected pregnancy of the subject.)

És sok gond van egy ilyen gyerekkel, egy ilyen pici gyerekkel, ugye?

'And, there is a lot of trouble with such a child, such a little child, isn't there?'

Hát mondom, én már majdnem elfelejtettem

*[azt, hogy mennyi gond van egy ilyen pici gyerekkel*DISC*]. Olyan régen volt '77.*
[how much trouble there is with such a little child]

*Hát bizony, hogy[sok gond van egy ilyen pici gyerekkel]*DISC*.*
                    [there are many problems with such a little child]

*Nagyon sok törődés, meg hát csak övele kell tényleg lenni, pár hónapos korában csak nem [lehet otthagyni*ENC*] [egy ilyen pici gyereket*DISC*].*
        [can be left alone]   [such a little child]

'Well, as I say, I have already nearly forgotten about [how much trouble there is with such a little child]. '77 was so long ago. Well, there is really [so much trouble with such a little child]. (S)he needs a lot of care, and, well, you have to really be just with her/him, when (s)he is only a few months old [such a little child] cannot [be left alone].'

*Nem lehet otthagyni [egy ilyen pici gyereket*DISC*].*

        [such a little child]

'[Such a little child] cannot be left alone.'

Csak ővele. Csak arra kell fordítani mindent.

'You have to care just for her/him. You have to devote all your attention just to her/him.'

Hát most majd beletanulsz újból

*[abba, hogy mennyi gond van egy ilyen pici gyerekkel*DISC*].*

[how much trouble there is with such a little child]

'Well, you will learn [how much trouble there is with such a little child] again now.'

One can argue that encyclopaedic knowledge cannot be defined unambiguously and whatever is marked by ENC is only one of the possibilities available. This, however, does not present a problem for the analysis provided here: a speaker uses these kinds of implicit arguments if (s)he is convinced that there is a preferable identification of implicit arguments or the differences existing in the communicative partner's encyclopaedic knowledge are not significant.

It can also be the case that the extended context makes possible more than one interpretation for implicit arguments. The speaker intends to produce a verbal stimulus to which the hearer can assign the intended pragmatically acceptable interpretation. The pragmatically acceptable interpretation is the first interpretation which is consistent with the cognitive principle of relevance (Blakemore 1992: 74). Let us analyse (201).

(201)   (The subject is speaking about her childhood.)

Először   Kemenespusztán   laktunk,   fönn
first   Kemenespuszta.SUP   lived.INDEF.1PL   up

*Kemenesen.   Kilenc   éves   voltam   [Ø*subj*],   hogy*
Kemenes.SUP   nine   year.old   was.INDEF.1SG   that

*leköltöztünk   [Ø*subj*] onnét [ ].   Télen   ilyen   szekérrel*
PVB.moved.INDEF.1PL   from.there in.winter such cart.INS

hordtak   *[Ø_{subj}]* *még* *akkor* *bennünket [ ].*
carried.INDEF.3SG   still   then   us.ACC

'First we lived in Kemenespuszta, at Kemenes. I was nine years old when we moved from there down to the village. Then in winter we were carried by a cart.'

Iskolába.

school.ILL

'To school.'

Iskolába.   *Nyáron*   *vagyis*   *tavasszal*   *meg*   *kora*
school.ILL   in.summer   or.rather   in.spring   and   early

ősszel   *meg*   *biciklivel*   *jártunk*   *le [ ].*
in.autumn   and   bicycle.INS   went.INDEF.1PL   PVB

'To school. In summer, or rather in spring and in early autumn, we rode down by bicycle.'

In the second utterance of (201), the implicit locative argument *[a faluba]* 'to the village' of the verb *leköltözik* 'move down' can be identified by means of an encyclopaedic assumption – near to Kemenespuszta there is a village named Kemenesmagasi in the valley – to which the context is extended. In the third utterance, the encyclopaedically extended context allows several possibilities of identifying the lexically unrealised argument of the verb *hord* 'carry': e.g. *[a faluba]* 'to the village', *[iskolába]* 'to school', *[orvoshoz]* 'to the doctor'. The choice from between the possibilities *a faluba* and *iskolába* is motivated by what the relevant interpretation will be. If these two identifications are relevant, then one has to examine which of these two identifications will be more relevant, i.e. which yields more contextual effects. In the first case, the implicit argument can be identified with the help of an assumption which derives from the preceding utterance, and it will be coreferential with the preceding implicit argument. This latter implicit argument is already recovered because of the extension of the context with the above-mentioned encyclopaedic assumption. The repeated occurrence of this implicit argument in the third utterance results in the relevant assumption that the informant and her companions were carried by cart to the village. But the exact place and goal of movement are left unknown. However, if we choose the second possibility, the assumption that the informant and her companions were carried to school in the village is accessible. Extending the context with an encyclopaedic assumption identifies the implicit argument in this case: the children who live in Kemenespuszta also go to school. The identification of the implicit argument as school not only gives precisely the place where the subject and her companion were taken, but also means that the goal of the movement –

studying – is inferable from it. Since the choice of school yields more contextual effects than the choice of village, this identification is more relevant, i.e. it results in the pragmatically acceptable interpretation. In the exchange, the communicative partner asks for a confirmation as to whether her/his identification is correct by producing the utterance *Iskolába* 'To school'. We should note that the choice of doctor will also be relevant, but the conversation must be continued in a different direction. Similarly to (200) and (201), I provide the implicit arguments identifiable by context extension in brackets in (202) to illustrate the analysis.

(202) *Először Kemenespusztán laktunk, fönn Kemenesen. Kilenc éves voltam, hogy*

*leköltöztünk onnét [a faluba*ENC*]. Télen ilyen ilyen szekérrel hordtak még akkor*

　　　　　 [to the village]

*Bennünket [iskolába*ENC*].*

　　　　 [to school]

'First we lived in Kemenespuszta, at Kemenes. I was nine years old when we moved from there down [to the village]. Then in winter we were carried by a cart [to school].'

Iskolába.

'To school.'

Iskolába. Nyáron vagyis tavasszal meg kora ősszel meg biciklivel jártunk le

*[iskolába*DISC*].*

[to school]

'To school. In summer, or rather in spring and in early autumn we rode down by bicycle.'

Extending the utterance context of implicit arguments with information from the observable physical environment mainly involves pragmatic inferential procedures, but not exclusively, as we have seen in (196) in the case of the implicit subject argument of the verb *adsz* 'give.INDEF.2SG', where the grammatical decoding of the verbal suffix *-sz* results in the identification of the implicit subject argument as a second person subject identical with the addressee, and pragmatic inferential processes recover the particular person of the addressee in the particular physical context, i.e. Santa Claus.

Extending the utterance context of implicit arguments with information from the previous discourse also includes both grammatical decoding and pragmatic inferential processes. In other words, the recovering of the antecedent of a zero discourse anaphor is based on the interaction between grammatical and pragmatic factors as we have seen in Section 5.2. The identification of zero discourse anaphors by means of this latter type of context extension operates in the same way as the zero anaphor resolution in utterances. Thus the behaviour of zero anaphors in Hungarian language use is not influenced by whether the antecedent can be found in the same utterance in which the zero anaphor itself is located, or in the preceding discourse.

Extending the utterance context of implicit arguments with information from encyclopaedic knowledge involves mainly pragmatic inferential processes. If the consideration of the encyclopaedic information under the conceptual address of lexemes in the immediate utterance context which involves implicit arguments does not yield a relevant interpretation, the context can be extended with further information from encyclopaedic knowledge. We have seen this kind of context extension in (197)–(202).

Conversations examined in this section contain not only implicit subject and direct object arguments, but adverbials as well. As we have seen, they can be analysed similarly to implicit subject and direct object arguments. The analyses in this section focused on the types of context extension and not on the types of implicit arguments. As to direct object arguments identifiable in the third (C) manner, transitive verbs with implicit direct object arguments are conjugated both for the indefinite and definite forms. In the first two (A) and (B) manners, they are conjugated only for the indefinite form. In the next section, let us discuss and summarise how indefinite/definite conjugations participate in the licensing and identification of implicit direct object arguments in all three manners.

5.4 The role of indefinite/definite conjugations in the occurrence of transitive verbs with implicit direct object arguments in all three manners

In Sections 4.2.1 and 5.2.2 exemplifying the various types of occurrences of Hungarian verbs with and without direct object arguments, I referred to the two types of conjugations, namely, the indefinite and definite. As I have mentioned, the inflections of indefinite conjugations mark only the number and the person of the subject, while the inflections of definite conjugation also mark the person of the direct object argument in addition to the number and the person of the subject. Since intransitive verbs cannot have direct object arguments, they can only be conjugated for the indefinite form, which determines only the number and the person of the subject. From the objectlessness of intransitive verbs it follows that they cannot occur with an implicit direct object argument, either. In contrast, transitive verbs can be conjugated for both indefinite and definite forms, and they can occur with both explicit and implicit direct object arguments. Recall from Section 4.2.1 that – according to some Hungarian grammatical traditions – if a transitive verb is conjugated for the indefinite form, then only the number and the person of the subject is determined, as in the case of the intransitive verbs: *vár-ok* 'I wait', *vár-sz* 'you wait', *vár-Ø* '(s)he waits', *vár-unk* 'we wait', *vár-tok* 'you wait', *vár-nak* 'they wait' (Tompa 1961: 482). But if a transitive verb is conjugated for the definite form, then in addition to the number and the person of the subject, it is also marked that the action denoted by the particular verb refers to a second person direct object (*téged* 'you.SG.ACC', *titeket* 'you.PL.ACC') or a third person direct object (*őt* 'him.ACC/her.ACC', *őket* 'them.ACC', *a fiút* 'the boy.ACC', *a lányokat* 'the girls.ACC', etc.; Tompa 1961: 482; Velcsov 1968: 174; Bokor 1991: 254): *vár-lak* 'I wait for you (singular or plural)', *vár-om* 'I wait for her/him, etc.', *vár-od* 'you wait for her/him, etc.', *vár-ja* '(s)he waits for her/him, etc.', *vár-juk* 'we wait for her/him, etc.', *vár-játok* 'you wait for her/him', *vár-ják* 'they wait for her/him'.

However, as was mentioned in Section 4.2.1, there is another view in the Hungarian grammatical tradition which assigns the *-lak/-lek* inflections to the indefinite conjugation instead of the definite one on the basis of the parallelism between the forms *vár-lak téged* 'I wait for you' and *vár-Ø téged* '(s)he waits for you' (Kiefer 1998: 218) as well as the functional division of labour between the forms *vár-ok* 'I wait' and *vár-lak* 'I wait for you' (Kugler 2000b: 109). These two latter forms together indicate the types of direct object arguments which are separately selected by the other first and second person indefinite suffixes. For example, disregarding the possibility of the use of implicit direct object arguments, the first person plural *vár-unk* can occur with both a third and second person direct object, while the first person singular *vár-ok* can only be used with a third person direct object argument and *vár-lak* with a second person direct object argument. Pete (1998: 137) also considers that the *-lak/-lek* suffixes belong to the indefinite conjugation in addition to the two traditionally distinguished forms of indefinite conjugation for *ik*-verbs and *ik*-less verbs.[14]

The use of indefinite/definite conjugations in the case of transitive verbs is determined by mostly semantic and/or syntactic criteria according to the Hungarian grammatical tradition. If transitive verbs occur with an explicit indefinite object (see (a) examples in (90)–(94) in Section 4.2.1, e.g. *Mária egy kiflit eszik* 'Maria is eating a croissant') or they occur in verbal phrases brought under the same form as complex predicates in which the direct object argument is incorporated and not determined (see the (c) examples in (90)–(94), e.g. *Mária kiflit eszik* 'Mária is eating croissants' in Section 4.2.1), they are conjugated for the indefinite forms. Otherwise, transitive verbs are conjugated for the definite forms, i.e. if they occur with a definite object as in the (b) and (e) examples in (90)–(94), e.g. *Mária eszi a kiflit* 'Mária is eating the croissant' and *Mária eszi [Ø]* 'Mária is eating [Ø]'.

Syntactic constraints guiding the use of indefinite/definite conjugations in the case of transitive verbs do not need to be discussed in detail here, but it is worth mentioning that there are at least two approaches to this question in the Hungarian grammatical tradition (Németh T. and Bibok 2001). The first approach (Tompa 1961; Velcsov 1968; H. Molnár 1962; Rácz 1968; Bokor 1991; Kálmánné Bors 1991; Balogh 2000) emphasises the indefiniteness/definiteness of the object argument from a logical-psychological point of view, allowing that the first and second person personal pronouns are also definite, but that when they appear in the object position, they can be used with the verbal forms of the indefinite conjugation. Furthermore, as we have seen above, in the case of the first person subject, the verbal form occurring with the second person personal pronominal object is assigned to the definite conjugation by Tompa (1961) and Velcsov (1968). The polite personal pronouns (*ön* 'you.SG', *önök* 'you.PL', *maga* 'you.SG', and *maguk* 'you.PL') as well as the reflexive pronouns (*magam* 'myself', *magad* 'yourself', *maga* 'himself/herself/itself', *magunk* 'ourselves', *magatok* 'yourselves', and *maguk* 'themselves') also raise some problems. Tompa (1961) and Velcsov (1968) consider these pronouns in object position to be third person definite objects. Although the personal pronouns *ön* 'you.SG', *önök* 'you.PL', *maga* 'you.SG', and *maguk* 'you.PL' are logically also definite, and can be categorised as second person personal pronouns from the logical-psychological point of view, similarly to the second person personal pronouns *te* 'you.SG' and *ti* 'you.PL' (Temesi 1961: 240; Velcsov 1968: 44), they do not require the indefinite conjugation as do *te* 'you.SG' and *ti* 'you.PL', but rather demand the definite conjugation. Thus, in terms of grammatical agreement, they behave as third person personal pronouns. The reflexive pronouns can only be connected to the verbs conjugated for the definite forms independently of the person. Bartos (2000: 740) establishes that it is not trivial, either, that intransitive verbs must be conjugated for the indefinite forms. If the definiteness feature of the objects determines what kind of forms the verbs must be conjugated for, then – in the case of the absence of an object – there are no criteria to decide what kind of conjugation must be applied. Thus, the approach based on only the semantic feature of indefiniteness/definiteness of the object has not proposed a satisfactory explanation for the use of indefinite/definite conjugations; it is necessary to find another, more plausible account.

The more general and adequate syntactic treatment suggested by É. Kiss (1998: 89–91) and Bartos (2000: 753–754) differs from the approach discussed above, since it uses categorical differentiation rather than meaning differentiation in order to grasp the factors governing the use of indefinite/definite conjugations. In the case of objects in the DP category, verbs are conjugated for the definite forms, otherwise they require the indefinite conjugation. However, É. Kiss (2003) emphasises that, in accordance with Bartos's (2000) suggestion in the generative grammatical tradition, the first and second person direct objects cannot be treated as being more indefinite than the third person objects. In other words, there is no reason to consider that the first and second person personal pronouns are indefinite NPs rather than definite DPs. However, if the first and second person personal pronouns are also in the DP category, it is problematic why the third person verbs are conjugated for the indefinite forms with the first and second person personal pronouns in the object position (see (203)), why the second person verbs are conjugated for the indefinite forms with the first person personal pronouns in the object position (see (204)), and why the first person plural verbs are conjugated for the indefinite forms with the second person personal pronouns in the object position (see (205); É. Kiss 2003).

(203)   a.   *ő*   *lát*   *engem/minket*
             (s)he   sees.INDEF   me.ACC/us.ACC
             '(s)he can see me/us'

        b.   *ők*   *látnak*   *engem/minket*
             they   see.INDEF.3PL   me.ACC/us.ACC
             'they can see me/us'

        c.   *ő*   *lát*   *téged/titeket*
             (s)he   sees.INDEF   you.SG.ACC/you.PL.ACC
             '(s)he can see you.SG/you.PL'

        d.   *ők*   *látnak*   *téged/titeket*
             they   see.INDEF.3PL   you.SG.ACC/you.PL.ACC
             'they can see you.SG/you.PL'

(204)   a.   *te*   *látsz*   *engem/minket*
             you.SG   see.INDEF.2SG   me.ACC/us.ACC
             'you.SG can see me/us'

        b.   *ti*   *láttok*   *engem/minket*
             you.PL   see.INDEF.2PL   me.ACC/us.ACC
             'you.PL can see me/us'

(205)   *mi* *látunk*   *téged/titeket*
        we   see.INDEF.1PL   you.SG.ACC/you.PL.ACC
        'we can see you.SG/you.PL'[15]

As to the occurrence of the first person verb with the second person object, É. Kiss (2003) also considers the *-lak/-lek* inflection highly problematic and indicates that there is no consensus in the Hungarian grammatical tradition as to whether it must be assigned to the indefinite or the definite conjugations. É. Kiss

(2012: 194) goes even further, saying that the *-lak/-lek* suffix belongs neither to the definite nor the indefinite conjugation.

É. Kiss (2003, 2013) suggests a functional semantic feature of prominence for the object in addition to the categorical one in order to explain the problematic verbal agreement with the first and second person direct objects. She starts out from Comrie's (1980) observation concerning the inverse verb forms in some Siberian languages, namely in Chukchi, Koryak, and Kamchadal. On the basis of agreement between verbs and their subject and direct object arguments in these languages, Comrie (1980) formulates a principle based on the animacy hierarchy of participants in the events denoted by the verbs. The animacy hierarchy goes from the first person to the third person and from the singular forms to the plural ones. In other words, the first person is more animate than the second, the second person is more prominent than the third, and all persons in singular are more animate than persons in plural. The agreement between the verbs and their subjects and objects is guided by the constraint in (206):

(206)   Inverse agreement constraint: An object agreeing with a verb must be lower in the animacy hierarchy than the subject agreeing with the same verb.

Without going into details of this particular animacy hierarchy, it can be summarised that two strategies are applied in these languages to avoid a violation of the inverse agreement constraint (Comrie 1980): either an inverse prefix is connected to the verb or the verb agrees only with the subject, as if it were an intransitive verb.[16] É Kiss (2013: 8) argues that this latter strategy is applied in Hungarian as well. É Kiss establishes that in Hungarian the speaker is at the top of the animacy hierarchy, the other participants in the discourse are at the intermediate level, and non-participants in discourse are at the least animate level. In accordance with this animacy hierarchy in Hungarian, É. Kiss (2013: 8) formulates the Hungarian version of the inverse agreement constraint:

(207)   *INVERSE AGREEMENT CONSTRAINT* (for Hungarian)
        An object agreeing with a verb must be lower in the animacy hierarchy than the subject agreeing with the same verb, unless both the subject and the object represent the lowest level of the animacy hierarchy.

To obtain the inverse agreement constraint, the Hungarian language blocks verbal agreement with an object more animate than the subject, thus the definite conjugation is not available in cases involving the third person subject and first/second person object, the second person subject and first person object, and the first person plural subject and second person object (É. Kiss 2013: 9). Notice that these are the cases when a definite object occurs with the indefinite conjugation.

As É. Kiss (2013: 9) highlights, the inverse agreement strategy does not rule out agreement between the verb and the object in the case of the first person singular subject and the second person object by applying the *-lak/-lek* inflection in which the *-l* element can be conceived of as an object agreement morpheme on the basis of historical linguistics considerations.[17] Although the inverse agreement constraint in (207) correctly predicts the distribution of the agreement between objects and verbs, it does not reveal the motivation underlying the attested distribution (É. Kiss 2013: 9).

É. Kiss (2013: 9–18) attempts to clarify the function of the object-verb agreement by overviewing the relevant literature concerning object-verb agreement in Uralic languages and concludes that Dalrymple and Nikolaeva's (2011) proposal recovers the motivation underlying the inverse agreement hypothesis. Uralic languages originally have a typical SOV sentence structure, in which verbal agreement with the object marks the secondary topic role. In a typical Uralic SOV sentence type, the primary topic role is obligatorily borne by the subject. Since the subject always has a topic role, the object can only function as a secondary topic or as a focus, in the former case eliciting verbal agreement (Nikolaeva 2001). The inverse agreement constraint prohibits the secondary topic being at a higher level on the animacy hierarchy than the primary topic.[18] É. Kiss (2013: 16) argues that, although Hungarian is no longer an SOV language, it retains the inverse agreement constraint as a linguistic fossil. Without going into the details of the history of the marking of the secondary topic by verbal agreement in Hungarian as revealed by É. Kiss (2013: 17), it can be summarised that, when the secondary topic becomes marked by verbal agreement, the inherent primary topic status of the first and second persons was manifested as the inverse agreement constraint blocking the marking of first and second person objects as a secondary topic.[19] É. Kiss (2013: 17) assumes that by the end of the twelfth century Hungarian sentence structure had changed from the Uralic SOV sentence-type to Topic Focus V X*, and the topic was encoded by movement into a designated left-peripheral position. É. Kiss concludes that agreement between the primary topic and the verb grammaticalised as an obligatory subject-verb agreement, while agreement between the secondary topic and verbs grammaticalised as an obligatory definite object-verb agreement. In the case of the third person subject and first/second person object, and the second person subject and first person object combinations, the inverse agreement constraint fossilised as a gap in the definite object-verb agreement. Thus, taking into account both the changes in the grammatical encoding of the information structure of Hungarian sentences recovered by É. Kiss (2013) and the inverse agreement constraint provides a satisfactory explanation for the problematic cases in the verbal agreement system, i.e. why a verb is not conjugated for the definite form, but is instead conjugated for the indefinite form if it has a third person subject and a first/second person object, or a second person subject and first person object.

Although Nikolaeva (2001), Dalrymple and Nikolaeva (2011), and É. Kiss (2013) all highlight the role of discourse/pragmatic factors such as animacy/prominence/salience in the formulation of the Hungarian verbal agreement system, it is worth emphasising again that discourse/pragmatic and grammatical factors together, in an intensive interaction, can provide an account of the functioning of the object-verb agreement system in Hungarian. At this point it must also be noted that when Nikolaeva (2001), Dalrymple and Nikolaeva (2011), and É. Kiss (2003, 2013) rely on discourse/pragmatic factors in their generative grammatical explanations, they incorporate discourse/pragmatic factors into the grammatical account of sentences of language. Thus their practice also supports the view according to which grammar and pragmatics interact. This practice contradicts the latent background assumption of generative grammar which holds that grammar is an autonomous component of the human mind (see Sections 1.2.1 and 1.2.2).

Wéber (2011) and Tolcsvai Nagy (2014) also argue against the purely semantic or syntactic explanation of the choices between the indefinite/definite conjugations based only on the formal indefinite/definite nature of the grammatical object, taking into consideration functional, cognitive, and pragmatic factors. Wéber (2011) considers the two inflectional paradigms as functional alternatives based on the speaker's decisions. In other words, she supposes that the use of indefinite/definite conjugations depends on the speaker's intention(s) regarding how (s)he determines the object in the ongoing discourse. Wéber (2011: 189) convincingly argues that any account of the difference between indefinite/definite conjugations which is independent of the speaker's intentions and the functions of indefinite/definite conjugations in communication cannot be adequate. Let us consider, for instance, the indefiniteness/definiteness of the object, which has been preferred as an important feature in the majority of the literature so far. In Wéber's opinion, the indefiniteness/definiteness of the clausal object is the consequence of the speaker's determination of the object and is not merely a syntactic or semantic feature as, for example, Coppock and Wechsler (2012) and Coppock (2013: 345) assume. They suppose that if the referential argument of a phrase has a familiar/new lexical specification, then the [+DEF]/[−DEF] semantic feature is assigned to it and this feature also governs the conjugation. The feature of the indefiniteness/definiteness of the clausal object has been taken into account in the various approaches which concentrate only on the syntactic, morphosyntactic, and semantic properties of sentences and not on utterances of language use. Overviewing the literature, Tolcsvai Nagy (2014: 578–580) also concludes that there are explanations which, although they refer to semantic and pragmatic factors of animacy/prominence/salience or foregrounding, consider the contribution of these factors to the use of indefinite/definite conjugations only secondary, since they concentrate mainly on the formal properties of sentences of language.

If one takes into account utterances in language use, as Wéber (2011) and Tolcsvai Nagy (2014) suggest, a more complex approach can be formulated in the description of the two conjugations in Hungarian. Wéber (2011: 199) supposes that the main functional difference between the two inflectional paradigms can be grasped in terms of whether the speaker wants to direct her/his hearer's attention to a new entity in the discourse or a previously introduced one. Grammatical and pragmatic devices for making this functional difference explicit include the intransitivity/transitivity of verbs, the non-optionality/optionality of the object argument, the lexical meaning of verbs, the person of the object, and the discourse context. Notice that the functional differentiation of the indefinite/definite conjugations suggested by Wéber (2011) is based on the information structure of utterances in discourse. As we have seen above, Nikolaeva (2001), Dalrymple and Nikolaeva (2011), and É. Kiss (2003, 2013) also emphasise the role of the information structure, but they attempt to describe the two types of conjugation in Hungarian in sentences of language, as is required in the generative grammatical tradition. However, since Nikolaeva (2001), Dalrymple and Nikolaeva (2011), and É. Kiss (2003, 2013) explicitly refer to discourse/pragmatic factors of animacy/prominence/salience, they de facto rely on utterances of discourse, though their utterances come from their intuition or some grammar book sources and always have a linguistic structure *ls* as do all well-formed sentences of the Hungarian language. Although Wéber's (2011) approach and the accounts proposed by Nikolaeva (2001), Dalrymple and Nikolaeva (2011), and É. Kiss (2003, 2013) differ from each other in their grammatical tradition and technical apparatus, they share a very important point, namely that they all consider the main governing factor of the functioning of Hungarian conjugation systems the information structure of utterances in discourse contexts.

Tolcsvai Nagy (2014: 580) remarks that all explanations in the literature treated above focus exclusively on the relationship between the subject and object in various building block models and do not take into account other complements. Instead of such models, he proposes a description which involves the investigation of the role of the broader complement structure of indefinite/definite conjugations,[20] in particular the conceptual domains of the non-subject complements known as landmarks in the network model of holistic cognitive linguistics (Langacker 1987). Tolcsvai Nagy (2014: 580) assumes that the two complex schemas in the case of first and second person subjects and objects are connected to subjectification, and in all persons to epistemic grounding. He considers a finite verb with its complements (2014: 581) a complex structure instantiated in utter-ances of language use. In their semantic structure, verbs include two schematic figures (Langacker 1987). These schematic figures are exemplified by nominals as the main participants of the event expressed by the clause in which verbs occur. One of the schematic figures is the primary one, which is the focus of attention and called the trajector. The trajector is construed in relation to the other sche-matic figure, the secondary one, called the landmark, within the temporal rela-tion of verbs (Langacker 1987; Tolcsvai Nagy 2014: 580). A finite verb with the indefinite inflection can take landmarks with various case suffixes (see (208a–d)) and can also occur in a clause which does not contain elaborated landmarks (see (208e)). However, if a finite verb is conjugated for the definite form, it obliga-torily takes a definite object (see (209a–b)). Let us investigate Tolcsvai Nagy's (2014: 581–582) modified examples in (208)–(209). The order of the examples and some complements have been changed here so as to have verb forms with the indefinite conjugation in (208) and with the definite conjugation in (209), and the utterance in (209c) has been added to Tolcsvai Nagy's list.

(208)   *Mit*   *csinálsz?*
          what.ACC   do.INDEF.2SG
          'What are you doing?'

    a.   *Várok*   *valakit.*
          wait.INDEF.1SG   someone.ACC
          'I am waiting for someone.'

    b.   *Várok*   *valamit.*
          wait.INDEF.1SG   something.ACC
          'I am waiting for something.'

    c.   *Várok*   *valakire.*
          wait.INDEF.1SG   someone.SUB
          'I am waiting for someone.'

    d.   *Várok*   *valamire.*
          wait.INDEF.1SG   something.SUB
          'I am waiting for something.'

    e.   *Várok [ ].*
          wait. INDEF.1SG
          'I am waiting for [someone/something].'

(209)   *Mit*   *csinálsz?*
             what.ACC   do.INDEF.2SG
             'What are you doing?'

   a.   *Várom*   *a*   *postást.*
         wait.DEF.1SG   the   postman.ACC
         'I am waiting for the postman.'

   b.   *Várom*   *a*   *soromat.*
         wait.DEF.1SG   the   my.turn.ACC
         'I am waiting for my turn.'

   c.   *Várom [   ].*
         wait.DEF.1SG
         'I am waiting for [someone/something].'

Tolcsvai Nagy (2014: 582) proposes that we examine the semantic nature of indefinite/definite conjugations by looking at the complement domains of Hungarian verbs. The functions of the two inflectional paradigms can be characterised by describing the intentionality/directionality in the verbs' inherent lexical meanings. The nominal which elaborates the trajector of the verb, prototypically the subject, directs its action toward the other figure, i.e. the landmark in the conceptually mapped event structure. In (208) the verb form *várok* 'wait.INDEF.1SG' occurs with the elaborated trajector, namely the first person singular subject complement in the nominative case, representing the speaker. Landmarks can be any entity which fulfils the conceptual constraints imposed by the verb *vár* 'wait'; syntactically they are object or adverbial complements, see (208a–b) and (208c–d), respectively.[21] In (208e) there is no elaborated landmark; syntactically the verb form *várok* occurs without any object or adverbial complements. Tolcsvai Nagy (2014: 582) emphasises that landmarks of *várok* 'wait.INDEF.1SG' are indefinite in the sense that they profile a non-prototypical thing; they are not necessarily identifiable for the speaker and the hearer. Although the landmarks of *várok* 'wait.INDEF.1SG' in (208a–d) – i.e. *valakit* 'someone.ACC', *valamit* 'something. ACC', *valakire* 'someone.SUB', *valamire* 'something.SUB' – can be non-identifiable for the speaker and the hearer,[22] this does not necessarily mean that they profile a non-prototypical thing. In the case of (208e), the verb form *várok* can occur with implicit syntactic complements precisely because its landmarks are not elaborated, since there is no need to elaborate them because they are not the focus of attention. The landmarks not expressed lexically must be a prototypical thing for the verb *vár* 'wait', otherwise they must have been lexicalised, as we have seen in

Chapter 4 (see also García Velasco and Portero Muñoz 2002; Goldberg 2005a, b).

In (209) the verb form *várom* 'wait.DEF.1SG' occurs with the elaborated trajector, i.e. the first person singular subject complement in the nominative case, representing the speaker. Landmarks can be any entity which fulfils the conceptual constraints imposed by the verb form; the syntactically obligatory landmark is the grammatical object supplied with the accusative case morpheme, while the other landmarks assist in the construction of the setting (Tolcsvai Nagy 2014: 583). The landmark syntactically realisable as a direct object in (209) must be necessarily identifiable for both the speaker and the hearer.

Tolcsvai Nagy (2014) also analyses the verb *vár* 'wait' supplied with the *-lak/-lek* morpheme. In the case of *várlak* 'wait.1SG.2OBJ',[23] the trajector is the same as with *várok* 'wait.INDEF.1SG' and *várom* 'wait.DEF.1SG', but the landmark syntactically realisable as a compulsory direct object is the particular addressee(s) in the discourse. This second person direct object can be expressed by the second person singular or the second person plural personal pronouns or it can be lexically unrealised (210).

(210)   *Mit*   *csinálsz?*
          what.ACC   do.INDEF.2SG
          'What are you doing?'

   a.   *Várlak*   *téged.*
          wait.1SG.2OBJ   you.SG.ACC
          'I am waiting for you.SG.'

   b.   *Várlak*   *titeket.*
          wait.1SG.2OBJ   you.PL.ACC
          'I am waiting for you.PL.'

   c.   *Várlak*   *[téged/titeket].*
          wait.1SG.2OBJ   you.SG/PL
          'I am waiting for [you.SG/PL].'

The landmark in (210) can be considered definite, since it is an easily identifiable participant in discourse for both the speaker and the hearer. Thus, following Tolcsvai Nagy's (2014) thinking, the *-lak/-lek* form can be assigned to the definite conjugation.

Focusing on the complement schemas of the verb *vár* 'wait', as well as their instantiations in the two Hungarian verbal inflectional paradigms, Tolcsvai Nagy (2014: 583–584) highlights non-symmetric functional differences which do not originate in the syntax; instead, they have a semantic nature connected to the landmarks of verbs. Of course, these differences have their impact on the elaboration of landmarks. The indefinite conjugation activates a wider and more variable semantic domain of schematic figures than the definite conjugation. For instance, the forms *várok valakit/valamit* 'I am waiting for someone/something' and *várok valakire/valamire* 'I am waiting for someone/something' are formal alternatives in the indefinite conjugation (see (208a–d)) without any essential functional difference, since the case suffix of both the object complement *valaki-t/valami-t* 'someone/something.ACC' and the adverbial complement *valaki-re/valami-re* 'someone/something.SUB' indicates spatial relations, according to Tolcsvai Nagy (214: 583). In both cases the process itself is profiled, i.e. the action denoted by the verb is the focus of attention and landmarks are less prominent. In contrast with this, the definite conjugation indicates that the landmark obligatorily expressed by the direct object is more prominent than the process (Tolcsvai Nagy 2014: 583), i.e. the focus of attention is not only on the action itself. Notice that the explanation for the functioning of indefinite/definite conjugations suggested by Tolcsvai Nagy (2014) is based on the same principle as the accounts of implicit direct object arguments suggested by García Velasco and Portero Muñoz (2002) and Goldberg (2005a, b) as well as the approach applied in the present book. These otherwise rival treatments are similar in the sense that they all rely on the speaker's evaluation of the situation, i.e. whether the speaker directs the hearer's attention to the action denoted by the verb, or to the participants of the action. In the first case, the action is considered more prominent, while in the second case the participants of the action are more salient. This direction of the hearer's attention on the basis of what information structure the speaker assigns to the utterance can be expressed linguistically by various tools. These tools involve the use of indefinite/definite conjugations and implicit direct object arguments in Hungarian.

Adding Tolcsvai Nagy's (2014) cognitive grammatical explanation to the above-discussed generative grammatical approach developed by É. Kiss (2003, 2013) and the functional treatment by Wéber (2011), one can compare these three rival approaches to indefinite/definite conjugations. It is worth emphasising again that, although their theoretical background and latent background assumptions are different, they share the view that the information structure of utterances motivated by the prominence/salience/animacy of the participants in the situation and the process denoted by the verb governs the use of indefinite/definite conjugations. Starting from the interpretation side, the indefinite/definite conjugations indicate what kind of information structure a speaker's utterances have if they include a verb conjugated for the indefinite or definite forms.

The indefinite/definite conjugations also have an influence on occurrences of Hungarian transitive verbs with implicit direct object arguments. If a transitive verb is conjugated for the indefinite form, it can be used with implicit direct object arguments, although not in the same way as when it is conjugated for the definite form. From the point of view of the interpretation, we can say that the indefinite vs definite forms indicate what manner of the occurrence of verbs with implicit arguments can be taken into consideration to identify the lexically unrealised direct object argument. In principle, the indefinite conjugation allows transitive verbs in all persons to occur with implicit direct object arguments in all three manners. Consider the utterances in (211)–(213) cited from Németh T. and Bibok's (2001: 88–89) study which is devoted to a detailed analysis of the influence of these morphosyntactic features in Hungarian language use on the occurrence of verbs with implicit direct object arguments. In these utterances the verb *lát* 'see' conjugated for the indefinite form occurs with singular third person subjects and singular third person implicit direct objects. However, as illustrated above in this section and Section 5.1.2, transitive verbs conjugated for the indefinite form of all persons can also occur with first and second person implicit direct objects.

(211)   *A*   *kéthetes*   *kiscica*   *már*   *lát.*
the   two.week.old   little.kitten.NOM   already   sees.INDEF
'The little two-week old kitten can already see.'

(212)   *Az*   *iskolás*   *szemüveget*   *kapott,*   *és*   *azóta*
the   schoolchild.NOM   glasses.ACC   got.INDEF.3SG   and   since.then
lát.
sees.INDEF
'The schoolchild got glasses, and since then she can see.'

(213)   (A naughty boy asks his mother.)
Honnan   *tudod,*   *hogy*   *mit*   *csinálok?*
from.where   know.INDEF.2SG   that   what.ACC   do.INDEF.1SG
'How do you know what I am doing?'

Tudod,   *hogy*   *anya*   *hátrafelé*   *is*   *lát.*
know.INDEF.2SG   that   Mum.NOM   backwards   also   sees.INDEF
'You know that Mum can also see backwards.'

In (211) the verb *lát* 'see' is used with an implicit direct object argument in the first (A) manner. The utterance in (211) refers not only to the physical act of seeing, but also necessarily includes the physical act of seeing something. The lexical-semantic representation of *lát* puts a selection restriction on the type of the direct object argument according to which it must be visually perceptible.

Thus, the little kitten can see the visually perceptible world around it. In (212) the implicit direct object argument of *lát* may be identified in the second (B) manner. The information stored under the conceptual addresses of the lexemes *iskolás* 'schoolchild' and *szemüveg* 'glasses' in (212) makes accessible an assumption about what and who a child should see in her/his school environment as well as another encyclopaedic assumption that glasses can correct inadequate sight. Following from these pieces of information, one concludes that the schoolchild who has got glasses can see the blackboard or the teacher. In other words, the lexically unrealised direct object can be identified with the blackboard or the teacher. And, finally, in (213) the implicit direct object argument of the verb *lát* can be identified in the third (C) manner. The immediate utterance context of (213) may be extended with encyclopaedic information about child care, i.e. with information that mothers automatically monitor the environment around their children, as well as from the physical context in which the mother suspects what the son is doing behind her back. Extending the utterance context with these pieces of information, the implicit direct object can include the son's naughty behaviour behind the mother's back.

However, not all transitive verbs conjugated for the indefinite form can occur with implicit direct object arguments in all three manners. The occurrences with implicit direct object arguments also depend on which group a verb belongs to according to the classification of Hungarian verbs in terms of the manners in which they can be used with implicit arguments. As indicated in Section 3.2 and Chapter 6, Hungarian verbs can be classified into three groups in this respect. These three groups generally classify Hungarian verbs independently of whether subject, indirect object, or adverbial arguments are taken into account. In other words, on the basis of their occurrences with all kinds of implicit arguments, Hungarian verbs can be classified into three groups in the same way. However, in this section I concentrate only on the classification of transitive verbs. Transitive verbs in the first group can occur with lexically unrealised direct object arguments in all three manners. Besides *lát* 'see' above, e.g. the verbs *eszik* 'eat', *iszik* 'drink', *takarít* 'clean', and *szánt* 'plough' belong to the first group (see also verbs in (106) in Section 4.2.2). Transitive verbs in the second group can be used with implicit direct object arguments in the second (B) and third (C) manners. For instance, the verbs *ad* 'give', *büntet* 'punish', *gyűjt* 'collect', and *cserél* 'change' are included in this group. As illustrated in Section 5.2, these verbs can occur with implicit direct objects in the second (B) manner if the encyclopaedic information of their immediate utterance context licenses it. Furthermore, they can also occur with implicit direct object arguments in the third (C) manner, if their extended context provides the information necessary for the identification of their implicit direct object arguments. However, considering zero object anaphors in utterance and discourse contexts, all transitive verbs can be used in both the second (B) and third (C) manners. The third group contains verbs which license implicit arguments only in the third (C) manner by extending their immediate utterance contexts (see the verbs *tologat* 'push' in Section 2.1, *elolvas* 'PVB.read' in Section 4.2.2, *beüt* 'PVB.punch' in Section 5.1.1, and *otthagy* 'PVB.leave' in Section 5.3).

The indefinite conjugation licences the occurrence of transitive verbs with implicit direct object arguments in interaction with the above typology of transitive verbs. If a transitive verb conjugated for the indefinite form belongs to the first group, then it can occur with implicit direct object arguments in all three manners. If a transitive verb conjugated for the indefinite form belongs to the second group, then it can occur with implicit direct object arguments in the second (B) and third (C) manners, and if a transitive verb conjugated for the indefinite form belongs to the third group, then it can occur with implicit direct object arguments only in the third (C) manner.

Various approaches to indefinite/definite conjugations treated above in this section share the opinion that the information structure of utterances intended by the speaker motivates what kind of conjugation is used. If the speaker directs the hearer's attention to the action denoted by the verb, it means that the action is more prominent/salient than the participants of the action. Therefore, the participants in the action can be left in the background. If a transitive verb is conjugated for the indefinite form and occurs with an implicit direct object argument, this lexically unrealised direct object is in the background and it can only have a typical interpretation, unless it cannot be left implicit (see Sections 4.2, 5.2, and 5.3). To put it another way, a transitive verb conjugated for the indefinite form can only be used with an implicit direct object argument if it is a typical one according to our encyclopaedic knowledge, which is either built into the lexical-semantic representation of the verb in question or is accessible in the immediate utterance context or the extended context.

If the speaker directs the hearer's attention to the participants of the action instead of the action itself, the participants are the most prominent/salient. The accounts of indefinite/definite conjugations discussed above agree that the definite conjugation requires the prominent/salient presence of an entity in the context. Following from this, verbs conjugated for the definite form can occur with implicit direct object arguments only if there is a saliently present entity in the context with which the lexically unrealised direct object argument can be identified. This identification cannot happen in the first (A) manner, since lexical-semantic representations of verbs cannot contain prominent/salient contextual information. Although they can constrain their arguments by selection restrictions, characteristic manners of actions, and prototypical structures of selected categories, they cannot include particular contextual information. The second (B) manner cannot identify a salient implicit direct object argument either, since it takes into consideration the typical encyclopaedic information stored under the conceptual addresses of the lexemes of the immediate utterance context. Transitive verbs occurring with lexically unrealised direct objects in this way are also conjugated for the indefinite forms, as I have attested to in Sections 5.1.2 and 5.2. The third (C) manner takes into consideration further, particular contextual information by extending the immediate utterance context of implicit arguments with information from the physical context c_{phys} or the previous discourse c_{disc} or further encyclopaedic knowledge c_{enc}. Thus, implicit direct object arguments with definite readings required by the definite conjugation can only be interpreted in the third (C) manner. This third manner can generally license Hungarian transitive verbs to occur with implicit direct object arguments, since all three groups provide the third (C) manner for the transitive verbs included in them.

The results of the analyses of the occurrence of transitive verbs with implicit direct object arguments in Hungarian language use can be summarised in the following four tables.

Table 1. The occurrence of transitive verbs in the first group conjugated for the indefinite forms with implicit direct object arguments

Singular/plural subjects	Verbal form	Singular/plural implicit arguments	Manners of identification		
			First (A) manner	Second (B) manner	Third (C) manner
1SG	*látok*	3rd person	+	+	+
1SG	*látlak*	2nd person	+	+	+
2SG	*látsz*	3rd person	+	+	+
		1st person			+
3SG	*lát*	3rd person	+	+	+
		2nd person			+
		1st person			+
1PL	*látunk*	3rd person	+	+	+
		2nd person			+
2PL	*láttok*	3rd person	+	+	+
		1st person			+
3PL	*látnak*	3rd person	+	+	+
		2nd person			+
		1st person			+

Table 2. The occurrence of transitive verbs in the second group conjugated for the indefinite forms with implicit direct object arguments

Subjects	Verbal form	Implicit direct object arguments	Manners of identification		
			First (A) manner	Second (B) manner	Third (C) manner
1SG	*cserélek*	3rd person		+	+
1SG	*cseréllek*[24]	2nd person	+	+	+
2SG	*cserélsz*	3rd person		+	+
		1st person			+
3SG	*cserél*	3rd person		+	+
		2nd person			+
		1st person			+
1PL	*cserélünk*	3rd person		+	+
		2nd person			+
2 PL	*cseréltek*	3rd person		+	+
		1st person			+
3 PL	*cserélnek*	3rd person		+	+
		2nd person			+
		1st person			+

Table 3. The occurrence of transitive verbs in the third group conjugated for the indefinite forms with implicit direct object arguments

Subjects	Verbal form	Implicit direct object arguments	Manners of identification		
			First (A) manner	Second (B) manner	Third (C) manner
1SG	*tologatok*	3rd person			+
1SG	*tologatlak*[25]	2nd person	+	+	+
2SG	*tologatsz*	3rd person			+
		1st person			+
3SG	*tologat*	3rd person			+
		2nd person			+
		1st person			+
1PL	*tologatunk*	3rd person			+
		2nd person			+
2PL	*tologattok*	3rd person			+
		1st person			+
3PL	*tologatnak*	3rd person			+
		2nd person			+
		1st person			+

Table 4. The occurrence of transitive verbs in all three groups conjugated for the definite forms with implicit direct object arguments

Singular/plural subjects	Verbal form	Singular/plural implicit arguments	Manners of identification		
			First (A) manner	Second (B) manner	Third (C) manner
1SG	*látom*	3rd person			+
	cserélem				+
	tologatom[1]				+
2SG	*látod*	3rd person			+
3SG	*látja*	3rd person			+
1PL	*látjuk*	3rd person			+
2PL	*látjátok*	3rd person			+
3PL	*látják*	3rd person			+

1. The verbs *lát, cserél,* and *tologat* behave in all persons in the same way, therefore, I only provide the suitable forms of *lát* in all persons.

As to the interpretation mechanisms, it can be concluded that if a verb is inflected for the indefinite conjugation, then we try to find the necessary information to construct the relevant interpretation, firstly, in the lexical-semantic representation of the verb, secondly, in its immediate context, and, thirdly, in its extended context. If a verb is inflected for the definite conjugation, then its implicit direct object argument can only be identified in the third manner with the help of the extended context.

CHAPTER 6

Summary and conclusions

In this final chapter I aim to briefly summarise the results and conclusions of the study reported on in this book. The main aim of the book was to discuss what factors can license occurrences of verbs with implicit subject and direct object arguments in Hungarian language use, as well as what factors guide their interpretation mechanisms. The individual chapters of the book had their own sub-aims, the achievement of which resulted in new findings in comparison to the previous treatments of implicit arguments in Hungarian (language use). By involving the term *language use* in brackets, I intend to indicate that many previous works on the use of Hungarian verbs with lexically unrealised arguments were sentence-oriented approaches. The object-theoretical and, at the same time, metatheoretical decision I took to study implicit arguments in language use had various advantages. Firstly, I could analyse implicit arguments in utterances in a complex approach, assuming an intensive interaction between grammatical (including lexical-semantic and morphosyntactic), general pragmatic, and particular contextual factors. Secondly, I could examine those occurrences of implicit subject and direct object arguments which were not available to the previous sentence-oriented approaches, widening the scope of the research into implicit arguments in Hungarian language use. Consequently, I was able to take into account data from those data sources (e.g. written and spoken corpora and thought experiments) which were not taken into account by sentence-oriented explanations, as well as integrating data from various data sources in the analyses. Thirdly, I was able to reveal the underlying pragmatic motivation of the use of verbs with implicit arguments and the guiding principle of their identification (see below in this section). Furthermore, I also reflected on my research from a metatheoretical point of view to shed light on how the methodological decisions necessarily influenced the process of research into implicit arguments in Hungarian language use and the formulation of conclusions. All these factors increased the explanatory power of the proposals put forward in the individual chapters.

After the introductory Chapter 1, in Chapter 2 I briefly overviewed the previous types of explanations for the occurrences of verbs with lexically unrealised arguments in various languages and different frameworks. I concluded that purely syntactic, pragmatic, and lexical-semantic explanations could not provide an adequate account. I agreed with current treatments that more complex approaches were necessary, treatments which took into consideration different factors in the licensing and interpretation of lexically unrealised arguments. By applying metatheoretical considerations based on Kertész and Rákosi's (2012) model of plausible argumentation, I examined complex frameworks to understand how they integrated grammatical and pragmatic constraints into their explanations, what common properties they had and how they differed in their latent background assumptions and theory formation. Although these rival explanations were formulated in different theoretical frameworks, I established that they could be compatible in some respects. Through this critical evaluation of the rival complex explanations, I prepared for the introduction of my approach.

In Chapter 3, I defined what I meant by implicit arguments and compared my definition to those of other researchers, indicating what approaches my conception was similar to and what approaches it differed from. I assumed three manners of occurrences of implicit arguments in Hungarian language use which were discussed in Chapters 4 and 5 in detail.

In Chapter 4, I investigated the first (A) manner of the occurrence of verbs with implicit subject and direct object arguments, i.e. I concentrated on the lexical-semantic properties of verbs in an interaction with other grammatical requirements, and general pragmatic and particular contextual factors. In Section 4.1 I first provided a new explanation for the occurrences of verbs of natural phenomena (e.g. *esteledik* '[for evening to] close in', *villámlik* '[for lightning to] strike', *havazik* 'snow', *szállingózik* 'snow softly', *esik* '[for precipitation to] fall') with explicit and implicit subject arguments in Hungarian language use. I started out from a wide spectrum of data from various direct sources neglected by previous approaches and attested that verbs of natural phenomena were not subjectless as the Hungarian grammatical tradition supposed. I proposed a rich lexical-semantic representation with a subject position for the verbs of natural phenomena on the basis of which their use with both explicit and implicit subjects as well as metaphorical and non-metaphorical occurrences can be explained in a unified way. Verbs of natural phenomena constrain their subject argument very strictly by means of selection restrictions, information about the characteristic manner of natural events, and the prototypical structure of categories. The lexical-semantic representation of these verbs can be interpreted in two ways. Either it is only the natural events denoted by the verbs which occupy the focus of attention, or their subjects do as well. When only natural events are the focus of attention, the subject arguments can be left implicit. This implicit subject argument can be identified with the information provided by the constraints the selection restriction imposes on the subject argument as background information. Given that what can fill the subject position is strictly or even uniquely constrained by the selection restrictions, the subject argument should not be lexically realised. Therefore, the economic and default occurrence of verbs of natural phenomena is their use with implicit subjects. At the same time, if the subject argument is also the focus of attention or the particular subject argument is not the prototype of the category required by the selection restriction, or the speaker wants to refer to a specific token of the category, then the subject argument must be explicitly expressed. Sometimes the background information in the lexical-semantic representation of a verb of natural phenomena cannot by itself permit an argument to be left implicit. In these cases the lexical-semantic representation of the verb interacts with the context. The suggested new analyses of occurrences of verbs of natural phenomena with implicit and explicit subjects proved more plausible than the previous occurrences, on the basis of the newly introduced data from various direct sources as well as on the basis of the theoretical solutions applied.

In Section 4.1, I analysed another class of verbs as well, namely verbs of work (e.g. *vet* 'sow', *arat* 'harvest', *szánt* 'plough', *takarít* 'clean', *operál* 'operate on') which can be used with implicit subject arguments, not only because of the pro-drop characteristics of Hungarian, but because of their lexical-semantic properties and contextual information. I proposed two rival accounts for the subjectless use of verbs of work relying on the first (A) and second (B) manners. The first explanation assumes an encyclopaedically rich lexical-semantic representation for verbs of work which licenses their occurrences with implicit subjects in interaction with the particular context. The second explanation suggests a poorer lexical-semantic representation as well as an interaction between the pieces of encyclopaedic information stored under the conceptual address of verbs of work and other lexemes in the utterances. As to the first explanation, the encyclopaedic information concerning the type of subject argument is built into the lexical-semantic representations of these verbs as selection restrictions with which the implicit subject in the subjectless use can be identified in a particular context. As for the second explanation, the encyclopaedic information concerning the type of subject arguments has not yet been built into the lexical-semantic representations. Instead, the encyclopaedic information regarding the typical subject argument is stored under the verb's conceptual address which also becomes available in the course of interpretation. In this case, the verb's lexical-semantic representation, the general encyclopaedic information about the typical subject and the encyclopaedic information stored under the conceptual address of other lexemes in immediate utterance contexts interact in the identification of the unlexicalised subject arguments. The main difference between the two accounts is the extent to which the lexical-semantic representation and the context participate in the meaning construction of utterances.

The proposed rival explanations are advantageous and novel on several counts. Firstly, both can account for a subjectless use of verbs of work which cannot be accounted for by the pro-drop characteristics of Hungarian alone. Secondly, they treat occurrences of verbs of work with implicit subjects similarly to uses of verbs of natural phenomena with implicit subjects and also to uses of verbs with implicit direct objects (see Section 4.2). Thirdly, the suggested types of lexical-semantic representations reveal how and to what extent the general encyclopaedic information can be built in, and how particular contextual information influences the lexicalisation of the subject arguments in utterances. Fourthly, the analysis based on the three manners of the occurrence of verbs with implicit arguments can be extended to zero subject arguments which have been considered indefinite or general subjects in the Hungarian grammatical tradition, thus providing a new, more plausible analysis for them. However, comparing these two rival explanations, it can be established that the first account based on the first (A) manner has a greater explanatory power, since it can account for the subjectless one-word utterances including verbs of work, while the second explanation based on the second (B) manner cannot.

In Section 4.2, I turned to the examination of implicit direct object arguments, and investigated how the lexical-semantic properties of verbs license their occurrences and guide their interpretation mechanisms in an interaction with morphosyntactic constraints and contextual factors. As in the case of verbs of natural phenomena and verbs of work, I focused particularly on the role of selection restrictions, the characteristic types of actions denoted by transitive verbs, and the prototypical structure of implicit arguments which can constrain their direct object arguments very strongly. Transitive verbs (e.g. *eszik* 'eat', *iszik* 'drink', *vedel* 'swill', *süt* 'bake', *mos* 'wash') which can occur with implicit direct object arguments in the first (A) manner have a rich lexical-semantic representation which can be interpreted in two ways. If only the actions or events designated by the verbs are the focus of attention, the direct object arguments can be left lexically unrealised. The information concerning whether the arguments in question are of a particular type or a token of a type or a unique token involved in the selection restrictions can also be accessed as background information. In the case of verbs whose lexical-semantic representation involves a unique selection restriction placed on direct object arguments, these arguments not only can be left implicit but must be (e.g. *gyón* 'confess', *meggyón* 'PVB.confess' above).

Although the particular constraint a verb imposes on its arguments can be considered an idiosyncratic lexical-semantic property of the verb, the property that a verb places a selection restriction on its arguments predicts that the verb can be used with implicit arguments in the first (A) manner without a larger context. By itself, however, information stored in the lexical-semantic representations of a verb is not sufficient to license the verb's occurrence with an implicit direct object argument. One has to take into consideration morphosyntactic (indefinite/definite conjugations) and pragmatic (general pragmatic and particular contextual) factors to a necessary extent. Thus, the assumption that the use and identification of implicit arguments should be conceived of as a phenomenon at the grammar-pragmatics interface has also been proven in the case of the occurrence of verbs with implicit direct object arguments.

In Chapter 5, I turned to the second (B) and third (C) manners of the occurrences of implicit subject and direct object arguments in Hungarian language use and studied the influence of the immediate utterance context with its grammatical requirements and extended context. In Section 5.1, I examined, firstly, implicit subject arguments as zero anaphors, a kind of implicit argument with its own syntactic position in the structure of utterances, and exophoric pronominal subjects in utterance and discourse contexts. On the basis of the analyses of zero subject anaphors and exophoric pronominal subjects, I concluded, on the one hand, that the use or interpretation predicted by grammar can be considered only a typical, default one that emerges due to the lack of any specific context, and, on the other hand, that grammar (e.g. syntactic, morphosyntactic, and semantic constraints) and pragmatics (general pragmatic knowledge and particular contextual information from the observable physical context c_{phys}, from encyclopaedic knowledge c_{enc}, and the previous parts of discourse c_{disc}) interact intensively (perhaps, in multiple ways) in the licensing and recovering of zero subject anaphors and exophoric pronominal subjects.

In Section 5.1, I also studied zero object anaphors and exophoric pronominal objects. I introduced new data sources such as written and spoken corpora, my intuition and other native speakers' as well as my own, thought experiments. Relying on the results of thorough and systematic analyses of various kinds of examples and theoretical considerations, I came to the conclusion that in Hungarian language use transitive verbs can occur not only with zero singular pronominal objects, as the majority Hungarian grammatical tradition has stated, but with plural ones as well, both anaphorically and exophorically. In Hungarian language use we can assume zero plural object pro-forms in all persons. Their use and interpretation are guided mainly by pragmatic factors and grammatical and semantic constraints. In many cases, grammar cannot explain their occurrence; moreover, they should not occur, according to sentence grammar. However, particular contexts can override the grammatical constraints and license the use and guide the interpretation of zero plural pronominal objects. Thus, the investigation of zero objects yielded the same conclusion as the research into zero pronominal subjects. In other words, the use or interpretation predicted by grammar at sentence level can be considered only a typical, default one which emerges due to the lack of any specific context. In particular contexts, this use or interpretation can be modified or even overridden.

From the methodological point of view, it should be emphasised that the introduction of data from new data sources into the research resulted in strong evidence for the hypothesis that verbs can be used with zero plural pronominal objects in Hungarian language use, as well as against the hypothesis that states that they cannot. Thus, the integration of data from various direct data sources had strengthened the plausibility of the hypothesis that transitive verbs can also occur with plural zero pronominal objects in Hungarian language use.

In Section 5.2, I investigated the role of the encyclopaedic information immediately accessible under the conceptual addresses of the words included in the utterances in which the verbs themselves were involved. As to the occurrence of transitive verbs in the second (B) manner, I also analysed the morphosyntactic properties of the utterances with implicit direct object arguments. Verbs in these utterances are conjugated for the indefinite form as in the first (A) manner. What is the focus of attention is the pure activity reading of transitive verbs, as in the first (A) manner. Implicit arguments in these utterances do not have their own positions in the syntactic structures of the sentences uttered; they are not zero anaphors or exophoric zero pronouns. They can be identified with the help of the encyclopaedic information stored under the conceptual address of the lexemes in the immediate utterance context. However, I provided an alternative, neo-Gricean pragmatic analysis by applying I(nformativeness)-implicatures. The occurrence of an implicit argument induces a pragmatic inference that the situation must be typical; otherwise they cannot be left lexically unrealised.

Both explanations highlight the role of encyclopaedic information, but they differ in the extent to which they consider it conventionalised. If we consider implicit direct object arguments used in this manner, the interaction between grammatical constraints required by indefinite/definite conjugations and typical encyclopaedic information must be emphasised in the meaning construction of the utterances which contain them. This interaction has a crucial role in both alternative accounts, namely both in the explanation according to which the encyclopaedic information is supposed to be stored under the conceptual address of the lexemes in the utterances, and in the proposal according to which an I-implicature is assumed, since in both cases the verb should be conjugated for the indefinite form.

In Section 5.3, I dealt with the third (C) manner; more precisely, how the context extended with the information from the observable physical environment and encyclopaedic knowledge can influence the use and interpretation of implicit subject and direct object arguments in Hungarian language use. Moreover, I showed that the study could be extended to implicit adverbial arguments which were analysed similarly in various spoken discourses. The main conclusion of this section was that, in the third (C) manner, context extensions and grammatical requirements license the use of implicit arguments together. In other words, the licensing factors and interpretation mechanisms involve both grammatical coding-decoding procedures and pragmatic inferential procedures. As to direct object arguments identifiable in the third (C) manner, transitive verbs with implicit direct object arguments can be conjugated both for the indefinite and definite forms. In the first two (A) and (B) manners, they should be conjugated only for the indefinite form.

Since the indefinite/definite conjugations play an important role in the licensing and identification of implicit direct object arguments in all three manners, I examined their role thoroughly in Section 5.4. I attested that, if a transitive verb is conjugated for the indefinite form, it can be used with an implicit direct object argument in all three manners. However, I emphasised that the real use also depends on the place the verb in question occupies in the typology of transitive verbs regarding their occurrence with implicit direct object arguments. If a transitive verb is conjugated for the definite form, it can only be used in the third (C) manner, regardless of which group of transitive verbs it belongs to. I also summarised the results of the analyses of the occurrence of transitive verbs with implicit direct object arguments in Hungarian language use in four tables.

The existence of three manners in which verbs can occur with implicit arguments in Hungarian language use does not mean that every verb can be used only in one manner. From this perspective, Hungarian verbs can be classified into three groups, as was outlined in Section 5.4 when the interaction between the indefinite/definite conjugations and the typology of transitive verbs was discussed. The classification can be extended to all Hungarian verbs independently of what kind of implicit arguments, i.e. subject, direct object or adverbial, they can occur with. In the present book I focused on the occurrence of verbs with implicit subject and direct object arguments, therefore, the typology is illustrated mainly by verbs which can be used with these kinds of lexically unrealised arguments, but not exclusively, since, especially in Section 5.3, implicit adverbial arguments from spoken discourses were also exemplified in detail. Furthermore, there are verbs such as verbs of work which can be used not only with one kind of implicit arguments, namely with implicit subjects, but also with direct objects in the same manner.

Group 1 contains verbs that can be used with implicit arguments in all three manners. This group involves those verbs which were dealt with in Chapter 4 when discussing the first (A) manner. For instance, Hungarian verbs of natural phenomena in (214) and verbs of work in (215), which can be used with implicit subject arguments, belong to Group 1.

(214)   *esteledik* '[for evening to] close in', *alkonyodik* '[for dusk to] set in', *sötétedik* '[for dark to] grow', *hajnalodik* '[for day to] break, dawn', *virrad* 'dawn', *dereng* 'dawn', *tavaszodik* '[for spring to] come', *fagy* 'freeze', *olvad* 'thaw', *villámlik* '[for lightning to] strike', *dörög* 'thunder', *borul* 'cloud over', *havazik* 'snow', *szállingózik* 'snow softly', *esik* '[for precipitation to] fall', *zuhog* 'pour', *szakad* 'pour', *ömlik* 'pour', *szemerkél* 'drizzle', *csepereg* 'sprinkle', *csorog* 'trickle'

(215)   *vet* 'sow', *arat* 'harvest', *szánt* 'plough', *takarít* 'clean', *operál* 'operate on', *gyógyít* 'treat', *ápol* 'care for', *szerel* 'mend, repair', *kézbesít* 'deliver', *oktat/tanít* 'teach'

Transitive verbs in (106) in Section 4.2.2, repeated here for convenience as (216), which can be used with implicit direct object arguments, are also included in Group 1.

(216)   *eszik* 'eat', *etet* 'make eat', *fal* 'devour', *zabál* 'devour/gobble', *rág* 'chew', *nyel* 'swallow', *iszik* 'drink', *itat* 'make drink', *vedel* 'swill', *bámul* 'gaze', *ír* 'write', *rajzol* 'draw', *fest* 'paint', *süt* 'bake', *mos* 'wash', *áztat* 'soak', *öblít* 'rinse', *vasal* 'iron', *mosogat* 'do dishes', *takarít* 'clean', *törölget* 'dry, dust', *varr* 'sew', *ás* 'dig', *gyomlál* 'weed', *permetez* 'spray', *kapál* 'hoe', *locsol* 'water', *szánt* 'plough', *vet* 'sow', *kaszál* 'scythe', *arat* 'harvest', *fej* 'milk', *épít* 'build', *fúr* 'drill', *farag* 'carve', *foltoz* 'patch', *stoppol* 'darn', *tereget* 'hang up [to dry]', *szárogat* 'dry', *fon* 'spin', *köt* 'knit', *sző* 'weave', *vásárol* 'shop', *kézbesít* 'deliver', *gyógyít* 'treat', *operál* 'operate on', *tanít* 'teach', *gyón* 'confess', etc.

Verbs of natural phenomena in (214) and verbs of work in (215) can occur with lexically unrealised subject arguments, and transitive verbs in (216) with direct object arguments not only in the first (A) manner but also in the second (B) and third (C) manners. Let us take the verb *eszik* 'eat' from (216) to illustrate all three possibilities. For the first (A) manner, consider (217), for the second (B) manner, (218).

(217)   A   *férjem*   *eszik.*
        the   my.husband.NOM   eats.INDEF
        'My husband is eating.'

(218) A   *férjem*   *fogta*   a   *tányért*   *és*   *a*
       the   my.husband.NOM   took.DEF.3SG   the   bowl.ACC   and   the

       kanalat,   *és*   *evett.*
       spoon.ACC   and   ate.INDEF.3SG
       'My husband took the bowl and the spoon and ate.'

In (217) the action denoted by the verb *eszik* 'eat' is the focus of attention, and the lexically unrealised direct object argument is available as background information provided by the selection restriction in the lexical-semantic representation of the verb *eszik* 'eat'. The implicit direct object argument must be of the type FOOD. The identification of the implicit argument with the category FOOD results in a relevant interpretation.

In (218) the lexical-semantic representation of *eszik* 'eat' by itself does not yield a relevant interpretation. In (218) one knows more about the implicit direct object argument than that it must be of the type FOOD by taking into account the rest of the utterance, i.e. the immediate utterance context. The encyclopaedic information stored under the conceptual addresses of *tányér* 'bowl', *kanál* 'spoon', and *eszik* 'eat' make immediately accessible an assumption such as the following: adult people typically eat liquid food, e.g. soup or vegetable stew, from a bowl with a spoon (a little child may eat other dishes with a spoon). So the relevant interpretation of (218) may be that 'my husband took the bowl, the spoon and he ate soup or vegetable stew or something similar from the bowl with the spoon'.

The verb *eszik* 'eat' can also occur with implicit direct object arguments in the third (C) manner. In this case the identification of a lexically unrealised direct object argument is made by extending the immediate utterance context, as in (219).

(219) *Mi*   *történt*   a   *csokoládémmal?*
       what.NOM   happened.INDEF.3SG   the   my.chocolate.INS
       'What happened to my chocolate?'

       A   *gyerekek*   *ettek*   a   *szobádban.*
       the   children.NOM   ate.INDEF.3PL   the   your.room.INE
       'The children were eating in your room.'

The implicit direct object argument in the second utterance can be identified by extending the immediate utterance context with information from the preceding utterance. Thus, it turns out to be coreferential with the noun *csokoládé* 'chocolate', which is of the type FOOD. A similar interpretation was assigned to (26) and

(39) in Section 2.3, where the coreferentiality was explained by a special kind of referentiality, namely cumulative reference. The indefinite conjugation also supports this kind of interpretation.

Group 2 includes verbs which can occur with implicit arguments in both the second (B) and the third (C) manners. This group can be illustrated, for instance, by the verbs in (220).

(220)   *ad* 'give', *adományoz* 'donate', *ajándékoz* 'give a present', *teleszór* 'PVB.scatter', *megjavít* 'PVB.repair', *megjavíttat* 'PVB.make repair', *kijavít* 'PVB.mend', *kijavíttat* 'PVB.make mend', *megcsinál* 'PVB.repair/mend', *megcsináltat* 'PVB.have repaired/ mended', *megszerel* 'PVB.repair', *megszereltet* 'PVB.have repaired', *szerepel* 'play a role', *győz* 'win', *nyer* 'win', *veszt* 'lose', *veszít* 'lose', *kap* 'get', *cserél* 'change, trade', *büntet* 'punish', *gyűjt* 'collect', *oszt* 'distribute', *juttat* 'distribute', *vesz* 'buy', *vásárol* 'buy'

Some of these verbs were discussed in Section 5.2 (and also in Németh T. 2001, 2008a, 2012; Bibok and Németh T. 2001). One remark seems to be in order in connection with this group of verbs. The enumerated verbs can be used with implicit arguments in the second (B) manner taking into account the encyclopaedic information stored under the conceptual addresses of the lexemes in the immediate utterance context. However, if one considers zero anaphors in utterances, all verbs can occur with lexically unrealised arguments in the second (B) manner.

The verbs belonging to **Group 3** can occur with implicit arguments only in the third (C) manner, i.e. only if the implicit arguments can be identified by extending their immediate utterance contexts. Such occurrences were presented in detail in Section 5.3 (and also in Németh T. 2001, 2008a, 2012; Bibok and Németh T. 2001). This group includes verbs like those in (221).

(221)   *tologat* 'push', *tesz* 'put', *lakik* 'dwell', *bánik* 'use', *elolvas* 'PVB.read', *tűnik* 'seem', *bízik* 'trust', *elmélyül* 'PVB.become absorbed', *átfut* 'PVB.sweep over', *elrepül* 'PVB. fly away', *felpróbál* 'PVB.try on', *lök* 'push', *beüt* 'PVB.punch in', *elfelejt* 'PVB.forget', *otthagy* 'PVB.leave', *beletanul* 'PVB.learn', etc.

An interesting implication can be identified on the basis of the order of licensing mechanisms (see Section 3.2). If a verb can be used with an implicit argument in the first (A) manner, then it can also occur with it in the second (B) manner, and also in the third (C) manner, i.e. A → B → C. While there are verbs which can be used with implicit arguments only in the third (C) manner, it is this manner in which every Hungarian verb can be used with lexically unrealised arguments.

One has to realise that the lexical-semantic representation of the verbs in Group 1 is rich enough to license and identify implicit arguments in the first (A) manner. These verbs place strict constraints on the type or properties of their arguments by means of selection restrictions, characteristic manners of actions, and prototypical structures of categories. The lexical-semantic representation of the verbs in the second group is poorer, i.e. less specific, and that of the verbs in the third group is even poorer, i.e. even less specific. The relevant interpretation of utterances containing verbs with implicit arguments can be obtained by taking into consideration larger and larger contexts with their grammatical requirements moving from Group 1 to Group 3. As to the implicit direct object arguments, if a transitive verb is inflected for the indefinite conjugation, then we try to find the necessary information to construct the relevant interpretation, firstly, in the lexical-semantic representation of the verb, secondly, in its immediate utterance context, and, thirdly, in its extended context. This order of interpretation mechanisms is applied in the identification process of implicit subject and adverbial arguments, as well. However, if a transitive verb is inflected for the definite conjugation, then its implicit direct object argument can be identified only in the third (C) manner without monitoring the first (A) and the second (B) manners (see Section 5.4).

On the basis of this order of licensing mechanisms, it can be predicted that if the lexical-semantic representation of a verb in Group 2 or Group 3 becomes rich, i.e. specific enough to identify the lexically unrealised argument by itself, the verb may move to Group 1. The enrichment of the lexical-semantic representation of a verb can occur by means of the lexicalisation of some elements of the context.

In connection with the formulation of the three manners of occurrences of Hungarian verbs with implicit arguments, I have referred to the cognitive principle of relevance (see Section 3.2). According to the cognitive principle of relevance (Sperber and Wilson 1986/1995: 260), human cognition tends to be geared towards the maximisation of relevance, i.e. to achieve more cognitive effects with less processing effort. In language use, speakers try to produce optimally relevant utterances to ensure that the hearer can achieve adequate contextual effects with the least processing effort. The universal cognitive principle of relevance guides and explains the licensing and interpretation of implicit arguments in a twofold way. Firstly, if an argument can be used implicitly in one of the three manners, it should be left lexically unrealised in a particular context, since with the use of the implicit form a speaker can achieve the same effects as with the explicit form, but with less processing effort. Secondly, in the course of interpretation the hearer attempts to form an adequate interpretation in a particular context starting from the lexical-semantic representation of the verb in the first (A) manner. If this does not result in a relevant interpretation, then (s)he turns to the second (B) and after that to the third (C) manner. Thus, the order of interpretation mechanisms is also relevance-based.

It must be emphasised that the order of interpretation mechanisms also involves important implications: ~A → B, ~B → C. These implications indicate that the interpretation mechanisms of implicit arguments are really controlled by an economy balance. In other words, they are guided by the requirement to take into account lexical-semantic, grammatical, and contextual information only to a necessary extent.

On the basis of the critical evaluations of the previous literature on implicit arguments (see Chapter 2), analyses and classification of a wide spectrum of data from various direct sources, and theoretical explanations (see Chapter 3 to Chapter 5), all of which were guided and supported by systematic metatheoretical considerations, it can finally be concluded that, in Hungarian, verbs do not vary as to whether they can be used with implicit arguments or not, but they vary as to the manner in which they can occur with such arguments. In other words, they vary in terms of the lexical and grammatical constraints which are placed on them, and in what contexts they can be used with lexically unrealised arguments in Hungarian language use. A similar claim can be generalised with respect to various languages (see Chapter 2). Languages do not vary as to whether they allow verbs to occur with implicit arguments, but they vary depending on the lexical, grammatical, and pragmatic constraints placed on them, as well as the contexts in which these verbs can occur with implicit arguments. Although the cognitive principle of relevance guides the licensing and interpretation processes of implicit arguments, the variety of the occurrences of implicit arguments does not rest solely on the presumption of relevance, but on the different lexical, grammatical, and pragmatic properties of a particular language and its use, as well as on their various interactions. So, it is only via a close co-operation that a grammar and an adequate pragmatic theory can account for the occurrences and identification mechanisms of implicit arguments.

Endnotes

1 Introduction

1. Example (6) comes from my 310-minute long spoken language corpus. For a more detailed characterisation of the corpus, see Section 1.2.3.
2. The discussion of the metatheoretical and methodological issues of the research into implicit arguments is based on Németh T. 2014b and Németh T. 2017a.
3. The theories and frameworks mentioned in the course of characterisation of the various groups only illustrate the particular groups. I do not aim to give a detailed overview of all current approaches. For a more detailed presentation of the approaches referred to, see, e.g., Engdahl 1999; Verschueren 1999; Levinson 2000; Goldberg 2005a, b; Ariel 2008, 2010.
4. For a detailed evaluation of the similar (and dissimilar) features of the multi-componential view of concept representation in relevance theory initiated by Sperber and Wilson (1986/1995), see Bibok 2004.
5. For a detailed treatment of the differences of formal and functional linguistic theories, see, e.g., Newmeyer 1998; Darnell, Moravcsik, Noonan, Newmeyer, and Wheatley 1998.
6. The exceptions are Pléh's and his colleagues' experiments and analyses in which they investigate zero anaphors in Hungarian (Pléh 1994, 1998; Pléh and Radics 1978; Pléh and McWhinney 1987). In the course of their work, Pléh and his colleagues assumed that pragmatic factors can influence grammatical requirements in the licensing and interpretation of implicit arguments, and their findings have supported their hypothesis.
7. For the discussion of the linguistic data and evidence in the previous decades, see, e.g., Labov 1975; Ringen 1975; Ross 1979; Schütze 1996.
8. In the second, new version of the Hungarian National Corpus, a spoken-language corpus is also available at http://clara.nytud.hu/mnsz2-dev/.
9. According to Kertész and Rákosi (2009, 2012), indirect sources are those from which one can obtain plausible statements by means of inferences.

10. For a detailed analyses of Hungarian verbs of natural phenomena, see Section 4.1.1.
11. A more detailed characterisation of my spoken corpus, see Németh T. 1996: 41–42.
12. Although I also relied on data from the Hungarian National Corpus (corpus.nytud.hu/mnsz), I did not aim to conduct a frequency-based statistical analysis of the occurrence of implicit subject and direct object arguments, since there is no annotation in the Hungarian National Corpus concerning the occurrences of verbs with implicit arguments. Consequently, my investigation was rather corpus-informed than corpus-driven (Tognini-Bonelli 2001).
13. This kind of classification is determined by the functions of data and the methods applied in the research. However, the problem of classification goes beyond the scope of the present book.
14. As I have mentioned above, data from the minimal pair and thought experiments can also be considered as introspective data.
15. The validity of the hearer's meaning construction of the speaker's utterances can also be questionable.
16. For a detailed discussion of thought experiments and the relationship between thought experiments and real experiments see Kiefer and Kertész (2013).

2 Explanations of the occurrence of verbs with implicit arguments

1. Levin's (1993) seminally important work on English verb classes and alternations is another important source for the studies of argument realisations in English and contrastive analyses of English and other languages including the Hungarian language. Although in some places of this book I make some remarks on the distinction between the argument realisations in English and Hungarian, in my research I did not have the aim of carrying out a contrastive analysis.
2. For further discussion and some particular examples, see Section 2.4.
3. The insufficiency of the purely pragmatic explanations of implicit arguments through conversational implicatures does not mean that the Gricean maxims cannot be involved in an account for implicit arguments. For such an analysis of zero anaphors, a subtype of implicit arguments, see Levinson 2000; Huang 2004.
4. Iten et al. (2005) as well as Pethő and Kardos (2009) criticise pragmatic approaches in a similar way.
5. For more detailed analyses of purely syntactic and pragmatic approaches, see the literature referred to in Sections 2.1 and 2.2.
6. Fillmore (1986) deals with the omission of non-subject complements, especially with the omissibility of direct object complements. He does not use

the term *implicit argument*, instead he speaks about *null/zero* complements. The term *complement* can mean not only a syntactic constituent, but also a semantic one as indicated in Section 1.1. In discussing Fillmore's thinking I also use his terminology, in addition to the terms *implicit arguments* and *lexically unrealised arguments*.

7. Goldberg (1995: 59) takes a similar position in investigating verbal argument structures in the framework of construction grammar.
8. The non-demonstrative deductive inferences are discussed in great detail by Sperber and Wilson (1986/1995: 65–117).
9. The sign * indicates that (41) is unacceptable and the sign ? indicates the acceptability of (42) is questionable. I added these signs to Groefsema's examples in order to make them mirror her acceptability judgments.
10. As will be seen later, the solution proposed by Saeboe (1996) is not valid for every zero argument that has a definite interpretation.
11. (45a, b) and (46a, b) are Saeboe's (1996: 194) examples, but my explanations of them differ from Saeboe's. The interpretation in (46c) is my own.
12. Saeboe (1996: 204–205) analyses the use of *erkränken* 'become sick' with implicit arguments in much detail.
13. These three problems are discussed by Saeboe (1996).
14. Gillon (2012) does not make explicit what distinction can be made between the terms *context* and *cotext*. I will return to this point later in this section.
15. For a detailed discussion of these empirical difficulties, see Gillon (2012: 316–335).
16. Gillon (2012: 325) extends the lexicon to a set of constituents which are simple English clauses with only a proper noun and do not contain any clauses or modifiers.
17. As can be seen in Section 2.4, my evaluation of Groefsema's (1995) and Iten et al.'s (2005) approaches differs from the evaluation presented by Gillon (2012). I do not consider Groefsema's (1995) account purely pragmatic and the explanation provided by Iten et al. (2005) purely metaphysical; instead, each of them is considered a complex approach.
18. I do not aim to overview all recent complex approaches to implicit arguments; instead, I will only refer to some elements which I will use in the construction of my explanation.
19. Similar claims are made by Ariel (1991), when she places the referring expressions on an accessibility scale on the basis of their linguistic cues.
20. For the discussion of the occurrence of null subjects in English, see Section 2.1 as well.
21. Cote (1996: 83) refers to the discourse units on the same topic as discourse packages. She introduces this new term to avoid confusion with terms such as *subject* and *topic*.

22. Cote (1996: 84) does not indicate lexically unrealised subjects in square brackets. She leaves square brackets empty.

23. We have seen earlier in Section 2.3 that not every DNC-verb (e.g. *win, lose*) requires an antecedent for its null object argument, and there are INC-verbs that allow their implicit direct object arguments to have an antecedent.

24. Cote does not rule out the existence of a true transitive–intransitive alternation, but she does not use it herself. The possible discourse effects of implicit arguments (e.g. the addition of a new member, a change in the saliency of an existing member) should be distinguished from the effects of intransitive uses of verbs.

25. (54)–(56) are Cote's examples.

26. According to Sperber and Wilson (1986/1995: 270), presumption of optimal relevance means that, on the one hand, the ostensive stimulus is relevant enough for it to be worth the addressee's effort to process it, and, on the other hand, the ostensive stimulus is the most relevant one compatible with the communicator's abilities and preferences.

3 Occurrences of implicit arguments in Hungarian

1. Zero anaphors are zero pronouns that have an antecedent in the utterance or discourse context which they can be coreferential with; see Section 4.1.2 as well as Section 5.1.

2. The term *pragmatic evidence* includes both general pragmatic factors and particular contextual properties.

3. For the criticism of this kind of approaches to the occurrence of verbs with indefinite or definite implicit arguments, cf. Goldberg 2013.

4. Categorisation and examples with references are cited here from Vicente and Groefsema's work (2013: 109).

5. For a detailed analysis of the argument structure of adjectives, see Meltzer-Asscher 2011. The definition can also be extended to nouns which have an argument structure, see, e.g., Hungarian nouns *igény* 'need', *válasz* 'answer, response', *hála* 'gratitude', *lehetőség* 'possibility', *győzelem* 'victory', *félelem* 'fear'. It must be noted that the definition in (57) can be extended not only to adjectives such as *ready* and nouns with an argument structure, but to all types of words which logically behave as predicates.

6. For example, Collins Cobuild English dictionary for advanced learners (Sinclair 2001: 1264) defines the verb *rain* as follows: 'When rain falls, you can say that **it is raining**'. And the noun *rain* is defined as 'Rain is water that falls from the clouds in small drops'.

7. Perry (1986) also argues that *rain* always occurs with location, and Taylor (2001) suggests a lexically determined locative argument.

8. Zouhar (2011: 245–248), who criticises Recanati's (2002: 319–320) views on

occurrences of the verb *open* used without and with an instrumental argument, assumes that the verb *open* in both kinds of occurrences is a three-place predicate with three syntactically realisable arguments. His argument is also valid for the verb *kill*. Recanati (2002: 319–320) also proposes a third argument for the verb *open* with an instrumental constituent, but in a different way. He offers a syntactically optional modifier, which introduces a particular feature of the circumstances, such as time or place of utterances. A circumstantial operator transforms an n-place predicate into an n+1 place predicate via variadic functions. Variadic functions are functions between relations where the output relations differ from the input ones by their decreased or increased adicity. Cf., e.g., *Jane took out her key and opened the door* vs *Jane took out her key and opened the door with the key*. This solution creates a new argument slot in the second utterance which is filled by *the key*. It is not necessary that an utterance explicitly contains a syntactically optional modifier. A context can also provide a suitable variadic function transforming a binary relation into a ternary relation with a third argument filling the new argument position. Cf. *Jane took out her key and opened the door [with the key]*. Recanati considers such a case a manifestation of free enrichment. However, it must be emphasised that this kind of free enrichment operates through a syntactic operation which has a semantic consequence. Thus, it differs from other types of free enrichment which are only contextually determined and have an exclusively inferential nature. This means that the process which supplies the verb *open* with the third argument can rather be considered saturation. Zouhar (2011: 245–248) goes even further and argues that there are no truly unarticulated constituents with free enrichment; instead, he proposes that all unarticulated constituents can be explained in terms of saturation, but he discusses only those cases which can be treated as lexically determined arguments.

9. However, the information provided by *in the garden* can be analysed in another way: namely, it can be considered a generalised conversational implicature, more precisely, a Levinsonian I-implicature (Levinson 2000). For a more detailed discussion of the role of I-implicatures in interpretation processes of utterances, see Section 4.2.4 as well as 5.2.

4 First (A) manner: the role of the lexical-semantic representation of verbs

1. These examples of metaphorical use can be found in the *Magyar Nemzeti Szövegtár* (Hungarian National Corpus, corpus.nytud.hu/mnsz), see Oravecz, Váradi, and Sass (2014).

2. *Magyar grammatika* argues that it is also characteristic of verbs in the first group that they cannot have other complements either. The only exception mentioned by this grammar is the verb *esteledik* '[for evening to] close in',

which can have an optional adverbial complement *ránk* 'upon us'. However, on the one hand, this optional adverbial complement can appear with other verbs which have a meaning expressing the passing of days and seasons as well, e.g. *ránk alkonyodik* 'evening is closing in on us', *ránk hajnalodik* 'day is breaking on us', *ránk sötétedik* 'it is getting dark on us', *ránk virrad* 'dawn is breaking on us', and *ránk tavaszodik* 'spring is breaking on us'. And, on the other hand, the adverbial complement in question can occur with this group of verbs of natural phenomena in other forms as well, see *Jól rátok esteledett* 'Evening has really closed on you', *Addig dolgoztak, míg rájuk virradt* 'They worked until dawn broke on them'. I want to thank Anna Fenyvesi for drawing my attention to these two examples.

3.   Komlósy (1994, 2001) and Tóth (2001) (see subsequently in this section) use the term *weather verb* but I prefer using the term *verb of natural phenomena* because of its wider scope.

4.   Since (60a–c) are Komlósy's (1994: 160–161) examples, I have cited them with the glosses he provided.

5.   However, morphological complexity is not considered a definitive property of the Hungarian weather verbs by Komlósy (1994).

6.   Komlósy (1994: 160) argues that adjectival stems might be conceived as nouns in the roots of weather verbs based on the morphologically unmarked adjective → noun derivation in Hungarian.

7.   These examples of metaphorical and non-metaphorical use can be found in the *Magyar Nemzeti Szövegtár* (Hungarian National Corpus, corpus.nytud. hu/mnsz). In note 1 of this chapter, I also referred to this source of metaphorical use.

8.   For the verbs' behaviour in participial adjunct clauses, see also Sárik (1998).

9.   For the problems of classification of direct data sources, see Németh T. (2010) and Section 1.2.3.

10.   In Section 4.2.2, I will discuss the role of the unique selection restriction in the use of verbs (e.g. *meggyón* 'PVB.confess') with direct object arguments in Hungarian in detail.

11.   *Esteledik a nap* (24-hour time unit) and *esteledik az idő* are dialectal variants.

12.   The present section does not aim to confront these solutions. This can be the task of another argumentation cycle.

13.   Of course, the information from the weather forecast may also influence the use of *szállingózik* 'snow softly' with implicit subject argument as a previous discourse context.

14.   In winter the prototype of precipitation can be snow.

15.   For a further discussion of null and cognate objects, see Lavidas 2013.

16.   In Section 3.1.2 it was argued that the verb *rain* can have a locative argument

in its lexical-semantic representation in addition to the subject argument (see also ((75))). A similar lexical-semantic representation with a locative argument can be assumed in the case of the verb *havazik* 'snow' for similar reasons.

17. Implicit subject arguments in (81a) can be considered more acceptable when they are morphologically derived from the respective verbs of work and/or when the work is of a traditional type, e.g. *vet* 'sow', *arat* 'harvest', and *szánt* 'plough'. (Investigating the Hungarian verbs of natural phenomena in the previous Section 4.1.1, I also highlighted the role of morphological derivation of the subject argument from the particular verb of natural phenomena). Here I do not aim to examine the overall morphological structure of the subject arguments of verbs of work; instead, I have attempted to analyse less traditional types of verbs of work, e.g. *operál* 'operate on', *szerel* 'mend, repair', and *kézbesít* 'deliver'. Hadrovics (1969) and Nyomárkay (1972) have listed many traditional verbs of work. However, it is without question that these issues of acceptability need further investigation.

18. Relying on Fillmore's (1986: 97) work, Gillon (2012: 353) mentions that the English verb *bake* denotes only the event of baking bread and pastry when it is used with implicit complements, but when it is used with explicit complements, these complements can denote potatoes, hams, and other things as well. In other words, the verb *bake* can occur with an implicit complement, only if it is bread or pastry, i.e. such a restriction must be imposed on the omitted direct object complement. If the object of baking differs from this restriction, the verb *bake* must be used with an explicitly expressed direct object complement. Cf. also (122) below in Section 4.2.4.

19. The other term for the indefinite conjugation is *general conjugation*. I do not want to discuss the rationale underlying the use of terms *indefinite* and *general conjugation*, I use the term *indefinite conjugation* following my previous work (Németh T. 2001, 2010; Bibok and Németh T. 2001).

20. For a discussion of the accounts of indefinite/definite conjugations, see, e.g., Németh T. and Bibok 2001, Coppok 2013, and Section 5.4.

21. A similar claim is made by Groefsema (1995: 139–141), Cote (1996: 5), and García Velasco and Portero Muñoz (2002) with regard to the English verb *eat*. The act of eating necessarily involves something that is being eaten, which is why the sentence *John was eating* expresses really *John was eating something* and not only that John was engaged in the physical activity of eating. Alberti (1998: 219, 225) also shares this opinion, analysing the corresponding Hungarian verb *eszik* 'eat'. For the detailed analysis of verbs of eating and drinking in various languages, see Newman (2009).

22. Jackendoff (1990) also proposes a set of formation rules to form concep-

tual representations. Since from the point of view of the focus of the present section the selection restrictions have the main role, I refrain from a more detailed characterisation of conceptual representations.

23. In (112) and below in (114a), I indicate the case inflections of the implicit second and third arguments of the verbs *itat* 'make drink' and *etet* 'feed' in order to differentiate them more easily.

24. For the interaction between verbs' lexical-semantic representations and aspectual properties, see Pustejovsky (1995); García Velasco and Portero Muñoz (2002), and Goldberg (2005b).

25. For the particular use of lexical stereotypes, see Gergely and Bever's (1986) as well as Bibok's (1996, 1998, 2000) analyses.

26. The lexical-semantic representation of *iszik*₁ 'drink' in (129a) is the same as the lexical-semantic representation of *iszik* in (124b) and (102b) in Section 4.2.2.

27. The role of encyclopaedic pieces of information stored under the conceptual addresses of the lexemes in the immediate utterance context in the use of verbs with implicit arguments will be discussed in Section 5.2.

5 Second (B) and third (C) manners: grammatical constraints and the role of the immediate utterance context and the extended context

1. This section is partly based on Németh T. 2017b.

2. The other terms used for the phenomenon of cataphor are as follows: counter-unidirectional anaphor, anticipatory anaphor, forward-looking anaphor, prospective anaphor, and cataphoric reference (Huang 2012: 46).

3. Analysing occurrences of verbs of natural phenomena and verbs of work with implicit subject arguments in Sections 4.1.1 and 4.1.2, we have seen that not all kinds of implicit subjects are pro-drop phenomena. These verbs can occur with implicit subject arguments in the first (A) manner, i.e. they are not projected into the syntactic structure of utterances but are available through lexical-semantic representations of the verbs as background information.

4. Not only in the case of zero anaphors do the grammatical constraints and pragmatic factors interact, but also in all cases of anaphors. For a complex analysis of anaphors in various languages, see Huang 2004.

5. In addition to the alternation of subjects, there is even a change in the chronological order of events described by the two utterances of (147b) if our background knowledge also contains information – as it does in Hungary – that, in public, Santa Claus goes up to and gives candy to those children who recite a poem or sing a song.

6. In Section 5.3 I will return to this conversation.

7. É. Kiss's (2012: 195) example cited here with its original gloss and transla-

tion. É. Kiss uses the abbreviation PRT (= particle) instead of PVB (= preverb) applied in the present study and she does not indicate that the verb *elbújik* 'PVB.hides.INDEF' is conjugated for the indefinite form.

8. More precisely, the use of plural pronominal objects involves VP-deletion with the V raised out of VP into T (É. Kiss 2012: 194). VP = verb phrase, V = verb, T = tense.

9. Pléh's (1994, 1998) and Dankovics's (2001, 2005) psycholinguistic experiments have the same result, namely that grammar cannot explain all pro-forms in Hungarian language use.

10. Like categories in general, the category of donation also has a prototypical structure.

11. Not only this second (B) manner of the occurrence of verbs with lexically unrealised arguments but also the first and the third manner can be extended to adverbial implicit arguments. Cf. also the utterance in (189).

12. I refrain from a formalisation of the semantic representation of *nagymama* here. The definition of *nagymama* and the problem relating to it are treated in detail in Stillings et al. 1987: 65–68.

13. The missing arguments in square brackets in (197) and (198) will be provided in (199) and (200).

14. In the indefinite conjugations, the *ik*-verbs (e.g. *esz-ik* 'eat', *isz-ik* 'drink', *szök-ik* 'escape'), which in the present tense third person singular forms are supplied with the *ik*-suffix, receive what is otherwise the definite suffix *-om/-em/-öm* in the first person singular forms instead of the indefinite suffix *-ok/-ek/-ök*. However, in colloquial Hungarian the latter suffixes are also frequently used with the *ik*-verbs (*esz-ek, isz-ok, szök-ök* instead of *esz-em, isz-om, szök-öm*; Fenyvesi 1998: 290).

15. The examples in (203)–(205) are É. Kiss's (2003) examples.

16. In this case the verbs are supplied with a detransitivising morpheme (Comrie 1980).

17. For a more detailed analysis of the history of the *-lak/-lek* inflection, see É. Kiss (2012, 2013).

18. If an object is more animate, i.e. more salient than the subject, it can only be presented as a focus (É. Kiss 2013: 16).

19. As É. Kiss (2013: 16) discusses, an object more animate/prominent than the primary topic could only function as a focus. Since first and second person objects are inherently more animate than a third person object, they could not bear the role of the secondary topic.

20. Tolcsvai Nagy (2014) uses the term *general conjugation* instead of the term *indefinite conjugation*. In order to be coherent in the critical evaluation of the literature concerning the two inflectional paradigms, I apply the term *indefinite conjugation* in the treatment of Tolcsvai Nagy's (2014) approach as well.

21. Tolcsvai Nagy (2014: 582) lists the complements *valahol* 'somewhere' and *valamiért* 'something.CAUS', in addition to the landmarks in (208a–d). Another potential landmark can be assumed in the case of the verb *vár*, namely *valamiért* 'something.CAU'.

22. The landmarks of *várok* 'wait.INDEF.1SG' in (208a–d) can be specifically identifiable for the speaker and non-identifiable for the hearer.

23. I do not want to discuss here whether the *-lak/-lek* inflection belongs to the indefinite or definite paradigm, because Tolcsvai Nagy (2014: 583) does not provide an explicit reference to one or the other paradigm. But when he characterises the landmark which must be realised as a grammatical object as compulsory, he highlights that it is definite, since it refers to the current addressee.

24. The inflection *-lak/-lek* makes it possible to use the transitive verbs in all three manners independently of which group the verb at issue belongs to.

25. The inflection *-lak/-lek* makes it possible to use the transitive verbs in all three manners independently of which group the verb at issue belongs to.

References

Alberti, Gábor (1998) Argument hierarchy and reflexivization. *Acta Linguistica Hungarica* 45(3–4): 215–251. https://doi.org/10.1023/A:1009661026350

Allerton, David J. (1975) Deletion and proform reduction. *Journal of Linguistics* 11(2): 213–237. https://doi.org/10.1017/S0022226700004540

Allerton, David J. (1982) *Valency and the English Verb.* New York: Academic Press.

Alsina, Alex (1992) On the argument structure of causatives. *Linguistic Inquiry* 23(4): 517–555.

Ariel, Mira (1991) The function of accessibility in a theory of grammar. *Journal of Pragmatics* 16(5): 443–463. https://doi.org/10.1016/0378-2166(91)90136-L

Ariel, Mira (2008) *Pragmatics and Grammar.* Cambridge: Cambridge University Press. https://doi.org/10.1017/CBO9780511791314

Ariel, Mira (2010) *Defining Pragmatics.* Cambridge: Cambridge University Press. https://doi.org/10.1017/CBO9780511777912

Bach, Kent (1994) Conversational implicature. *Mind & Language* 9(2): 124–162. https://doi.org/10.1111/j.1468-0017.1994.tb00220.x

Balogh, Judit (2000) A tárgy [The object]. In Borbála Keszler (ed.) *Magyar grammatika* [Hungarian Grammar] 414–422. Budapest: Nemzeti Tankönyvkiadó.

Bartos, Huba (1997) On 'subjective' and 'objective' agreement in Hungarian. *Acta Linguistica Hungarica* 44(3–4): 363–384.

Bartos, Huba (2000) Az inflexiós jelenségek szintaktikai háttere [The syntactic background of inflectional phenomena]. In Ferenc Kiefer (eds.) *Strukturális magyar nyelvtan 3. Morfológia* [Structural Hungarian Grammar 3. Morphology] 653–762. Budapest: Akadémiai Kiadó.

Bibok, Károly (1996) Problema konceptual'noj semantiki russkogo i vengerskogo jazyka [Problem of conceptual semantics of Russian and Hungarian]. *Voprosy Jazykoznanija* (2): 156–165.

Bibok, Károly (1998) A *hív* és a *küld* igék konceptuális szemantikai vizsgálata [The conceptual semantic investigation of verbs *hív* 'call' and *küld* 'send']. *Magyar Nyelv* 94(4): 436–446.

Bibok, Károly (2000) Conceptual semantic investigations in Russian and Hungarian. In Endre Lendvai (ed.) *Applied Russian Studies in Hungary* 15–32. Pécs: Krónika.

Bibok, Károly (2004) Word meaning and lexical pragmatics. *Acta Linguistica Hungarica* 51(3–4): 265–308. https://doi.org/10.1556/ALing.51.2004.3-4.3

Bibok, Károly (2008) Az igék szemantikája és a szintaktikai alternáció [The semantics of verbs and syntactic alternation]. In Ferenc Kiefer (eds.) *Strukturális magyar nyelvtan 4. A szótár szerkezete* [Structural Hungarian Grammar 4. Structure of the Lexicon] 23–70. Budapest: Akadémiai Kiadó.

Bibok, Károly (2009) Az evidencia problémája az elméleti nyelvészetben [The problem of evidence in theoretical linguistics]. Talk presented at the conference *Kutatócsoportjaink* [Our research groups], Szeged.

Bibok, Károly (2010) From syntactic alternations to lexical pragmatics. In Enikő Németh T. and Károly Bibok (eds.) *The Role of Data at the Semantics-Pragmatics Interface* 261–304. Berlin and New York: Mouton de Gruyter. https://doi.org/10.1515/9783110240276.261

Bibok, Károly and Németh T., Enikő (2001) How the lexicon and context interact in the meaning construction of utterances. In Enikő Németh T. and Károly Bibok (eds.) *Pragmatics and the Flexibility of Word Meaning* 289–320. Amsterdam: Elsevier.

Bierwisch, Manfred (1983) Semantische und konzeptuelle Repräsentation lexikalischer Einheiten. In Rudolf Růžička and Wolfgang Motsch (eds.) *Untersuchungen zur Semantik.* (Studia grammatica 22) 61–99. Berlin: Akademie Verlag.

Bierwisch, Manfred (1996) How much space gets into language? In Paul Bloom, Mary A Peterson, Lynn Nadel, and Merrill F. Garrett (eds.) *Language and Space* 31–76. Cambridge, MA: MIT Press.

Blackwell, Sarah (2001) Testing the neo-Gricean pragmatic theory of anaphora: The influence of consistency constraints on interpretation of coreference in Spanish. *Journal of Pragmatics* 33(6): 901–941. https://doi.org/10.1016/S0378-2166(01)80034-5

Blakemore, Diane (1992) *Understanding Utterances.* Oxford: Blackwell.

Bokor, József (1991) Szóalaktan [Morphology]. In Anna Jászó A. (ed.) *A magyar nyelv könyve* [The Book of Hungarian Language] 234–271. Budapest: Trezor.

Borg, Emma (2005) Saying what you mean: Unarticulated constituents and communication. In Reinaldo Elugardo and Robert Stainton (eds.) *Ellipsis and Non-Sentential Speech* 237–262. Dordrecht: Kluwer Academic Publishers.

Borsley, Robert D. (ed.) (2005) Special issue on data in theoretical linguistics. *Lingua* 115/11.

Brennan, Susan E., Friedman, Marylin W., and Pollard, Carl J. (1987) A centering approach to pronouns. *Proceedings of the 25th Annual Meeting of the ACL* 155–162. https://doi.org/10.3115/981175.981197

Bresnan, John (1995) Lexicality and argument structure. Paper presented at *Paris Syntax and Semantics Conference,* 12 October 1995. Retrieved on 10 May 2013 from http://www.stanford.edu/~bresnan/paris.pdf

Bresnan, John (2001) *Lexical-Functional Syntax.* Oxford: Blackwell.

Camacho, José A. (2013) *Null Subjects.* Cambridge: Cambridge University Press. https://doi.org/10.1017/CBO9781139524407

Capone, Alessandro (2008) Belief reports and pragmatic intrusion (the case of null appositives). *Journal of Pragmatics* 40(6): 1019–1040. https://doi.org/10.1016/j.pragma.2008.02.008

Carston, Robyn (1988) Implicature, explicature, and truth-theoretic semantics. In Ruth Kempson (ed.) *Mental Representations. The Interface between Language and Reality* 155–181. Cambridge: Cambridge University Press.

Carston, Robyn (2002) *Thoughts and Utterances: The Pragmatics of Explicit Communication.* Oxford: Blackwell. https://doi.org/10.1002/9780470754603

Carston, Robyn (2009) The explicit/implicit distinction in pragmatics and the limits of communication. *International Review of Pragmatics* 1(1): 35–62. https://doi.org/10.1163/187731009X455839

Carston, Robyn (2010) Explicit communication and 'free' pragmatic enrichment. In Belén Soria and Esther Romero (eds.) *Explicit Communication. Essays on Robyn Carston's Pragmatics* 217–287. Basingstoke: Palgrave. https://doi.org/10.1057/9780230292352_14

Chomsky, Noam (1957) *Syntactic Structures.* The Hague: Mouton.

Chomsky, Noam (1977) *Essays on Form and Interpretation.* New York: North Holland.

Chomsky, Noam (1981) *Lectures on Government and Binding: The Pisa Lectures.* Dordrecht: Foris.

Chomsky, Noam (1986) *Knowledge of Language: Its Nature, Origin and Use.* New York: Praeger.

Chomsky, Noam (1995) *The Minimalist Program.* Cambridge, MA: MIT Press.

Comrie, Bernard (1980) Inverse verb forms in Siberia: Evidence from Chukchee, Koryak and Kamchadal. *Folia Linguistica Historica* 1(1): 61–74.

Coppok, Elizabeth and Wechsler, Stephen (2012) The objective conjugation in Hungarian: Agreement without phi-features. *Natural Language & Linguistic Theory* 30(3): 699–740. https://doi.org/10.1007/s11049-012-9165-5

Coppok, Elizabeth (2013) A semantic solution to the problem of Hungarian object agreement. *Natural Language Semantics* 21(4): 345–371. https://doi.org/10.1007/s11050-013-9096-7

Cornish, Francis (2005) Null complements, event structure, predication and anaphora: A functional discourse grammar account. In John Lachlan Mackenzie and María de los Ángeles Gómez González (eds.) *Studies in Functional Discourse Grammar* 21–47. Bern: Peter Lang.

Cote, Sharon A. (1996) *Grammatical and Discourse Properties of Null Arguments in English.* PhD dissertation. Philadelphia: University of Pennsylvania.

Culicover, Peter W. and Jackendoff, Ray (2005) *Simpler Syntax.* Oxford: Oxford University Press. https://doi.org/10.1007/s11049-012-9165-5

Cummins, Sarah and Roberge, Yves (2005) A modular account of null objects in French. *Syntax* 8(1): 44–64. https://doi.org/10.1111/j.1467-9612.2005.00074.x

Dalrymple, Mary and Nikolaeva, Irina (2011) *Objects and Information Structure.* Cambridge: Cambridge University Press. https://doi.org/10.1017/CBO9780511993473

Dankovics, Natália (2001) Anaforikus viszonyok finn, észt és magyar összetett mondatokban pszicholingvisztikai szempontból [Anaphoric relations in Finnish, Estonian, and Hungarian compound sentences from the psycholinguistic point of view]. *Nyelvtudományi Közlemények* 98: 120–142.

Dankovics, Natália (2005) A szórend szerepe az anafora-feldolgozásban [The role of word order in anaphor resolution]. In Judit Gervain, Kristóf Kovács, and Mihály Racsmány (eds.) *Az ezerarcú elme: Tanulmányok Pléh Csaba 60. születésnapjára* [The Thousand Face Mind. Studies on the Occasion of Csaba Pléh's 60th Birthday] 117–134. Budapest: Akadémiai Kiadó.

Darnell, Michael, Moravcsik, Edith, Noonan, Michael, Newmeyer, Frederick J., and Wheatley, Kathleen (eds.) (1998) *Functionalism and Formalism in Linguistics*. Amsterdam: John Benjamins.

Dik, Simon Cornelis (1985) Formal and semantic adjustment of derived constructions. In A. Machtelt Bolkestein, Casper de Groot, and John Lachlan Mackenzie (eds.) *Predicates and Terms in Functional Grammar* 1–28. Dordrecht: Foris.

Dörnyei, Zoltán (2007) *Research Methods in Applied Linguistics: Quantitative, Qualitative, and Mixed Methodologies*. Oxford: Oxford University Press.

Dowty, David (1981) Quantification and the lexicon: A reply to Fodor and Fodor. In Teun Hoekstra, Michael Moortgrat, and Harry van der Hulst (eds.) *The Scope of Lexical Rules* 79–106. Dordrecht: Foris.

Dowty, David (2003) The dual analysis of adjuncts/complements in categorial grammar. In Ewald Lang, Claudia Maienborn, and Cathry Fabricius Hansen (eds.) *Modifying Adjuncts* 33–66. Berlin: Mouton de Gruyter.

Ehlich, Konrad (1982) Anaphora and deixis: Same, similar, or different? In Robert J. Jarvella and Wolfgang Klein (eds.) *Speech, Place and Action: Studies in Deixis and Related Topics* 315–338. Chichester: John Wiley.

É. Kiss, Katalin (1985) Az anaforikus névmások értelmezéséről [On the interpretation of anaphoric pronouns]. *Általános Nyelvészeti Tanulmányok* 16: 155–187.

É. Kiss, Katalin (1998) Mondattan [The syntax]. In Katalin É. Kiss, Ferenc Kiefer, and Péter Siptár (eds.) *Új magyar nyelvtan* [New Hungarian Grammar] 15–184. Budapest: Osiris Kiadó.

É. Kiss, Katalin (2002) *The Syntax of Hungarian*. Cambridge: Cambridge University Press.

É. Kiss, Katalin (2003) A szibériai kapcsolat, avagy miért nem tárgyasan ragozzuk az igét 1. és 2. személyű tárgy esetén [The Siberian connection, or why we do not conjugate the verb for the definite form in the cases of its occurrence with 1st and 2nd person object]. *Magyar Nyelvjárások* 41: 321–327.

É. Kiss, Katalin (2012) Null pronominal objects in Hungarian: A case of exaptation. *Acta Linguistica Hafniensia* 44(2): 192–206. https://doi.org/10.1080/03740463.2013.779077

É. Kiss, Katalin (2013) The inverse agreement constraint in Uralic languages. *Finno-Ugric Languages and Linguistics* 2(1): 2–21.

Elbourne, Paul (2008) Implicit content and the argument from binding. In Tova Friedman (ed.) *Proceedings of Semantics and Linguistic Theory XVIII* (SALT 18) 284–301. Ithaca, NY: Cornell University, CLC Publication. https://doi.org/10.3765/salt.v18i0.2489

Engdahl, Elisabet (1999) Integrating pragmatics into the grammar. In Lunella Mereu (ed.) *Boundaries of Morphology and Syntax* 175–194. Amsterdam: John Benjamins. https://doi.org/10.1075/cilt.180.12eng

Fenyvesi, Anna (1998) Inflection. In István Kenesei, Anna Fenyvesi, and Robert Vago, *Hungarian* 191–351. London and New York: Routledge.

Fillmore, Charles J. (1986) Pragmatically controlled zero anaphora. *Berkeley Linguistic Series* 12: 95–107. https://doi.org/10.3765/bls.v12i0.1866

Fodor, Jerry (1983) *The Modularity of Mind.* Cambridge, MA: MIT Press.

Fodor, Jerry and Fodor, Janet Dean (1980) Functional structure, quantifiers and meaning postulates. *Linguistic Inquiry* 11(4): 759–769.

García Velasco, Daniel and Portero Muñoz, Carmen (2002) *Understood Objects in Functional Grammar.* (Working papers in functional grammar 76) Amsterdam: University of Amsterdam.

Gazdar, Gerald (1979) *Pragmatics: Implicature, Presupposition and Logical Form.* New York: Academic Press.

Gergely, György and Bever, Thomas G. (1986) Related intuitions and the mental representation of causative verbs in adults and children. *Cognition* 23(3): 211–277. https://doi.org/10.1016/0010-0277(86)90035-1

Gillon, Brendan S. (2006) English relational words, context sensitivity and implicit arguments. Retrieved on 2 October 2013 from http://semanticsarchive.net/Archive/jkZjU1O/implicit-argument.pdf

Gillon, Brendan S. (2012) Implicit complements: A dilemma for model theoretic semantics. *Linguistics and Philosophy* 35(4): 313–359. https://doi.org/10.1007/s10988-012-9120-2

Glaude, Herby and Zribi-Hertz, Anne (2014) Verb cognates in Haitian creole. *The Linguistic Review* 31(2): 241–294. https://doi.org/10.1515/tlr-2014-0003

Goldberg, Adele (1995) *Constructions: A Construction Grammar Approach to Argument Structure.* Chicago: The University of Chicago Press.

Goldberg, Adele (2005a) Argument realization: The role of constructions, lexical semantics and discourse factors. In Jan-Ola Östman and Mirjam Fried (eds.) *Construction Grammars: Cognitive Grounding and Theoretical Extensions* 17–43. Amsterdam: John Benjamins.

Goldberg, Adele (2005b) Constructions, lexical semantics and the correspondence principle: Accounting for generalizations and subregularities in the realization of arguments. In Nomi Erteschik-Shir and Tova Rapoport (eds.) *The Syntax of Aspect* 215–236. Oxford: Oxford University Press.

Goldberg, Adele (2013) Arguments structure constructions versus lexical rules or derivational verb templates. *Mind & Language* 28(4): 435–465. https://doi.org/10.1111/mila.12026

Gordon, Peter C., Grosz, Barbara, J., and Gilliom, Laura A. (1993) Pronouns, names, and the centering of attention in discourse. *Cognitive Science* 17(3): 311–347. https://doi.org/10.1207/s15516709cog1703_1

Gregoromichelaki, Eleni, Cann, Ronnie, and Kempson, Ruth (2013) On coordination in dialogue: Sub-sentential talk and its implications. In Laurence Goldstein (ed.) *Brevity*, 53–73. Oxford: Oxford University Press.

Grice, Herbert Paul (1975) Logic and conversation. In Peter Cole and Jerry Morgan (eds.) *Syntax and Semantics 3. Speech Acts* 41–58. New York: Academic Press.

Grimshaw, Jane and Vikner, Sten (1993) Obligatory adjuncts and the structure of events. In Eric J. Reuland and Werner Abraham (eds.) *Knowledge and Language 2. Lexical and Conceptual Structure* 143–155. Dordrecht: Kluwer Academic Publishers. https://doi.org/10.1007/978-94-011-1842-2_7

Groefsema, Marjolein (1995) Understood arguments: A semantic/pragmatic approach. *Lingua* 96(2–3): 139–161. https://doi.org/10.1016/0024-3841(95)00002-H

Groot, Casper de (1985) Predicates and features. In Alide Machtelt Bolkestein, Casper de Groot, and John Lachlan Mackenzie (eds.) *Predicates and Terms in Functional Grammar* 71–84. Dordrecht: Foris.

Hadrovics, László (1969) *A funkcionális magyar mondattan alapjai* [Foundations of Hungarian Functional Syntax]. Budapest: Akadémiai Kiadó.

Haegeman, Liliane (1991) *Introduction to Government and Binding Theory*. Oxford: Blackwell.

Haegeman, Liliane and Guéron, Jacqueline (1999) *English Grammar: A Generative Perspective*. Oxford: Blackwell.

Haegeman, Liliane and Ihsane, Tabea (1999) Subject ellipsis in embedded clauses in English. *English Language & Linguistics* 3(1): 117–145. https://doi.org/10.1017/S1360674399000155

Haegeman, Liliane and Ihsane, Tabea (2001) Adult null subjects in the non-pro-drop languages: Two diary dialects. *Language Acquisition* 9(4): 329–346. https://doi.org/10.1207/S15327817LA0904_03

Hale, Ken and Keyser, Samuel Jey (2002) *Prolegomena to a Theory of Argument Structure*. Cambridge, MA: MIT Press.

Hall, Alison (2008) Free enrichment or hidden indexicals? *Mind & Language* 23(4): 426–456. https://doi.org/10.1111/j.1468-0017.2008.00350.x

Hall, Alison (2009) Subsentential utterances, ellipsis, and pragmatic enrichment. *Pragmatics & Cognition* 17(2): 222–250. https://doi.org/10.1075/pc.17.2.02hal

H. Molnár, Ilona (1962) A tárgy [Direct object]. In József Tompa (ed.) *A mai magyar nyelv rendszere: Leíró nyelvtan 2. Mondattan* [The Structure of Modern Hungarian Language: A Descriptive Grammar. Vol 2. Syntax] 147–161. Budapest: Akadémiai Kiadó.

Horn, Laurence Robert (1984) Toward a taxonomy for pragmatic inferences: Q- and R-based implicature. In Deborah Schiffrin (ed.) *Meaning, Form, and Use in Context* 11–42. Washington, DC: Georgetown University Press.

Huang, Yan (2000) Discourse anaphora: Four theoretical models. *Journal of Pragmatics* 32(2): 151–176. https://doi.org/10.1016/S0378-2166(99)00041-7

Huang, Yan (2004) Anaphora and the pragmatics–syntax interface. In Laurence Robert Horn and Gregory Ward (eds.) *The Handbook of Pragmatics* 288–314. Oxford: Blackwell.

Huang, Yan (2009) Anaphora, cataphora, exophora, logophoricity. In Keith Allan (ed.) *Concise Encyclopaedia of Semantics* 19–31. Amsterdam: Elsevier.

Huang, Yan (ed.) (2012) *The Oxford Dictionary of Pragmatics*. Oxford: Oxford University Press.

Hwang, Jena (2012) Making verb argument adjunct distinctions in English. *Colorado Research in Linguistics* 23: 1–21. Retrieved on 7 April 2014 from http://www.colorado.edu/ling/CRIL/Volume23_Issue1/paper_Hwang.pdf

Iida, Ryu, Inui, Kentaro, and Matsumoto, Yuji (2006) Exploiting syntactic patterns as clues in zero-anaphora resolution. *Proceedings of the 21st International Conference on Computational Linguistics and 44th Annual Meeting of the ACL*, 625–632. Sydney, July 2006. Association for Computational Linguistics. https://doi.org/10.3115/1220175.1220254

Iten, Corinne, Junker, Marie-Odile, Pyke, Aryn, Stainton, Robert, and Wearing, Catherine (2005) Null complements: Licensed by syntax or by semantics-pragmatics? *CLA Annual Conference Proceedings* (2005): 1–15. Retrieved on 13 December 2015 from http://works.bepress.com/robertstainton/97

Ivaskó, Lívia (2002) Az afáziás nyelvhasználat sikertelenségének okairól [Reasons of communicative failure in aphasic language use]. In Mihály Racsmány and Szabolcs Kéri (eds.) *Architektúra és patológia a megismerésben* [Architecture and Pathology in Cognition] 40–51. Budapest: Books in Print.

Jackendoff, Ray (1990) *Semantic Structures*. Cambridge, MA: MIT Press.

Jackendoff, Ray (2002) *Foundations of Language: Brain, Meaning, Grammar, Evolution*. Oxford: Oxford UniversityPress.

Kálmánné Bors, Irén (1991) Az egyszerű mondat [The simple sentence]. In Anna A. Jászó (ed.) *A magyar nyelv könyve* [The Book of Hungarian Language] 324–387. Budapest: Trezor.

Kasher, Asa (1986) Pragmatics and Chomsky's research program. In Asa Kasher (ed.) *The Chomskyan Turn* 122–149. Oxford: Blackwell.

Kaufmann, Ingrid and Wunderlich, Dieter (1998) Cross-linguistic patterns of resultatives. *Working Papers SFB Theorie des Lexikons* **109**. Düsseldorf: University of Düsseldorf.

Kepser, Stephan and Reis, Marga (eds.) (2005) *Linguistic Evidence: Empirical, Theoretical and Computational Perspectives*. Berlin and New York: Mouton de Gruyter. https://doi.org/10.1515/9783110197549

Kertész, András and Rákosi, Csilla (eds.) (2008a) *New Approaches to Linguistic Evidence: Pilot Studies*. Frankfurt am Main: Lang.

Kertész, András and Rákosi, Csilla (2008b) Megjegyzések a nyelvészeti adatok és evidencia problémájáról folyó vita jelenlegi állásához [Remarks on the current discussion on linguistic data and evidence]. *Magyar Nyelv* 104(3): 274–286, 104(4): 385–402.

Kertész, András and Rákosi, Csilla (2009) On current approaches to linguistic data and evidence. *Sprachteorie und germanistische Linguistik* 19(2): 125–170.

Kertész, András and Rákosi, Csilla (2012) *Data and Evidence in Linguistics: A Plausible Argumentation Model*. Cambridge: Cambridge University Press. https://doi.org/10.1017/CBO9780511920752

Kertész, András and Rákosi, Csilla (eds.) (2014) *The Evidential Basis of Linguistic Argumentation*. Amsterdam: John Benjamins. https://doi.org/10.1075/slcs.153

Keszler, Borbála (ed.) (2000) *Magyar grammatika* [Hungarian Grammar]. Budapest: Nemzeti Tankönyvkiadó.

Kiefer, Ferenc (1990) Noun incorporation in Hungarian. *Acta Linguistica Hungarica* 40(1–2): 149–179.

Kiefer, Ferenc (1998) Alaktan [Morphology]. In Katalin É. Kiss, Ferenc Kiefer, and Péter Siptár (eds.) *Új magyar nyelvtan* [New Hungarian Grammar] 185–289. Budapest: Osiris Kiadó.

Kiefer, Ferenc (2006) *Aspektus és akcióminőség: Különös tekintettel a magyar nyelvre* [Aspect and Aktionsart: With Special Regard to Hungarian Language]. Budapest: Akadémiai Kiadó.

Kiefer, Ferenc and Kertész, András (2013) From thought experiments to real experiments in pragmatics. In Alessandro Capone, Ferruccio Lo Piparo, and Marco Carapezza (eds.) *Perspectives on Philosophy and Pragmatics* 53–86. Berlin, Heidelberg, New York: Springer.

Kim, Kye-Sung, Park, Seong-Bae, Song, Hyu-Je, Park, Se Young, and Lee, Sang Jo (2010) Identification of non-referential zero pronouns for Korean–English machine translation. In Byoung-Tak Zhang and Mehmet A. Orgun (eds.) *PRICAI 2010: Trends in Artificial Intelligence. 11th Pacific Rim International Conference on Artificial Intelligence, Daegu, Korea, August 30–September 2, 2010. Proceedings* 112–122. Berlin and Heidelberg: Springer Verlag. https://doi.org/10.1007/978-3-642-15246-7_13

Komlósy, András (1992) Régensek és vonzatok [Predicates and complements]. In Ferenc Kiefer (ed.) *Strukturális magyar nyelvtan: Mondattan* [A Structural Grammar of Hungarian: Syntax] 299–527. Budapest: Akadémiai Kiadó.

Komlósy, András (1994) Complements and adjuncts. In Ferenc Kiefer and Katalin É. Kiss (eds.) *Syntax and Semantics 27. The Syntactic Structure of Hungarian* 91–178. New York: Academic Press.

Komlósy, András (2001) *A lexikai-funkcionális grammatika mondattanának alapfogalmai* [Basic Notions in the Syntax of Lexical-Functional Grammar]. Budapest: Tinta Könyvkiadó.

Kugler, Nóra (2000a) Az alany [The subject]. In Borbála Keszler (ed.) *Magyar grammatika* [Hungarian Grammar] 405–413. Budapest: Nemzeti Tankönyvkiadó.

Kugler, Nóra (2000b) Az igeragozás [The conjugation]. In Borbála Keszler (ed.) *Magyar grammatika* [Hungarian Grammar] 104–126. Budapest: Nemzeti Tankönyvkiadó.

Labov, William (1975) *What is a Linguistic Fact?* Lisse: The Peter de Ridder Press.

Laczkó, Krisztina (2003) A mutató névmások funkcionális vizsgálata [The functional examination of demonstrative pronouns]. *Magyar Nyelvőr* 127(3): 314–325.

Langacker, Ronald (1987) *Foundations of Cognitive Grammar 1. Theoretical Prerequisites.* Stanford, CA: Stanford University Press.

Lavidas, Nikolaos (2013) Null and cognate objects and changes in (in)transitivity. *Acta Linguistica Hungarica* 60(1): 69–106. https://doi.org/10.1556/ALing.60.2013.1.2

Leech, Geoffrey N. (1983) *Principles of Pragmatics.* London: Longman.

Lehmann, Christian (2004) Data in linguistics. *The Linguistic Review* 21(3–4): 175–210.

Lejtovicz, Katalin E. and Kardkovács, Zsolt T. 2007. Anaphora resolution. *Magyar Kutatók 8. Nemzetközi Szimpóziuma. 8th International Symposium of Hungarian Researchers on Computational Intelligence and Informatics* 227–237. Budapest: BMF.

Lengyel, Klára (2000) Az ige [The verb]. In Borbála Keszler (ed.) *Magyar grammatika* [Hungarian Grammar] 81–95. Budapest: Nemzeti Tankönyvkiadó.

Levin, Beth (1993) *English Verb Classes and Alternations: A Preliminary Investigation.* Chicago: The University of Chicago Press.

Levinson, Stephen C. (1983) *Pragmatics.* Cambridge: Cambridge University Press.

Levinson, Stephen C. (2000) *Presumptive Meanings: The Theory of Generalized Conversational Implicature.* Cambridge, MA: MIT Press.

Lyons, John (1979) *Semantics* I–II. Cambridge: Cambridge University Press.

Maleczki, Márta (1994) Bare common nouns and their relation to the temporal constitution of events in Hungarian. In Zoltán Bánréti (ed.) *Papers in the Theory of Grammar* 168–184. Budapest: Research Institute for Linguistics of the Hungarian Academy of Sciences.

Maleczki, Márta (2001) Indefinite arguments in Hungarian. In István Kenesei (ed.) *Argument Structure in Hungarian* 157–199. Budapest: Akadémiai Kiadó.

Martí, Luisa (2006) Unarticulated constituents revisited. *Linguistics and Philosophy* 29(2): 135–166. https://doi.org/10.1007/s10988-005-4740-4

Mel'čuk, Igor Aleksandrovič. (2012) *Semantics: From Meaning to Text.* Amsterdam: John Benjamins. https://doi.org/10.1075/slcs.129

Meltzer-Asscher, Aya (2011) *Adjectives and Argument Structure.* PhD-Dissertation. Tel-Aviv University. Retrieved on 5 April 2014 from http://humanities.tau.ac.il/linguistics_eng/images/stories/Aya_Meltzer-Asscher_PhD_2011.pdf

Mey, Jacob (1993) *Pragmatics: An Introduction.* Oxford: Blackwell.

Mitkov, Ruslan (2013) *Anaphora Resolution* (2nd edn). London: Routledge.

Mittwoch, Anita (1983) Backward anaphora and discourse structure. *Journal of Pragmatics* 7(2): 129–139. https://doi.org/10.1016/0378-2166(83)90048-6

Müller, Stefan and Wechsler, Stephen (2014) Lexical approaches to argument structure. *Theoretical Linguistics* 40(1–2): 1–76. https://doi.org/10.1515/tl-2014-0001

Nagy C., Katalin (2008) Data in historical pragmatics: A case study on the Catalan periphrastic perfective past. In András Kertész and Csilla Rákosi (eds.) *New Approaches to Linguistic Evidence* 171–197. Frankfurt am Main: Peter Lang.

Neale, Stephen (1990) *Descriptions.* Cambridge, MA: MIT Press.

Németh T., Enikő (1995) On the role of pragmatic connectives in Hungarian spoken discourse. In Brita Wårvik, Sanna-Kaisa Tanskanen, and Risto Hiltunen (eds.) *Organization in Discourse: Proceedings from the Turku Conference* 393–402. Turku: University of Turku = *Anglicana Turkuensia* 14.

Németh T., Enikő (1996) *A szóbeli diskurzusok megnyilatkozáspéldányokra tagolása* [Segmentation of Spoken Discourse into Utterance-Tokens]. Budapest: Akadémiai Kiadó = *Nyelvtudományi Értekezések* 142.

Németh T., Enikő (2000) Occurrence and identification of implicit arguments in Hungarian. *Journal of Pragmatics* 32(11). 1657–1682. https://doi.org/10.1016/S0378-2166(99)00114-9

Németh T., Enikő (2001) Implicit arguments in Hungarian: Manners of their occurrence and possibilities of their identification. In István Kenesei (ed.) *Argument Structure in Hungarian* 113–156. Budapest: Akadémiai Kiadó.

Németh T., Enikő (2004) The principles of communicative language use. *Acta Linguistica Hungarica* 51(3–4): 379–418. https://doi.org/10.1556/ALing.51.2004.3-4.7

Németh T., Enikő (2005) Az osztenzív-következtetéses kommunikációtól a verbális kommunikációig [From ostensive-inferential communication to verbal communication]. In Lívia Ivaskó (ed.) *Érthető kommunikáció* [Comprehensible Communication] 77–87. Szeged: Szegedi Tudományegyetem.

Németh T., Enikő (2006) Pragmatika [Pragmatics]. In Ferenc Kiefer (ed.) *Magyar nyelv* [The Hungarian Language] 222–261. Budapest: Akadémiai Kiadó.

Németh T., Enikő (2007) Grammatika és pragmatika viszonya az implicit argumentumok tükrében [The relationship between grammar and pragmatics in case of implicit arguments]. In Tamás Gecső and Csilla Sárdi (eds.) *Nyelvelmélet – nyelvhasználat* [Theory of Languge and Language Use] 188–197. Székesfehérvár: Kodolányi János Főiskola.

Németh T., Enikő (2008a) Az implicit alanyi és tárgyi argumentumok előfordulásának lexikai-szemantikai jellemzői [The lexical-semantic properties of the occurrence of implicit subject and direct object arguments]. In Ferenc Kiefer (ed.) *Strukturális magyar nyelvtan 4. A szótár szerkezete* [A Structural Grammar of Hungarian 4: The Structure of the Lexicon] 71–128. Budapest: Akadémiai Kiadó.

Németh T., Enikő (2008b) Verbal information transmission without communicative intention. *Intercultural Pragmatics* 5(2): 153–176. https://doi.org/10.1515/IP.2008.009

Németh T., Enikő (2010) How lexical-semantic factors influence the verbs' occurrence with implicit direct object arguments in Hungarian. In Enikő Németh T. and Károly Bibok (eds.) *The Role of Data at the Semantics–Pragmatics Interface* 305–348. Berlin: Mouton de Gruyter.

Németh T., Enikő (2012) Lexical-semantic properties and contextual factors in the use of verbs of work with implicit subject arguments in Hungarian. *Intercultural Pragmatics* 9(4): 453–477.

Németh T., Enikő (2014a) Hungarian verbs of natural phenomena with explicit and implicit subject arguments: Their use and occurrence in the light of data. In András Kertész and Csilla Rákosi (eds.) *The Evidential Basis of Linguistic Argumentation* 103–132. Amsterdam: John Benjamins.

Németh T., Enikő (2014b) Implicit arguments at the grammar–pragmatics interface: Some methodological considerations. *Argumentum* 10: 679–694.

Németh T., Enikő (2017a) Theoretical and methodological issues in the research into implicit arguments in Hungarian. In Stavros Assimakopoulos (ed.) *Pragmatics at its Interfaces* 149–174. Berlin: Mouton de Gruyter.

Németh T., Enikő (2017b) Zero subject anaphors and extralinguistically motivated subject pro-drop in Hungarian language use. In Piotr Cap and Marta Dynel (eds.) *Implicitness: From Lexis to Discourse* 95–118. Amsterdam: John Benjamins.

Németh T., Enikő and Bibok, Károly (2001) Az alanyi és a tárgyas ragozás szerepe az igei tárgyi argumentumok elhagyhatóságában [The role of indefinite and definite conjugations in the omissibility of verbal directs object arguments]. In Marianne Bakró-Nagy, Zoltán Bánréti, and Katalin É. Kiss (eds.) *Újabb tanulmányok a strukturális magyar nyelvtan és a nyelvtörténet köréből* [Recent Studies in Structural Hungarian Grammar and in the History of Language] 78–96. Budapest: Osiris Kiadó.

Németh T., Enikő and Bibok, Károly (2010) Interaction between grammar and pragmatics: The case of implicit arguments, implicit predicates and co-composition in Hungarian. *Journal of Pragmatics* 42(2): 501–524. https://doi.org/10.1016/j.pragma.2009.07.001

Newman, John (2009) *The Linguistics of Eating and Drinking.* Amsterdam and Philadelphia: John Benjamins. https://doi.org/10.1075/tsl.84

Newmeyer, Frederick J. (1998) *Language Form and Language Function.* Cambridge, MA: MIT Press.

Newmeyer, Frederick J. (2006) Negation and modularity. In Betty Birner and Gregory Ward (eds.) *Drawing the Boundaries of Meaning: Neo-Gricean Studies in Pragmatics and Semantics in Honor of Laurence R. Horn* 241–261. Amsterdam: John Benjamins. https://doi.org/10.1075/slcs.80.14new

Nikolaeva, Irina (2001) Secondary topic as a relation in information structure. *Linguistics* 39(1): 1–49. https://doi.org/10.1515/ling.2001.006

Nyomárkay, István (1972) Tárgyas igék tárgy nélkül [Transitive verbs without direct objects]. *Magyar Nyelv* 68(2): 198–209.

Oravecz, Csaba, Váradi, Tamás, and Sass, Bálint (2014) The Hungarian gigaword corpus. *Proceedings of LERC 2014*: 1719–1723.

Paradis, Michel (1998) The other side of language: Pragmatic competence. *Journal of Neurolinguistics* 11(1–2): 1–10. https://doi.org/10.1016/S0911-6044(98)00001-3

Penke, Martina and Rosenbach, Anette (2004) What counts as evidence in linguistics? An introduction. *Studies in Language* 28(3): 480–526. https://doi.org/10.1075/sl.28.3.03pen

Peral, Jesús and Fernández, Antonio (2000) Generation of Spanish zero pronouns into English. In Dimitris N. Christodoulakis (ed.) *Natural Language Processing – NLP 2000. Second International Conference. Patras, Greece, June 2000. Proceedings* 252–260. Berlin and Heidelberg: Springer Verlag. https://doi.org/10.1007/3-540-45154-4_24

Pereltsvaig, Asya (1999) Cognate objects in Russian: Is the notion 'cognate' relevant for syntax? *Canadian Journal of Linguistics* 44(3): 267–291. https://doi.org/10.1017/S0008413100017333

Perry, John (1986) Thought without representation. *Supplementary Proceedings of the Aristotelian Society* 60(1): 263–283. Accessed 28 May 2018 from http://john.jperry.net/cv/1986d.pdf

Perry, John (1998) Indexicals, contexts, and unarticulated constituents. In Dag Westerståhl et al. (eds.) *Computing Natural Language* 1–11. Stanford: CSLI Publication.

Pete, István (1998) A magyar igeragozás típusai [Types of Hungarian conjugation]. In László Büky and Márta Maleczki (eds.) *A mai magyar nyelv leírásának újabb módszerei 3.* [Current Methods in the Description of the Present-Day Hungarian] 133–148. Szeged: JATE.

Pethő, Gergely and Kardos, Éva (2009) Cross-linguistic evidence and the licensing of implicit arguments. *Oslo Studies in Language* 1(1): 33–61.

Pinker, Steven (1989) *Learnability and Cognition: The Acquisition of Argument Structure.* Cambridge, MA: MIT Press.

Pléh, Csaba (1994) Mondatközi viszonyok feldolgozása: Az anaphora megértése a magyarban. [Processing intersentential relations: Interpreting anaphors in Hungarian]. *Magyar Pszichológiai Szemle* 50(5–6): 287–320.

Pléh, Csaba (1998) *A mondatmegértés a magyar nyelvben* [Sentence Comprehension in Hungarian]. Budapest: Osiris Kiadó.

Pléh, Csaba and McWhinney, Brian (1987) Anaphora resolution in Hungarian. *Acta Linguistica Academiae Scientiarum Hungaricae* 37(1/4): 103–124.

Pléh, Csaba and Radics, Katalin (1978) Truncated sentence, pronominalization and the text. *Acta Linguistica Academiae Scientiarum Hungaricae* 28(1/2): 91–113.

Pollard, Carl and Sag, Ivan A. (1994) *Head-Driven Phrase Structure Grammar.* Chicago: The University of Chicago Press.

Pustejovsky, James (1995) *The Generative Lexicon.* Cambridge, MA: MIT Press.

Pustejovsky, James (1998) Generativity and explanation in semantics: A reply to Fodor and Lepore. *Linguistic Inquiry* 29(2): 289–311. https://doi.org/10.1162/002438998553752

Pusztai, Ferenc (ed.) (2003) *Magyar értelmező kéziszótár* [Concise Explanatory Dictionary of Hungarian]. Budapest: Akadémiai Kiadó.

Rácz, Endre (1968) Mondattan [Syntax]. In Endre Rácz (ed.) *A mai magyar nyelv* [The Present-Day Hungarian] 205–458. Budapest: Tankönyvkiadó.

Radford, Andrew (1988) *Transformational Grammar: A First Course.* Cambridge: Cambridge University Press. https://doi.org/10.1017/CBO9780511840425

Radford, Andrew (1997a) *Syntax: A Minimalist Introduction.* Cambridge: Cambridge University Press. https://doi.org/10.1017/CBO9781139166898

Radford, Andrew (1997b) *Syntactic Theories and the Structure of English: A Minimalist Approach.* Cambridge: Cambridge University Press. https://doi.org/10.1017/CBO9781139166706

Rappoport-Hovav, Malka and Levin, Beth (1995) The elasticity of verb meaning. In *IATL 2: Proceedings of the Tenth Annual Conference of the Israel Association for Theoretical Linguistics and the Workshop on the Syntax-Semantics Interface* 153–171.

Rappoport-Hovav, Malka and Levin, Beth (2001) An event structure account of English resultatives. *Language* 77(4): 766–797. https://doi.org/10.1353/lan.2001.0221

Recanati, Francois (2002) Unarticulated constituents. *Linguistics and Philosophy* 25(3): 299–345. https://doi.org/10.1023/A:1015267930510

Recanati, Francois (2004) *Literal Meaning.* Cambridge: Cambridge University Press.

Recanati, Francois (2007) It is raining (somewhere). *Linguistics and Philosophy* 30(1): 123–146. https://doi.org/10.1007/s10988-006-9007-1

Reinhart, Tanya (1985) *Anaphora and Semantic Interpretation.* London: Croom Helm.

Renkema, Jan (2004) *Introduction to Discourse Studies*. Amsterdam: John Benjamins. https://doi.org/10.1075/z.124

Rescher, Nicholas (1976) *Plausible Reasoning*. Assen and Amsterdam: Van Gorcum.

Rice, Sally (1988) Unlikely lexical entries. *Berkeley Linguistic Series* 14: 202–212. https://doi.org/10.3765/bls.v14i0.1797

Ringen, Jon (1975) Linguistic facts: A study of the empirical scientific status of transformational generative grammars. In David Cohen and Jessica R. Wirth (eds.) *Testing Linguistic Hypotheses* 1–41. Washington, DC: Hemisphere Publishing Corp.

Rizzi, Luigi (1986) Null objects in Italian and the theory of *pro*. *Linguistic Inquiry* 17(3): 501–557.

Roeper, Thomas (1987) Implicit arguments and the head–complement relation. *Linguistic Inquiry* 18(2): 267–310.

Ross, John Robert (1979) Where's English? In Charles J. Fillmore, Daniel Kempler, and William S-Y. Wang (eds.) *Individual Differences in Language Ability and Language Behavior* 127–163. New York: Academic Press. https://doi.org/10.1016/B978-0-12-255950-1.50014-7

Saeboe, Kjell (1996) Anaphoric presupposition and zero anaphora. *Linguistics and Philosophy* 19(2): 187–209. https://doi.org/10.1007/BF00635837

Sanders, José and Spooren, Wilbert (1997) Perspective, subjectivity, and modality from a cognitive linguistic point of view. In Wolf-Andreas Liebert, Gisela Redeker, and Linda Waugh (eds.) *Discourse and Perspective in Cognitive Linguistics* 85–112. Amsterdam and Philadelphia: John Benjamins. https://doi.org/10.1075/cilt.151.08san

Sárik, Pál (1998) A határozói igenevek néhány problémája [Some problems of adverbial participles]. *Magyar Nyelv* 94(4): 423–435.

Schütze, Carson T. (1996) *The Empirical Base of Linguistics: Grammaticality Judgments and Linguistic Methodology*. Chicago: The University of Chicago Press.

Scott, Kate (2006) When less is more: Implicit arguments and relevance theory. In Richard Breheny and Mary Pearce (eds.) *UCL Working Papers in Linguistics* 18: 139–170.

Scott, Kate (2013) Pragmatically motivated null subjects in English: A relevance theory perspective. *Journal of Pragmatics* 53: 68–83. https://doi.org/10.1016/j.pragma.2013.04.001

Searle, John R. (1969) *Speech Acts: An Essay in the Philosophy of Language*. Cambridge: Cambridge University Press. https://doi.org/10.1017/CBO9781139173438

Shopen, Tim (1973) Ellipsis as grammatical indeterminacy. *Foundations of Language* 10(1): 65–77.

Sinclair, John (ed.) (2001) *Collins Cobuild English Dictionary for Advanced Learners* (3rd edn). Glasgow: Harper Collins Publishers.

Sperber, Dan (2000) Metarepresentations in an evolutionary perspective. In Dan Sperber (ed.) *Metarepresentations: A Multidisciplinary Perspective* 117–137. Oxford: Oxford University Press.

Sperber, Dan and Wilson, Deirdre (1986/1995) *Relevance: Communication and Cognition*. Oxford: Blackwell.

Sperber, Dan and Wilson, Deirdre (2002) Pragmatics, modularity and mind-reading. *Mind & Language* 17(1–2): 3–23. https://doi.org/10.1111/1468-0017.00186

Stainton, Robert (2004) The pragmatics of non sentences. In Laurence Robert Horn and Gregory Ward (eds.) *The Handbook of Pragmatics* 266–287. Oxford: Blackwell.

Stainton, Robert (2006) *Words and Thoughts: Subsentences, Ellipsis, and the Philosophy of Language.* Oxford: Oxford University Press. https://doi.org/10.1093/acprof:oso/9780199250387.001.0001

Stanley, Jason (2000) Context and logical form. *Linguistics and Philosophy* 23(4): 391–434. https://doi.org/10.1023/A:1005599312747

Stillings, Neil, Feinstein, Mark H., Garfield, Jay L., Rissland, Edwina L., Rosenbaum, David A., and Weisler, Steven E. (1987) *Cognitive Science: An Introduction.* Cambridge, MA: MIT Press.

Taylor, Kenneth A. (2001) Sex, breakfast, and descriptus interruptus. *Synthese* 128(1–2): 45–61. https://doi.org/10.1023/A:1010349621943

Temesi, Mihály (1961) A névmás [The pronoun]. In József Tompa (ed.) *A mai magyar nyelv rendszere: Leíró nyelvtan 1. Bevezetés. Hangtan. Szótan* [The System of the Present-Day Hungarian Language: Descriptive Grammar 1. Introduction. Phonetics. Lexicology] 237–250. Budapest: Akadémiai Kiadó.

Tognini-Bonelli, Elena (2001) *Corpus Linguistics at Work.* Amsterdam and Philadelphia: John Benjamins. https://doi.org/10.1075/scl.6

Tolcsvai Nagy, Gábor (2001a) 3rd person anaphora in Hungarian. *Hungarian Studies* 15(2): 287–298.

Tolcsvai Nagy, Gábor (2001b) *A magyar nyelv szövegtana* [Textlinguistics of Hungarian]. Budapest: Akadémiai Kiadó.

Tolcsvai Nagy, Gábor (2014) General and definite verb inflection in Hungarian: A semantic approach. *Argumentum* 10: 576–587.

Tompa, József (1961) Az igeragozás [The conjugation]. In József Tompa (ed.) *A mai magyar nyelv rendszere: Leíró nyelvtan 1. Bevezetés. Hangtan. Szótan* [The System of the Present-Day Hungarian Language: Descriptive Grammar 1. Introduction. Phonetics. Lexicology] 482–511. Budapest: Akadémiai Kiadó.

Tóth, Ildikó (2001) Impersonal constructions and null expletives. In István Kenesei (ed.) *Argument Structure in Hungarian* 51–78. Budapest: Akadémiai Kiadó.

Velcsov, Mártonné (1968) Alaktan [Morphology]. In Endre Rácz (ed.) *A mai magyar nyelv* [The Present-Day Hungarian Language] 85–204. Budapest: Tankönyvkiadó.

Verschueren, Jef (1999) *Understanding Pragmatics.* London: Arnold.

Vicente, Begoña and Groefsema, Marjolein (2013) Something out of nothing? Rethinking unarticulated constituents. *Journal of Pragmatics* 47(1): 108–127. https://doi.org/10.1016/j.pragma.2012.12.009

Wéber, Katalin (2011) '*Rejtelmes kétféleség*': *A kétféle igeragozás elkülönülése a magyar nyelvben* ['Mysterious duality': Differentiation of the two conjugations in Hungarian]. PhD dissertation, Pécs: Pécsi Tudományegyetem, Nyelvtudományi Program, Alkalmazott Nyelvészeti Doktori Iskola.

Wharton, Tim (2003) Natural pragmatics and natural codes. *Mind & Language* 18(5): 447–477. https://doi.org/10.1111/1468-0017.00237

Wilson, Deirdre and Sperber, Dan (2002) Truthfulness and relevance. *Mind* 111(443): 583–632. https://doi.org/10.1093/mind/111.443.583

Wunderlich, Dieter (1972) *Linguistische Pragmatik.* Frankfurt: Athenäum.

Zouhar, Marián (2011) What is wrong with unarticulated constituents? *Human Affairs* 21(3): 239–248. https://doi.org/10.2478/s13374-011-0025-5

Subject index

CPSIA information can be obtained
at www.ICGtesting.com
Printed in the USA
LVHW050722221218
600626LV00004B/11/P